Approaches to Joyce's *Portrait*

APPROACHES

University of Pittsburgh Press

THOMAS F. STALEY

and

BERNARD BENSTOCK

Editors

TO JOYCE'S PORTRAIT

Ten Essays

Library of Congress Cataloging in Publication Data

Main entry under title:

Approaches to Joyce's Portrait.

Includes bibliographical references.
1. Joyce, James, 1882–1941. A portrait of the
artist as a young man.   I.   Staley, Thomas F.
II.   Benstock, Bernard.
PR6019.09P6432   823′.9′12   76-6670
ISBN 0-8229-3331-4

Grateful acknowledgment is made to those who granted permission to quote material in this book:

Excerpts from *Closing Time* by Norman O. Brown. Copyright © 1973 by Norton R. Potter, as Trustee. Reprinted by permission of Random House, Inc.

Excerpts from *Howl and Other Poems* by Allen Ginsberg. Copyright © 1956, 1959 by Allen Ginsberg. Reprinted by permission of City Lights Books.

Excerpts from *Wintering Out* by Seamus Heaney. Copyright © 1972 by Seamus Heaney. Reprinted by permission.

Excerpts from *A Portrait of the Artist as a Young Man* by James Joyce. Copyright 1916 by B. W. Huebsch; copyright renewed 1944 by Nora Joseph Joyce. Copyright © 1964 by the Estate of James Joyce. All rights reserved. Reprinted by permission of The Viking Press, Jonathan Cape Ltd., and The Society of Authors as the literary representative of the Estate of James Joyce. Excerpts from *A Portrait of the Artist as a Young Man* (Viking Critical Library Edition) by James Joyce. Copyright 1916 by B. W. Huebsch; copyright renewed 1944 by Nora Joseph Joyce. Copyright © 1964 by the Estate of James Joyce. Copyright © 1968 by The Viking Press, Inc. All rights reserved. Reprinted by permission of The Viking Press, Jonathan Cape Ltd., and The Society of Authors as the literary representative of the Estate of James Joyce.

Excerpts from *The Great Hunger* by Patrick Kavanagh. Copyright © 1942 by Patrick Kavanagh. Excerpts from *Tarry Flynn* by Patrick Kavanagh. Copyright © 1948 by Patrick Kavanagh. Both reprinted by permission of Mrs. Catherine Kavanagh, and Martin Brian & O'Keeffe, Ltd.

To Tom, Carrie, Mary, Timmy

and

To Kevin, Erika, Eric

Contents

Introduction

FEW NOVELS of the twentieth century have reached the level of total acceptability as has *A Portrait of the Artist as a Young Man*. Its stature is assured, and it is distinguished by its general availability and readability. It seems a most natural book for college students, finding its way into their hands even when not a part of their curriculum. Titles like *Ulysses* and *Finnegans Wake* conjure up overwhelming questions and suggest incongruities, anachronisms, strained associations, endless mysteries, but *A Portrait of the Artist as a Young Man* tells us exactly what it is and what its component parts are. The gap that usually exists between the "average" reader and the scholar-critic is minimal where *A Portrait* is concerned.

Not that Joyce's *Portrait* has been deprived of the full measure of scholarly attention. It is just that we never have the impression that it has been picked to death, or treated with hushed and reverential awe as a Great Classic. As portraiture it is intense and vivid, illuminating a way of life at the end of the nineteenth century, a unique social organism that is "British" Ireland, the mores and mannerisms of its bourgeois class, the peculiar nature of the Irish Catholic church and its educational systems, and the personality of a sensitive child growing into adolescence and manhood. The language of the novel, from its initial baby talk to the self-conscious verbalizations in the final diary entries, pleases because of its felicity and yet calls attention to itself because of its unusual precision. The rhythms of the novel, fluctuating between the rising development of heightened emotion and the crestfallen return to the mundane and seamy, suggest the dramatist as well as the poet. And the structure of the novel, advancing sequentially through isolated phases and special moments, indicates a virtuosity rarely expected from a short piece of prose fiction. But primarily it is that odd balance of the known world and an individual reaction to it which evokes the acceptance and astonishment that make a reading of the *Portrait* an exciting experience and a rereading a multiply valuable one.

Easy accessibility and an absence of notoriety have assured *A Portrait*'s solid reputation for almost six decades, and the classroom has provided a comfortable proving ground for ideas about it. *A Portrait* is certainly the one book by James Joyce most often taught, resulting in continuing interchange of points of view between the generation that can identify immediately and spontaneously with protagonist Stephen Dedalus and the generation distanced from the tyro artist to a degree comparable to that of author James Joyce in the process of composing. This might well account for the reasonable tone that often highlights essays on this novel: there is less need for ingenious theories to cover the lacunae or for argumentative defenses of pet interpretations. The concepts developed in *Portrait* criticism often reflect pretesting in the classroom and profit from fresh and youthful responses. Whereas *Ulysses* admirers form a coterie and *Wake* enthusiasts a cabal, *Portrait* readers form a community.

From that community *Approaches to Joyce's Portrait* offers ten new investigations. These critics have been asked to inspect *A Portrait of the Artist* from new perspectives, each focusing on one vital factor of the work. None of us can pretend to recapture the initial wonder of first looking into Joyce's *Portrait*, nor would we want to ignore the wealth of commentary that has informed and matured our rereadings of it, but by allowing each of us only a single lens we hope to have concentrated on our individual outlooks. Together the examiners form their own community; we maintain tenaciously the sharpness of our individual viewpoints yet contribute to a broader range of possible views.

Since a community functions best when each member responds with a complete commitment toward it and has total freedom of role within it, the editorial aim has been to pose to each contributor a particular approach, allowing each of us to follow our individually determined dictates. And we hoped that controversy and stimulating differences of opinion would emerge. When any two devotees write about Joyce this becomes an inevitability, and *Approaches to Joyce's Portrait* reveals both diversity of viewpoint and individuality of perspective. This editorial policy proved itself in our previous volume, *Approaches to Ulysses: Ten Essays* (Pittsburgh: University of Pittsburgh Press, 1970).

The first essay, Thomas F. Staley's, presents an overview of previous critical response to *A Portrait* and provides an informed discussion of the development of the scholarship surrounding the work. Establishing the reliability of the text itself is an important critical procedure, and Hans Walter Gabler presents here the latest findings on that difficult subject; nowhere else in *Portrait* commentary has there been so minute a tracking of Joyce's creative process at this early and formative juncture. And as Professor Gabler seeks to set the text of the *Portrait*, Breon Mitchell seeks to set the *Portrait* within the context of an important European tradition, the graphing of Stephen's development from childhood to manhood.

There are other roots as well as the *Bildungsroman* inherent in the makeup of Joyce's *Portrait*: Margaret Church argues for the thematic and structural importance of Giambattista Vico (known for his influence on the later *Wake* but hitherto ignored as a source for the early novel); Richard M. Kain examines the pervading force of Joyce's environment in providing the basic structure of Stephen Dedalus's world. James Naremore, in turn, extends this examination by analyzing the social forces at work within that world and Joyce's definite consciousness of those forces, and since Freud follows Marx as a natural continuum, Chester G. Anderson responds with the latest in the newly-reawakened area of psychoanalytic criticism of Joyce by probing the reverberations throughout Joyce's work of the childhood elements at the beginning of *A Portrait*.

The texture of the *Portrait* provides fertile ground for two commentators. Hugh Kenner concentrates on the relationship of texture to theme, advancing his renowned essay, "The *Portrait* in Perspective," (*Kenyon Review* 10 [Summer 1948]: 361–81) into a new dimension. Bernard Benstock looks at the symbolic components as they extend the range of meaning in this short novel. With Darcy O'Brien we return to the vast world of Stephen Dedalus's nation, placing Joyce within his Irish context, looking backward at Irish origins and forward to the modern Ireland foreseen by Joyce and affected by Joyce. Each commentator has helped to prove what has long been suspected: that the approaches to Joyce's *Portrait* are nearly infinite and that each leads into the heartland of a constantly rewarding experience.

Thomas F. Staley
Bernard Benstock

Approaches to Joyce's *Portrait*

Strings in the Labyrinth: Sixty Years with Joyce's *Portrait*

THOMAS F. STALEY

1

I. Introduction and Early Comments

IN AN ESSAY which marked the fiftieth anniversary of the book publication of *A Portrait*, Father William T. Noon wrote that "ideally, every true Joycean supposes, a reader of *A Portrait* should also have already read or be in the act of reading straight through all of Joyce's works."[1] This is an idealism brought about by near necessity, for *A Portrait* is so central to our interpretation of Joyce's art that nearly every extended study undertaken, even those which concentrate on the later work, has compared some aspect of its meaning and design to his later artistic vision. To recognize the seminal position of *A Portrait* in Joyce's canon is not to make inflated claims for it, but merely to confirm the degree to which intensive scholarly study in recent years has revealed the work's centrality. Extensive treatment of the novel within this context is attributable to two additional factors: the inherent unity of Joyce's work, and the fact that the important figure of Stephen Dedalus appears in *Stephen Hero, A Portrait, Ulysses*, and, if only as a blurred or philosophical extension or embodiment, as Shem, the penman, the artist figure in *Finnegans Wake. A Portrait*, of course, rests on its own merits, apart from Joyce's

3

other work; it remains his most widely read book; in and of itself it stands as an important and significant novel of the twentieth century. Its compelling richness and its technical accomplishments have prompted a wide critical discussion; many general studies of the modern novel have devoted entire chapters or significant portions of discussion to it.[2] But as we can see so well in retrospect, the novel's achievement, in spite of the respect it received, was not immediately apparent to everyone.

Edward Garnett, a reader for the British publishing house of Duckworth and Company, upon reading the manuscript of *A Portrait* commented that it was not "a book that would make a young man's reputation."[3] In his report Garnett went on to note that *A Portrait* was "too discursive, formless, unrestrained." When it was published the early reviews belied Garnett's opinions as has most of the criticism devoted to *A Portrait* over the past sixty years. As Marvin Magalaner has observed, "from its first appearance, the *Portrait* was recognized as a work of genius."[4]

The earliest commentary on *A Portrait*, beginning with Ezra Pound's various laudatory comments as it was being published serially in *The Egoist* and upon its book publication in 1916, placed the novel in the tradition of European realism, specifically French. Virginia Woolf, who was later to have her problems with *Ulysses*, also saw it as a work which "attempts to come closer to life," and H. G. Wells noted that the "interest of the book depends upon its quintessential and unfailing reality."[5] But another distinguishing element, the book's deliberate artistry, was also recognized and commented upon—both favorably and unfavorably. Wyndham Lewis, for example, who rarely read anything he liked, felt it to possess "far too tenuous an elegance for my taste."[6] On the whole, however, initial reception of *A Portrait* was favorable. It is important to recognize the various shades of response to the novel, for a number of these colorings influenced or were followed by the later interpretations. Because the novel seemed so "real" to early readers, a persistent assumption arose that the work was solely autobiographical with many interesting technical embellishments—an assumption which has died hard. The subtleties of Joyce's art, which established an extremely complex relationship between art and life, were not quickly understood and became realized only through the careful study of a number of scholars. Several of these early responses to *A Portrait*, collected by Deming, are especially valuable in assessing the literary climate when the novel was published.

The early impact of *A Portrait* was, however, rapidly submerged by the far more startling appearance of the installments of *Ulysses* which began in *The Little Review* in March of 1918; this event immediately shifted attention from the earlier work. Critical studies of *Ulysses*, later joined by those of *Finnegans Wake*, dominated Joyce studies until the late fifties. During that period *A Portrait* came increasingly to the attention of students and scholars alike, and appeared more frequently in college syllabi. The novel (perhaps in the strictest technical sense the only work by Joyce that can without hesitation be called a novel) has over the years achieved the critical importance and central place in Joyce scholarship that it so rightfully deserves. The quality and volume of scholarship devoted to the work over the past twenty years clearly reveal its individual significance and its centrality in Joyce's canon, and this present volume is further testimony to the wide range of interest which the novel still provokes among critics.

II. Texts and Bibliographies

A Portrait first appeared in book form in 1916, issued by the American publisher, B. W. Huebsch. It was published in England in 1917 with the American sheets; English printers refused to accept the responsibility of printing the manuscript. It ran serially in *The Egoist* from 2 February 1914 through 1 September 1915, in twenty-five installments. The text, as Slocum and Cahoon point out in *A Bibliography of James*

Joyce (New Haven: Yale University Press, 1953), pp. 95–96, is substantially the same as the text of the first edition with the exception of some corrected misprints and the opening pages of chapter 3, p. 115, line 9, to p. 116, line 5, which are omitted from *The Egoist* serialization.

The Viking Press has published a "definitive text" of *A Portrait* (New York, 1964) corrected from the Dublin holograph by Chester G. Anderson with editorial assistance by Richard Ellmann. This text is based upon a comparison of Joyce's final fair-copy holograph manuscript with all the texts published in England and the United States and with lists of corrections and changes noted by Joyce, some of which were never made in any of the published versions. It is important to note, however, that Anderson has disclaimed the description of this edition as definitive in a long essay that describes in detail the textual problems in *A Portrait*, "The Text of James Joyce's *A Portrait of the Artist as a Young Man*," (*Neuphilologische Mitteilungen* 65 [1964]: 160–200). A recent essay by Hans Walter Gabler, "Zur Textgeschichte und Textkritik des *Portrait* (in *James Joyces Portrait: das Jugendbildnis im Lichte neurer deutscher Forschung,* ed. Wilhelm Füger [Munich, 1972]), and his later essay in *Studies in Bibliography* (27 [1974]: 1–54) "Towards a Critical Text of James Joyce's *A Portrait of the Artist as a Young Man*" reveal many further textual corruptions and problems. The most extended study of the textual problems of *A Portrait* thus far is offered by Gabler in the present volume. Robert M. Adams has also discussed the *Portrait* text in *James Joyce: Common Sense and Beyond* (New York: Random House, 1966), and has offered reasons for preferring the 1924 Jonathan Cape edition. Although not a definitive text as we may have been led to believe, we can generally agree that the 1964 Viking edition represents a considerably better text than all previous *Portrait* editions. Leslie Hancock has compiled a computerized concordance to this edition, *Word Index to James Joyce's "Portrait of the Artist"* (Carbondale: Southern Illinois University Press, 1967). Chester G. Anderson has also edited *A Portrait* for the Viking Critical Library series (New York, 1968), including selections of criticism, detailed explanatory notes, and a selected bibliography. Heinemann has also published an edition of *A Portrait* (London, 1964) in their Modern Novel series, with an introduction and notes by J. S. Atherton.

The most easily accessible bibliography of secondary materials on *A Portrait* is that by Maurice Beebe, Phillip F. Herring, and A. Walton Litz in the Joyce number of *Modern Fiction Studies* (15 [Spring 1969]). A later bibliography has appeared in Germany compiled by Wilhelm Füger in his *James Joyces "Portrait."* The bibliography contains 455 secondary items and offers a special section listing translations of *A Portrait*. Robert H. Deming's *A Bibliography of James Joyce Studies* (Lawrence: University of Kansas Libraries, 1964) offers an annotated bibliography of studies through 1961. Marvin Magalaner and Richard M. Kain's *Joyce: The Man, The Work, The Reputation* (New York: New York University Press, 1956) is an important source for further study and offers as well an informative account of Joyce scholarship through the mid-fifties. For an extended treatment of research in Joyce studies see my essay in the new Modern Language Association publication, *Anglo-Irish Literature: A Review of the Research*, edited by Richard J. Finneran.

III. Biography and Background

The most valuable sources other than the novel itself for the serious study of *A Portrait* are two of Joyce's earlier works. In January of 1904 Joyce wrote a narrative essay, "A Portrait of the Artist," in which he stated his early intentions as a writer—intentions which remained constant through the various stages of the novel's composition.[7] Joyce concludes the first paragraph of the essay by stating that "a portrait is not an identificative paper but rather the curve of an emotion," a point cited again and again by critics. After this essay Joyce began a long autobiographical novel in the naturalistic tradition which he called *Stephen Hero* (1944; 2nd ed., New York: New Directions, 1955; 1963). Only one-fourth of the manuscript survives, and it was published posthumously. Whatever its own merits, it is an invaluable source for the study of *A Portrait*.

Biographical and background studies are also of special value. For example, much of what we know of Joyce's structural plans for the novel is revealed through biographical sources, most notably in Richard Ellmann's definitive biography, *James Joyce* (New York: Oxford University Press, 1959). It is fair to say that Ellmann's biography advanced all aspects of Joyce scholarship as well as widened interest in him far beyond the academic community. Little need be added to the general public praise which this book has received.

Excellent background material for the study of *A Portrait* is provided by Robert Scholes and Richard Kain in *The Workshop of Daedalus: James Joyce and the Raw Materials for "A Portrait of the Artist as a Young Man"* (Evanston: Northwestern University Press, 1965) and by Kain in *Dublin in the Age of William Butler Yeats and James Joyce* (Norman: University of Oklahoma Press, 1962). *The Workshop of Daedalus* is a source book which includes many of the early manuscript materials later incorporated in various degrees into *A Portrait*, including the early Epiphanies, those short sketches in which Joyce attempted to capture in words "memorable phases" of the apprehending artist. The volume also includes biographical sketches of Joyce by his Dublin contemporaries and selections from authors who influenced Joyce and gave aesthetic dimension to the novel. Kain's earlier volume on Dublin is especially valuable in providing the social and political background against which Joyce was writing.

Two works that treat Joyce's Catholic heritage and its influence on his work are Kevin Sullivan, *Joyce Among the Jesuits* (New York: Columbia University Press, 1958) and J. Mitchell Morse, *The Sympathetic Alien* (New York: Columbia University Press, 1959). While dealing with the same general subject, these volumes are quite different. Sullivan offers extremely close analysis of factual and primary materials, such as class records, grade reports, school catalogues, contemporary sketches of various faculty members whom Joyce knew, retreat manuals, textbooks, student themes, and the like, all of which help to provide a meticulous account of Joyce's academic career. Sullivan's study was one of the important works that shifted critical opinion away from the previously loose biographical assumptions made about Joyce from reading *A Portrait* and *Stephen Hero*. His work clearly revealed the essential difference between Joyce and his character Stephen Dedalus. Morse's book is more an intellectual and historical account of Joyce's artistic confrontation with the church fathers, such as Duns Scotus, Thomas Aquinas, William of Ockham, and Ignatius Loyola. The general tone as well as certain theses (perhaps more than the content itself) of Morse's book produced some rather sharp replies. Specifically, Morse's view of the Jesuits came under attack when a section of his book was earlier published in *PMLA*. His position was modified somewhat in the book, though the overall view he presents of Jesuits through his study remains harsh and unconvincing.

IV. Introductions and Collected Criticism

A number of volumes have been designed to provide help for the student or to make basic secondary material easily accessible. Don Gifford's *Notes for Joyce: "Dubliners" and "A Portrait"* (New York: Dutton, 1967), which extensively annotates allusions and nuances of vocabulary, especially late nineteenth-century Dublin slang, is a helpful little book; James Atherton's good introduction and sound notes make the Heinemann Educational Books edition of *A Portrait* a worthwhile text; the Viking Critical Library volume edited by Chester G. Anderson includes a valuable selection of critical and background material, as well as notes, along with Anderson's corrected text. My own *Critical Study Guide to Joyce's "A*

Portrait" (Totowa, N.J.: Littlefield, Adams, 1968) and Harvey
Peter Sucksmith's *James Joyce: "A Portrait"* (London: Edward
Arnold, 1973) are designed as starting points of critical explora-
tion for the beginner. Two collections of essays, *Portraits of an
Artist* (New York: Odyssey Press, 1962), edited by William E.
Morris and Clifford A. Nault, Jr., and *Joyce's "Portrait,"
Criticisms and Critiques* (New York: Appleton-Century-
Crofts, 1962) edited by Thomas E. Connolly, provide representative selections of studies on the work, but they are now
dated. A volume in the Twentieth Century Interpretations
series (Englewood Cliffs: Prentice-Hall, 1968), edited by William Schutte, provides several later essays but is more limited
and less satisfactory than either of the other two. Wilhelm
Füger's volume, mentioned earlier, although in German, is a
helpful addition to works of this type and includes an essay on
the text by H. W. Gabler as well as Rosemarie Franke's article
on the critical reception of *A Portrait* and of its German
translation in the German-speaking countries. The valuable
bibliography which the Füger book provides was discussed
previously. Nathan Halper's recent monograph *The Early
James Joyce* (New York: Columbia University Press, 1973), in
the Essays on Modern Writers series, is a good introduction to
Joyce generally and offers a concise analysis of his early
accomplishments in the context of the later work and cautions
the reader about various interpretative pitfalls. A new "case-
book" which is both well arranged and clearly presented is
"Dubliners" and "A Portrait" (London: Macmillan, 1973),
edited by Morris Beja. It provides a good index and a selected
annotated bibliography. A collection of original essays by
various hands intended primarily for students is *Dedalus on
Crete* (Los Angeles: Immaculate Heart College, 1957; 1964).
This volume is elementary, the articles originating in a campus-
wide symposium, at Immaculate Heart College, but they
represent a wide range of topics and disciplines. A distinguishing feature of the volume is that its cover design was one of the
first by Sister M. Corita.

V. Criticism

Because *A Portrait* is considered so central to all of Joyce's work, much of the best criticism can be found in general book-length studies of Joyce's entire canon. The pioneering study of Harry Levin, *James Joyce: A Critical Introduction* (Norfolk: New Directions, 1941; rev. and augmented ed., 1960) includes a chapter on the novel which remains an excellent starting point. Levin places the novel in the European tradition of the *Bildungsroman*, or, more specifically, the *Künstlerroman*, and also establishes its centrality in Joyce's canon. Later studies have also viewed the novel in the tradition of the *Bildungsroman*. Jerome Buckley in his *Season of Youth* (Cambridge, Mass.: Harvard University Press, 1974) sees Joyce as summing up, even as he transforms, the traditions of the nineteenth-century *Bildungsroman* in *A Portrait*. Buckley concludes that the ending of the novel, "like that of many another Bildungsroman, presents problems of indecision and inconclusiveness." Breon Mitchell, in his essay in the present volume, also views the novel as emanating from this tradition.

William York Tindall's *A Reader's Guide to James Joyce* (New York: Noonday Press, 1959) exerted considerable influence on Joyce studies. His chapter on *A Portrait* stresses the symbolic, allusive, and mythic elements, aspects which have since been dealt with in great detail by other critics. Tindall's influence is not seen in any particular critical position, but rather in the close attention paid to the text and in the careful scrutiny given to symbolic and thematic overtones throughout the novel.

An important but not well-known essay which examines the symbolic structure of *A Portrait* is Kenneth Burke's "Fact, Inference, and Proof in the Analysis of Literary Symbolism" (in Burke's *Terms for Order*, ed. Stanley E. Hyman and Barbara Karmiller [Bloomington: Indiana University Press, 1964], pp. 145-72). He treats the individual words of *A Portrait* as the basic "facts," and "the essay asks how to operate with these 'facts,' how to use them as a means of keeping one's inferences under control, yet how to go beyond them, for purposes of inference when seeking to characterize the motives and 'salient' traits of the work, in its nature as a total symbolic structure." Primarily theoretical, Burke's essay uses *A Portrait* as a test case for establishing a modus operandi for the analysis of literary symbolism, but in so doing it illuminates the symbolic network of the novel.

The major topics of critical interest have been the character of Stephen Dedalus, especially his relationship to the author; Stephen's aesthetic theories as they are propounded in the novel and their comparison with Joyce's own art; structure; problems of irony and point of view; symbolic elements; mythic framework; psychological elements; the novel's influence; and the traditions from which the novel emerged. These categories overlap, of course, but they represent workable divisions in organizing and describing the criticism devoted to the novel. Besides these specific areas of focus a number of broad studies have concentrated on the early development of Joyce's fiction, discussing *A Portrait* in relationship to *Dubliners* and more closely to *Stephen Hero*.

By implication nearly all the studies of *A Portrait* insist on or, at the very least, admit to the novel's centrality in Joyce's art. Robert Ryf's study, *A New Approach to Joyce* (Berkeley and Los Angeles: University of California Press, 1962), is the most insistent on this point. He sees the novel as presenting, in embryonic form, the themes and techniques which Joyce expanded upon in all his later work. His theory that Joyce uses Stephen's aesthetic theories in his later work has, of course, been largely and correctly discounted. However, Ryf's observations on certain cinematographic techniques employed in *A Portrait* are revealing. His study rightly attempted to correct or, better, redirect certain critical assumptions which had minimized the work, but his claims are far too strong and ignore the growing aesthetic subtleties and larger dimensions of the later work. Joyce's development required much sifting and sorting, much changing after false starts; there was more than mere sophisticated assimilation and a clean line of evolving aesthetic unity, a point which many later critics have established clearly.

The earlier work of Marvin Magalaner and Joseph Prescott is far more valuable on this point, especially in accounting for the technical development that led to *A Portrait*. Magalaner's *Time of Apprenticeship* (New York: Abelard Schuman, 1959) devotes more attention to *Dubliners,* but is a valuable study of Joyce's growing craftsmanship, of the painstaking care he took to achieve desired effects, and of how he assimilated influences from his reading and allowed them to shape his imagination. The way in which Joyce traversed the distance between art and reality through form and technique is Magalaner's central concern, and he produces abundant evidence from the early drafts of *Dubliners* and *Stephen Hero* to display Joyce's craftsmanship and growing accomplishments. Magalaner and Joseph Prescott, in *Exploring James Joyce* (Carbondale: Southern Illinois Press, 1964, make important observations on the nature of the relationship between *Stephen Hero* and *A Portrait,* especially on the form and craft which others have commented upon, but concentrate their discussions more narrowly on the aesthetic concepts and their refinements.

One persistent problem is the difficulty in accounting for the success of *Dubliners* and Joyce's growing recognition of the artistic failure of *Stephen Hero,* on which he worked simultaneously, a question which involves a number of formal narrative considerations: point of view, structure, and style. A recent study by Homer Obed Brown, *James Joyce's Early Fiction* (Cleveland: Case Western Reserve University Press, 1972), subtitled *The Biography of a Form,* treats this problem in detail. Brown argues that changes in the formal development of the early work make possible the later evolutions in style; Joyce's changing concept of the nature of reality accounts for the shift from the early realism of the first stories of *Dubliners* and *Stephen Hero* to "The Dead" and *A Portrait.* "The Dead" signals a crucial stage of Joyce's development,

Brown argues, for with it he was able for the first time to harmonize disparate visions of reality to fuse the cold and distant observer of a dead world and the symbolist poet who sought spiritual transcendence. The fixed outside world which the Stephen of *Stephen Hero* sees shifts in "The Dead" to the union we see with Gabriel Conroy, where the outer world dissolves as he realizes his oneness with it; in this integration the end of "The Dead" looks forward to the world of *A Portrait* with its organic unity "held together by a narrator who represents both sides of this dualism." As Hugh Staples has noted, many Joyce critics would agree with Brown's points, but most have previously explored this critical question from a biographical point of view rather than through the careful and logical analysis Brown has brought to bear.

The critical work of Hugh Kenner has raised some of the most cogent and, at the same time, debatable issues surrounding the interpretation of *A Portrait*. Kenner's study, *Dublin's Joyce* (London: Chatto and Windus, 1955; Bloomington: Indiana University Press, 1956) reflects comprehensive judgments related to Joyce's entire canon, and those sections dealing with *A Portrait* are extremely important to the development of criticism of the novel. The first chapter of his book is entitled "Double Writing," and here Kenner discusses Joyce's use of parody and its thematic effects. From this basis he establishes a thesis that the "controlling ideas" in Joyce's work are developed from his analogical vision which emanates from an essentially ironic conception; thus the fictional world of *Ulysses* (this also applies to *Dubliners* and *A Portrait*), for example, suffused with Joyce's irony, does not directly reveal the author's spiritual or, perhaps a better word, moral values. Rather, those values lie outside the work, drawn by the ironic implications in the work itself. Kenner's assessment of Stephen Dedalus offers a central focus of discussion. Kenner writes: "Joyce's irony goes deep indeed. . . . Stephen . . . is aware that he is Hamlet, but his awareness is put to the wrong uses. It provides him with no insight" (p. 209). Kenner's point throughout his argument is that spiritual values lie not in the world of Joyce's fiction but outside of it. Joyce has accomplished by the quality of his irony an abstraction that implies a clear moral connective. This moral vision grows out of the ironic treatment of his creation. The detached artist reveals the nature of his antipathy through technique, but a technique which forces interpretation of the world of his work. Kenner's view of Joyce's work leads him to an adverse position regarding Stephen, and he has thus been labeled the founder of the "Stephen haters."

The character of Stephen Dedalus is an interesting and provocative topic, but critical study is complicated by several issues which have created constant controversy and debate in Joyce studies, namely, Joyce's relationship to and attitude toward his young hero and the attendant questions of aesthetic distance, point of view, and the proximity of Stephen's aesthetics to Joyce's. Critical arguments have tied interpretations of Stephen to the nature of Joyce's irony. Besides Kenner, critics such as Tindall, Kenneth Burke, John V. Kelleher, and Denis Donoghue, among others, have considered this subject and reached varying conclusions. Chester G. Anderson has summarized the controversy in his critical edition of *A Portrait* (see pp. 446–54), and he includes essays by Wayne Booth and Robert Scholes which present summary views and offer representative opposing conclusions. The selection by Booth appeared originally in his influential *The Rhetoric of Fiction* (Chicago: University of Chicago Press, 1961). Booth concludes that the critical uncertainty surrounding Joyce's attitude toward Stephen's vocation, his aesthetics, and his villanelle reflects Joyce's own uncertainty; the text itself combines irony and admiration in unpredictable mixtures (p. 334). Scholes offers ample evidence that the text can yield a predictable mixture. Using both external and internal evidence, he concentrates on an analysis of the villanelle, refutes Booth's position, and also challenges the early position of Kenner (in *Dublin's Joyce*) which ascribes to Joyce an ironic vision of Stephen.

Another thorough and convincing challenge to Booth's arguments is offered by James Naremore in "Style as Meaning in *A Portrait of the Artist*" (*James Joyce Quarterly* 4 [Summer 1967]: 331–42). The topic is still treated frequently. An article by Thomas W. Grayson in the same issue of the *James Joyce Quarterly*, "James Joyce and Stephen Dadalus: The Theory of Aesthetics," suggests that the novel itself "serves to exorcize Stephen from the personality of Joyce, thereby permitting the emergence of the artist" (p. 311). One is tempted to suggest that the entire argument of Stephen's relationship to Joyce, the problem of point of view, and the ironic dimension of Joyce's art has gone through a Viconian cycle, that is, back to where it began but with a difference. In light of Grayson's, Scholes's, and Booth's arguments, one should recall Mark Schorer's seminal essay "Technique and Discovery" (*The Hudson Review* 1 [Spring 1948]: 67–87) to which Booth objects so strongly. Schorer described the aesthetic achievement of *A Portrait* in terms of technique. He argued that *A Portrait* "analyzes its material rigorously, and it defines the value and the quality of its experience not by appended comment or moral epithet, but by the texture of the style." Joyce's success, Schorer points out, was achieved by refining himself out of existence (a point Booth cannot accept, but which Grayson from a different perspective argues for fully); that is, by refusing any overt commentary on the content of the novel. It is by the texture of the style that Joyce defines the value and quality of experience in the novel.

Essays dealing with Stephen's aesthetic theory are abundant. A selection of the most helpful, although several are dated, are those by A. D. Hope, Irene Hendry Chayes, Geddee MacGregor, Haskell M. Block, Marshall McLuhan, Thomas E. Connolly, Maurice Beebe, and J. Mitchell Morse which appear in a special section of Connolly's *Joyce's "Portrait"* referred to above. William T. Noon's *Joyce and Aquinas* (New Haven: Yale University Press, 1957) is the most valuable source study on this subject.

The fullest treatment of subjects related to Stephen Dedalus is in Edmund L. Epstein's extensive study, *The Ordeal of Stephen Dedalus* (Carbondale: Southern Illinois University Press, 1971). Especially valuable in this study is the description of the way themes introduced in *A Portrait* are developed, refined, and expanded more fully in *Ulysses* and *Finnegans Wake*. Epstein's close and careful reading of the novel offers the best account thus far of the nature and source of Joyce's irony in the first section of chapter 4 of *A Portrait*, but this delineation is not sustained for the later portions of the novel. Epstein also offers an extended analysis of Stephen's lecture on aesthetics in chapter 5 in light of the King David figure, the mature artist in the *Wake*. He sketches the historical meaning of David as it may have come to Joyce, how Joyce embodied this historical and mythical figure in Stephen, especially its messianic aspects, and how he contributed facets of his own concept of King David as visionary. Epstein reads the ending as essentially optimistic—Stephen is confirmed in his vocation as an artist and is reaching for maturity as a man. He is careful to point out, however, the clear limitations in Stephen's character at the conclusion of the novel, seeing Stephen as being too confident of his own powers and not aware of how confused some of his ideas are.

Epstein's study concentrates, of course, on many psychological aspects of Stephen's nature, but it is not a formal psychoanalytical study such as Edward Brandabur's *A Scrupulous Meaness* (Urbana: University of Illinois Press, 1971), which focuses mainly on *Dubliners* and *Exiles*, but also offers commentary on *A Portrait*. Mark Shechner's *Joyce in Nighttown* (Berkeley and Los Angeles: University of California Press, 1974) is the most extended psychoanalytic study of Joyce's work to date. Chester G. Anderson's essay in this volume also concentrates on the psychological aspects of *A Portrait*.

Contrary to Booth's view, ambiguity remains a central aspect of life as well as of art, and Joyce's character, like Hamlet, reflects this. Kenner's early view that Stephen's weak-

nesses were not unintentional but rather poignant examples of
Joyce's irony enriched by a moral vision of the world is not
easily tenable today, and Kenner's own view has been modified (see *Windsor Review* 1 [Spring 1965]: 1–15 and his essay in
the present volume). Later criticism has moved away from the
simple dichotomies and thus closer to the complex reality that
Joyce attempts to reveal in *A Portrait*. Sympathy and irony are
somehow joined and it is toward the discernment of this
balance that the more recent distinguished criticism has
turned. S. L. Goldberg's *The Classical Temper: A Study of
James Joyce's "Ulysses"* (London: Chatto and Windus, 1961),
although it deals primarily with *Ulysses*, examines closely and
well Joyce's engagement in and distance from his characters,
and L. A. Murillo's *The Cyclical Night: Irony in James Joyce
and Jorge Luis Borges* (Cambridge: Harvard University Press,
1968) deals fully with the ironic dimension in Joyce's work and
its major function in his art. Further examination of the ironic
dimension can be found in F. Parvin Sharpless's excellent
essay, "Irony in Joyce's *Portrait*: The Stasis of Pity" (*James
Joyce Quarterly* 4 [Summer 1967]: 320–30).

Closely associated with discussions related to Stephen's
aesthetic theory is the critical debate over the term "epiphany"
and its meaning in Joyce's fiction. The term occurs in the mind
of Stephen Daedalus (as the name is spelled in *Stephen Hero*):
"By an epiphany he meant a sudden spiritual manifestation,
whether in the vulgarity of speech or of gesture or in a
memorable phase of the mind itself. He believed it was for the
man of letters to record these epiphanies with extreme care,
seeing that they themselves are the most delicate and evanes-
cent of moments."[8] William Noon, writing of the prominence
that the term has been given by critics, has ironically referred
to it as the "quasirubrical imperative of Joycean aesthetics."[9]
Early importance was given to the epiphany as a literary
technique by Irene Hendry in her essay "Joyce Epiphanies" (in
James Joyce: Two Decades of Criticism, ed. Seon Givens
[1948; New York: Vanguard Press, 1963]), in which she pointed

out that the theory of epiphany was central to Stephen Dedalus's entire literary theory and was applied far more extensively by Joyce himself in his work. Tindall, in *Reader's Guide to James Joyce* (New York: The Noonday Press, Inc., 1959), extended this analysis to include a symbolic function: "Plainly Stephen's epiphany or radiance, a shining out or showing forth, is what we call symbolism and his radiant object a symbol" (pp. 10-11). Dorothy Van Ghent in *The English Novel: Form and Function* (1953; New York: Rhinehart, 1959) took this position further by showing the epiphany's central relevance to the dialectical movements and structural elements in *A Portrait*. Florence L. Walzl in "The Liturgy of the Epiphany Season and the Epiphanies of Joyce" (*PMLA* 80 [September 1965]: 436-50) insists on an even greater centrality of the epiphany in Joyce's work. She and Robert Scholes engaged in a debate on the matter in a later issue of *PMLA* (82 [March 1967]: 152-54). Scholes had earlier debunked the claims of the epiphany's importance in his essay "Joyce and the Epiphany: The Key to the Labyrinth?" (*Sewanee Review* 72 [January-March 1964]: 65-77). For a particular example of the disagreement on Joyce's aesthetic theory and his use of source material, see the controversy between Scholes and John T. Shawcross stemming from Scholes's "James Joyce, Irish Poet," (*James Joyce Quarterly* 2 [Summer 1965]: 255-70) and Shawcross's "'Tilly' and Dante," (*James Joyce Quarterly* 7 [Fall 1969]: 61-64). See also Scholes's letter to the editor and Shawcross's reply (7 [Spring, 1970]: 281-83) and Scholes's later reply (8 [Winter 1971]: 192-93). Although this controversy is specifically related to Joyce's poetry, the opposing arguments are related to the aesthetic concerns of *A Portrait*. Morris Beja's *Epiphany in the Modern Novel* (Seattle: University of Washington Press, 1971) treats the conception and function of the epiphany in a number of modern writers, and his discussion of Joyce's use of the epiphany is a valuable analysis.

During his recovery from rheumatic fever Joyce decided to rewrite *Stephen Hero* completely, and he told his brother

Stanislaus in September of 1907 that he would write the book in five chapters. As Ellmann points out, it was at this time that Joyce discovered a "principle of structure." The drastic changes in organizational principle which Joyce employed in the version that became *A Portrait* have been the subject of much critical speculation, and structural studies of the novel abound. The early works of Kenner and Dorothy Van Ghent have been the most influential and still stand as essential reference points on the subject.

All of the studies agree that the central structural principle in the novel is informed and even controlled by Stephen's own spiritual growth and development. Thomas F. Van Laan, "The Meditative Structure of Joyce's *Portrait*" (*James Joyce Quarterly* 1 [Spring 1964]: 3–13), Robert J. Andreach, *Studies in Structure* (New York: Fordham University Press, 1964), and Sidney Feshbach, "A Slow and Dark Birth: A Study of the Organization of *A Portrait of the Artist as a Young Man*" (*James Joyce Quarterly* 4 [Summer 1967]: 289–300) all recognize Stephen's development as Joyce's central ordering device, but each points to external ordering principles which inform the structure. Van Laan notes the correspondence between the novel and Ignatius Loyola's *Spiritual Exercises* and Joyce's employment of his pattern of meditation and spiritual exercise. This offered a system of introspective focus in a design which integrated miscellaneous units into a meaningful whole. Andreach contends that the structure of *A Portrait* is built upon the stages of the fivefold Christian division of the spiritual life although Joyce reverses the order of the five stages and inverts the individual ones. Even with Joyce's obvious delight in reversing religious symbols, Andreach's pattern seems too neat and forces him to conclude his judgment of Stephen on a far too simplistic basis. Feshbach notes clearly in his intriguing essay that he does not account for what appears to him to be the implicit irony in the Joyce-Stephen relationship, but he sees the organization of the novel emanating from the traditional progression of the character called "the ladder of perfection" and that Joyce has made Stephen's soul the soul and form of the novel.

Three additional structural studies with different approaches are Evert Sprinchorn's "A Portrait of the Artist as Achilles," in *Approaches to the Twentieth-Century Novel,* ed. John Unterecker (New York: Crowell, 1965), pp. 9–50; Lee T. Lemon's *"A Portrait of the Artist as a Young Man:* Motif as Motivation and Structure" (*Modern Fiction Studies* 12 [Winter 1967–68]: 441–52); and Grant H. Redford's "The Role of Structure in Joyce's *Portrait"* (*Modern Fiction Studies* 4 [Spring, 1958]: 21–30). Redford's essay is the most similar to the three above; he suggests that the book's themes of search and rebellion are made meaningful through structure, and that "structure is the embodiment of an artistic proposition proclaimed by the central character himself as being basic to a work of art." Lemon bases his methodology on the work of the Russian Formalists, and thus argues that it is Joyce's adroit handling of the various motifs which reveals Stephen's development and subsequently unifies the novel. Sprinchorn, however, attempts to account for what he sees as Joyce's loss of sympathy for Stephen in chapter 5. His study offers an elaborate if somewhat pretentious explication of the chapter and further attempts to show its integration with the other four chapters and its consistency with the overall structural and symbolic pattern of the novel as a whole. Bernard Benstock's essay in this volume is the most extensive treatment thus far of the way in which the various levels of symbolism accent and extend meaning to develop the entire symbolic structure of the novel.

These structural studies afford an excellent example of the general evolution of criticism of *A Portrait,* in their move to a more qualified, but nevertheless more acute understanding of the relationship of character to author, technique to form, and design to content.

The novel's epigraph from Ovid, the obviousness of the hero's surname, and the frequent mythological allusions in the text itself make abundantly clear the mythic framework of *A*

Portrait. This aspect of the work has been discussed by a number of critics. The most extensive treatment has been Diane Fortuna's long essay entitled "The Labyrinth as Controlling Image in Joyce's *A Portrait*" (*Bulletin of the New York Public Library* 76 [1972]: 120–80), in which she traces with careful attention to archeological detail and mythic artifact the Daedalus myth together with its ritualistic associations. David Hayman's "Daedalian Imagery in *A Portrait*" (in *Hereditas: Seven Essays on the Modern Experience of the Classical*, ed. Frederick Will [Austin: University of Texas Press, 1964], pp. 31–54) is also a thorough study of the mythic framework of the novel which suggests the way myth gives dimension and force to Stephen's character. Perhaps it is a testament to the novel's originality that relatively little scholarship has been devoted to the literary influences on *A Portrait*. As any number of critics have pointed out, when Joyce abandoned the largely naturalistic framework of *Stephen Hero* for more formally controlled symbolic realism of *A Portrait*, he seemed to have left many of his literary debts behind. There have been, however, a number of comparative studies which have treated the similarities between *A Portrait* and other works such as Hayman's "*A Portrait* . . . and *L'Education sentimentale:* The Structural Affinities" (*Orbis Litterarum* 19 [1964]: 161–75); Dusoir Ilse Lind, "*The Way of all Flesh* and *A Portrait* . . . : A Comparison" (*Victorian Newsletter*, no. 9 [Spring 1956]: 7–10); and Joyce W. Warren, "Faulkner's Portrait of the Artist" (*Mississippi Quarterly* 19 [Summer 1966]: 121–31). Far more scholarship has been devoted to the influence of *A Portrait* on later works than to the influence of other works on Joyce in the writing of the novel.

Many of the essays which have dealt with Stephen's aesthetic discussions have pointed out the philosophical sources in the formulation of his theories. For example, Margaret Church's essay in this volume argues for the early use of Vico by Joyce. Source studies on *A Portrait* have been most revealing on the subject of the retreat sermon in chapter 3. Both James R.

Thrane in "Joyce's Sermon on Hell: Its Source and Its Background" (*Modern Philosophy* 57 [February 1960]: 172–98) and Elizabeth Boyd in "Joyce's Hell-Fire Sermons" (*Modern Language Notes* 75 [November 1960]: 561–71) have shown conclusively that the sermons which Father Arnall gives were borrowed by Joyce from Giovanni Pietro Pinamonti's *L'Inferno aperto al cristiano*, or *Hell Opened to Christians* in its nineteenth-century English translation. James Doherty has dealt further with this source in "Joyce and *Hell Opened to Christians*" (*Modern Philosophy* 61 [November 1963]: 110–19), and Eugene August has analyzed Arnall's use of scripture in his sermons in "Father Arnall's Use of Scripture in *A Portrait*" (*James Joyce Quarterly* [Summer 1967]: 275–79).

In the history of literary criticism sixty years is a very short time, but it gives enough perspective to estimate the permanent place that *A Portrait* has established in modern fiction. While neither so monumental as *Ulysses* nor so spectacular as *Finnegans Wake*, its achievement lies in the brilliant ordering and fulfillment of its art, the universal depth of its themes, and, as so much of the criticism devoted to it attests, the full realization of its purpose. Its artistic achievement is confirmed in the creation of the character of the artist-hero who possesses in various degrees the strengths and weaknesses of modern man which we are able to see and understand, to mock or praise. But in either mood he touches us; and if he did not, however perfect the novel's symmetry, *A Portrait* would be far less an achievement.

NOTES

1. Thomas F. Staley, ed. *James Joyce Today* (Bloomington: Indiana University Press, 1966), p. 59.

2. A sampling of such books which contain a chapter or extensive discussion devoted to *A Portrait*: William R. Mueller, *The Prophetic Voice* (1951); Margaret Church, *Time and Reality* (1962); John Edward Hardy, *Man in the*

Modern Novel (1964); Harold Kaplan, *The Passive Voice* (1966); Frederick J. Hoffman, *The Imagination's New Beginning* (1967); Louis D. Rubin, Jr., *The Teller in the Tale* (1967); Morris Beja, *Epiphany in the Modern Novel* (1971).

3. Robert H. Deming, ed. *James Joyce: The Critical Heritage*, vol. 1, 1902–27 (London: Routledge & Kegan Paul, 1970), p. 81.

4. Marvin Magalaner and Richard M. Kain, *Joyce: the Man, the Work, the Reputation* (New York: New York University Press, 1956), p. 102.

5. Deming, pp. 125, 87.

6. Deming, p. 120.

7. The most accessible publication of this essay is in the Viking Critical Library edition of Joyce's *A Portrait of the Artist as a Young Man*, ed. Chester G. Anderson (New York: Viking Press, 1968), pp. 257–66.

8. James Joyce, *Stephen Hero* (Norfolk, Connecticut: New Directions, 1963), p. 211.

9. Staley, ed., *Joyce Today*, p. 64.

The Seven Lost Years of
A Portrait of the Artist
as a Young Man

HANS WALTER GABLER   **2**

JAMES JOYCE WROTE and rewrote the novel that was to become *A Portrait of the Artist as a Young Man* in several phases between 1904 and 1914. In January 1904, he submitted the narrative essay "A Portrait of the Artist" to the Dublin literary magazine *Dana*.[1] Upon its rejection, he began to write *Stephen Hero*, planned to the length of sixty-three chapters. He was actively engaged upon it until the summer of 1905, when it broke off with chapter XXV.[2] It remained a fragment. In September 1907, when the plans for revision of the fragment had sufficiently matured in his mind, he began to write *A Portrait of the Artist as a Young Man* in five chapters. This reached the state of an intermediary manuscript during 1907 to 1911.[3] In 1913–14, the novel was completed. It is represented in its final state by the fair-copy manuscript in Joyce's hand now in the possession of the National Library of Ireland in Dublin. Moreover, complete textual versions or fragments of text from each of the major stages of the novel's ten-year progression are still extant and identifiable. But it is also true that by far the majority of the materials, the plans, sketches, or intermediate drafts which as a body would have borne witness of its emergence, must be assumed to be lost. Nevertheless, close survey and careful scrutiny of those which survive make it   *25* possible to indicate some of the essential aspects of the work's genesis. Paradoxically, it is the seven years from 1907 to 1914, during which the novel matured and ultimately reached its final form, that have remained most obscure in its textual history. It is on the novel's growth and Joyce's work during these years that the present essay attempts to shed light.

I

In the only surviving textually complete document of *A Portrait*, the Dublin holograph manuscript, several strata of composition may be distinguished.[4] Each manuscript leaf carries one column of text on its recto. There are 139 (−1)[5] handwritten pages of text in chapter I, 94 in chapter II, 129 in chapter III, 61 in chapter IV, and 175 in chapter V. Together with the separate leaves for title and motto, the manuscript comprises exactly 600 (−1) leaves inscribed in Joyce's hand. Another 8 leaves, 4 completely blank and 4 carrying the large roman numerals II to V in red crayon to number the chapters, serve as protective endpapers for the chapters and as chapter dividers. A total of 608 (−1) leaves therefore make up the manuscript, which since its accession to the National Library of Ireland in 1951 has been bound (and, alas, rather thoughtlessly bound, destroying evidence of the manuscript's original makeup) into two volumes: MS 920 contains chapters I and II, MS 921 chapters III–V. In their division, the volumes seem to correspond to two bundles (their labels being fragmentarily retained) in which the manuscript was given to the library by Harriet Weaver. The penciled numbering of the pages in chapters I–III, and perhaps part of that in chapter V, may be hers. Page totals for each chapter have been jotted in ink on the back of the protective endpapers of chapters II, III, and IV They give the page count in a manner also found in some of Joyce's later manuscripts, and may be his. Chapter IV has a page numbering which differs from that of the others, in large arabic numerals, mostly in ink, on the verso of the leaves. This numbering runs on without interruption through the first 13 leaves of chapter V. The sequence begins with "239" for the first text page in chapter IV, and, not counting the two leaves that divide the chapters (which are thus shown to be later insertions), it runs to "313" for fol. 13 of chapter V.[6]

For a stratification of the manuscript by which to distinguish the order of inscription, and at times of the composition of the text, this page count is the decisive bibliographical clue. It links all of chapter IV with the beginning of chapter V (for which the roman numeral V in ink over the text on leaf "301" clearly sets the opening) as an inscriptional continuum. It also indicates that, inscriptionally, pages "239" to "313" are the earliest section of the Dublin manuscript. The absence of a corresponding page numbering for chapters I–III suggests that these chapters were inscribed later, an assumption strengthened by the fact that not 238, but 362 manuscript text pages precede chapter IV in the Dublin holograph. Accordingly, it is easy to see that the continuous page count, a vestige apparently of a through numbering of the pages of some other manuscript, was abandoned as of no further consequence for the remainder of chapter V. Inscriptionally, therefore, this would also seem to be later than pages "239" to "313," though why the pattern breaks where it does is not readily discernible. Nor, of course, is it a foregone conclusion that chapters I–III in their entirety preceded all of the main body of chapter V in a relative chronology of inscription of the manuscript.

The page numbers "239" to "313" themselves, however—of this there can be little doubt—are Joyce's own. They accord fully with his numbering habits in the *Stephen Hero* manuscript.[7] To this the numbered pages in the Dublin holograph of *A Portrait* cannot have belonged, since they follow so clearly from the five-chapter plan of *A Portrait*. They were consequently written at some time after September 1907. Perhaps their text was not conceived before February 1909, though this depends on what precisely Ettore Schmitz (Italo Svevo) read of *A Portrait* in January–February 1909.[8] The actual pages

"239" to "313" belonged, I suggest, to the *Portrait* manuscript that narrowly escaped destruction in 1911, the "original" original which when rescued was sorted out and pieced together in preparation of the final manuscript,[9] and in which there were "pages . . . I could never have re-written" (*JJ* 325). Contrary to the view that the fourth and fifth chapters of the novel were not brought into shape until 1914, after Ezra Pound's enquiry about publishable material had rekindled Joyce's desire to complete the novel—supposedly while the early chapters were already getting into print[10]—the evidence of the Dublin manuscript indicates that, in 1911, when *A Portrait* was almost annihilated, Joyce had completed chapter IV and begun chapter V. Indeed, chapter IV, the only section of the Dublin holograph which has come down inscriptionally intact from the earlier manuscript, appears also to be the only part of the final text which represents without significant and extensive changes the novel in the textual state of 1911.

As applied to the pre-1911 leaves actually preserved in the Dublin manuscript, Joyce's posthumously reported remark about pages he could never have rewritten would seem to mean merely pages which he saw no further need to reinscribe. It is surely significant that chapter IV in the Dublin manuscript is the only chapter which to any marked extent shows traces of Joyce's revising hand. Consider the final heightening of the paragraph, steeped in the symbolism of Pentecost, which begins: "On each of the seven days of the week he further prayed that one of the seven gifts of the Holy Ghost might descend upon his soul" (148–49).[11] In the manuscript, it originally ended: "to whom, as God, the priests offered up mass once a year, robed in scarlet." This is revised to read: "robed in *the* scarlet *of the tongues of fire.*" Or consider how much denser and richer, how much more both threatening and alluring, becomes the passage which in the manuscript originally read:

No king or emperor on this earth has the power of the priest of God. No angel or archangel in heaven, no saint, not even the Blessed Virgin herself has the power of a priest of God, the power to bind and to loose from sin, the power, the authority, to make the great God of Heaven come down upon the altar and take the form of bread and wine. What an awful power, Stephen!—

By revisional amplification, this becomes:

No king or emperor on this earth has the power of the priest of God. No angel or archangel in heaven, no saint, not even the Blessed Virgin herself has the power of a priest of God, *the power of the keys*, the power to bind and to loose from sin, *the power of exorcism, the power to cast out from the creatures of God the evil spirits that have power over them*, the power, the authority, to make the great God of Heaven come down upon the altar and take the form of bread and wine. What an awful power, Stephen!—(158)

Correspondingly, Stephen, in his imaginings of priesthood, as originally worded

longed for the office of deacon at high mass, to stand aloof from the altar, forgotten by the people, his shoulders covered with a humeral veil, and then, when the sacrifice had been accomplished, to stand once again in a dalmatic of cloth of gold on the step below the celebrant. . . . If ever he had 'seen himself celebrant it was as in the pictures of the mass in his child's massbook, in a church without worshippers, at a bare altar . . . and it was partly the absence of a rite which had always constrained him to inaction.

But in the text as interlinearly revised in the manuscript, his longings and reflections are enriched and particularized in much detail. Also, as in the preceding passage, the revision results in greater syntactical as well as rhythmical complexity:

He longed for the *minor sacred* offices, *to be vested with the tunicle* of *sub*-deacon at high mass . . . his shoulders covered with a humeral veil, *holding the paten within its folds,* ~~and then,~~ *or,* when the sacrifice had been accomplished, to stand *as deacon* ~~once again~~ in a dalmatic of cloth of gold on the step below the celebrant. . . . If ever he had seen himself celebrant it was . . . in a church without worshippers, *save for the angel of the sacrifice,* at a bare altar . . . and it was partly the absence of an *appointed* rite which had always constrained him to inaction. (158–59)

Anyone familiar with Joyce's revisional habits in shaping *Ulysses* and *Finnegans Wake* will here recognize in rudimentary form the same patterns and procedures which reach such complexity in the processes of composition of the later works. Conversely, although the examples quoted are the only passages in which compositional revision clearly manifests itself in *A Portrait*, these examples, together with our general knowledge of Joyce's later working habits, make us more keenly aware of the likelihood of revision, perhaps even extensive revision, in the course of the emergence of *A Portrait* at lost stages of its textual development.

Pages "239" to "313," salvaged intact from the manuscript of 1911, will not have been the only pages which Joyce "could never have re-written." Such others as there were he apparently recopied, taking advantage in the process of the opportunity for revising and expanding his earlier text. Positive evidence derives from Ettore Schmitz's letter of 8 February 1909, that, for example, certain "sermons" as part of the third chapter then existed. Consequently, they were also in the manuscript of 1911. In one form or another they would textually seem to go back even to February or March of 1904. The notes for *Stephen Hero* at the end of the "Portrait" copybook testify to the plan for the inclusion in chapter XI (?) of "six lectures," in a sequence outlined as:

1) Introductory, evening before		1st Day
2) Death	⎫	
3) Judgement	⎭	2nd Day
4) Hell	⎫	
5) Hell	⎭	3rd Day
6) Heaven morning after		4th Day[12]

In *A Portrait*, by contrast, we have one introduction and three sermons on four consecutive evenings. Of the three sermons, the first, on death and judgment, is not given verbatim, but as reported speech, filtered through Stephen's mind. Only the second and third sermons are fully developed as insets of pulpit oratory. Hell is the subject of both of them; and despite the preacher's promise in his introduction to put before the boys "some thoughts concerning the four last things . . . death, judgment, hell and heaven" (109–10), there is in *A Portrait* no sermon on heaven. In the last part of chapter III, instead, heavenly mercy comes as an immediate and intensely personal experience to Stephen on the morning after the fourth day of the retreat: "The ciborium had come to him" (146). Revision, then, is indicated, not merely between the two extreme stages of, on the one hand, the outline plan for chapter XI of *Stephen Hero* and its unknown realization, and, on the other, the final version of chapter III of *A Portrait*, but also as a developmental process in the course of the emergence since 1907–08 of the third chapter of the five-chapter *Portrait*.

About the emergence not only of chapter III, but of the entire pre-1911 portion of the novel, further inferences are possible from Ettore Schmitz's letter. The only third-chapter matter it expressly mentions are "the sermons." It gives no indication of the chapter's conclusion. By its initial reference to a fragmentary ending of the text it is even open, I suggest, to the interpretation that the third chapter was unresolved in the sections of the work in progress that Joyce allowed his pupil and critic to read. Schmitz feels unable to submit a rounded opinion about the work partly for want of competence, but partly also because the text breaks off at a crucial moment: "when you stopped writing you were facing a very important development of Stephen's mind." At the same time, his letter appears to indicate that, in a discontinuous manner of composition, Joyce had by late 1908 or early 1909 already proceeded beyond chapter III in his rewriting of *Stephen Hero* into the five-chapter *Portrait*. For Schmitz continues: "I have already a sample of what may be a change of this mind described by your pen. Indeed the development of Stephen's childish religion to a strong religion felt strongly and vigorously or better lived in all its particulars (after his sin) was so important that no other can be more so."[13]

This is an obscure comment if referring to chapter III alone, and to nothing of *A Portrait* beyond it. It makes good sense, however, if considered as a reflection on the first section of chapter IV which precisely describes "a strong religion felt strongly and vigorously or better lived in all its particulars (after [Stephen's] sin)." Without a knowledge of the subsequent offer and rejection of priesthood and the culminating scene on the beach, Schmitz would not have grasped the ironic implications of the fourth chapter's opening section; nor would he have realized that Stephen's way lay toward art, not religion. But he saw accurately enough that Joyce was "facing a very important development of Stephen's mind." The reference to having a sample of Stephen's altered mind described by Joyce's pen suggests that Schmitz had read a textual fragment drafted for the continuation of the novel beyond the point where Joyce had "stopped writing." Together with the subsequent explicit mention of the sermons, it suggests that, as Schmitz read it, the third chapter ended with the sermons and the dejection and contrition they caused in Stephen, and that Joyce in 1909 had not yet formulated the last transitional section which by way of Stephen's confession, absolution, and communion links it to the opening of chapter IV.

With the hindsight of our reading experience, the thematic and narrative logic of that transition seems so clear that it is hard to conceive of any great problems encountered in the writing of it. However, several observations converge which may suggest that Joyce did not achieve it easily.[14] The most important of these derives physically from the Dublin manuscript itself and indicates that the end of chapter III as we now have it is a very late piece of writing. On fol. 100 of chapter III in the Dublin holograph, the communal prayer which concludes the last of the hell sermons ends, with Joyce's characteristic three asterisks marking the sectional subdivision, halfway down the page. Below, the final section opens with a clear paleographic break: the pen, the ink, the slope of the hand, and the typical letter formations which remain identical from here on for the last 29 leaves of the chapter are all distinctly different from the style of inscription of the preceding 100 pages, and particularly of that of the two hell sermons on fols. 40–100. If, as was argued earlier, the main body of chapter III was itself retranscribed after 1911 (and probably revised, and perhaps augmented, in the process), the evidence now shows that the final section was inscribed, and therefore added to the main transcription, at yet a later stage.

The completion of chapter III by the adding on of its final 29 manuscript pages cannot be positively dated. But it is perhaps worth pointing out once more[15] the late dispatch of the chapter III typescript to Ezra Pound in London, for *The Egoist*. It is at least possible that the end of this chapter was not entered in the fair-copy manuscript until the chapter was to be handed to the typist. If this was so, it would not necessarily mean that Joyce did not have a plan, notes, or a draft to fall back upon; that is, it would not entail the belief that the ending of chapter III held intrinsic difficulties which Joyce found insuperable until imminent publication forced him to overcome them. It might, however, indicate that Joyce, although he knew the direction which the transition to chapter IV was to take, after faircopying the third chapter to the end of the hell sermons, still failed to give final shape to the text for the concluding 29 pages, turning rather, perhaps, to a revision of chapters I and II, and to what must have been the even greater task of composing chapter V in its final shape. As will be seen, there is a distinct paleographic link between chapter III, fols. 40–100, and chapter V, fols. 112–120. It is conceivable, then, that the end of chapter III was among the latest sections to be inscribed in the Dublin holograph.

In a first draft, chapters I–III of *A Portrait* were written between September 1907 and 7 April 1908 (*JJ* 274). They are the chapters that Ettore Schmitz comments on in his letter of 8 February 1909. He praises the second and third chapters, but he criticizes the first: "I think it deals with events devoid of importance and your rigid method of observation and description does not allow you to enrich a fact which is not rich by itself. You should write only about strong things."[16] Richard

Ellmann believes that Joyce did not heed this criticism (*JJ* 283), but that, in my opinion, is far from certain. The physical evidence of the Dublin manuscript alone shows that not only were chapters I–III written out anew after the near destruction, in 1911, of the earlier *Portrait* manuscript; by inference from the page numbering in the leaves which survive from it, the initial chapters were also augmented by a total of 124 manuscript pages. Beyond a recopying of salvaged text, this bespeaks thorough, and probably extensive revision.[17]

We know from an entry in Stanislaus Joyce's diary that in September 1907, Joyce's plan for rewriting *Stephen Hero* was "to omit all the first chapters and begin with Stephen . . . going to school" (*JJ* 274). This was the way out of the difficulty over the first chapters of *Stephen Hero* which Joyce had commented on before to his brother.[18] The new conception was realized. In the first school episode, the incomplete alteration of the name Mangan to Moonan in the early pages of the Dublin manuscript demonstrates positively a copying from earlier papers.[19] That would put at least this episode of Stephen's illness at Clongowes among the matter contained in the 1911 manuscript, and hence probably into chapter I as read by Ettore Schmitz in 1909, and, consequently, as written between 8 September and 29 November 1907. No new chapters dealing with Stephen's childhood were written then or later to precede this beginning.

The first chapter of the novel as we now have it, however, opens with a brief section of great significance which on the narrative level relates Stephen's childhood. It represents the final expression of Joyce's original intention to encompass the earliest years in his hero's life. Its consummate artistry, resulting from a great concentration and condensation of thought, imagery, symbolism, and meaning, has often been admired and commented upon.[20] In the manifold attempts at elucidating the complexity of the opening of *A Portrait*, there seems to be an agreement that, to adopt Hugh Kenner's musical terminology, it functions as an overture anticipating the main themes and developments of the novel. As such, it gives every impression of having been written in view not only of the whole as planned, but of the whole of the subsequent composition as executed, or largely executed, in the details of its narrative progression and symbolism. Though no positive textual proof for this is available, I venture to suggest that the opening section of chapter I was written at a late stage of the textual genesis of the novel. It had found its shape and place by late 1913, of course, when from the Dublin holograph originated the novel's transmission into print via the typescript prepared from the manuscript. But the opening section with which we are familiar may have formed no part, and (though this is speculation only) may have had no textual equivalent or alternative in chapter I as read by Ettore Schmitz in 1909 and as contained in the manuscript of 1911.

A general paleographic impression gained from the Dublin holograph is that the final inscription of chapter II preceded that of chapter I. An assumption of this order of revision gains support from the observation that at some stage in the seven-year textual history of *A Portrait*, the Christmas dinner scene was moved from chapter II to chapter I. In the plan for chapter VIII of *Stephen Hero*, the episode, or a prototype of it, is firmly embedded in other matter which now goes into chapter II of *A Portrait*. It remained, as I have been able to show elsewhere, in chapter II surroundings when Joyce first rewrote *Stephen Hero* into *A Portrait*.

The novel's beginning was thematically unified by the transposition of this scene. By the immediate juxtaposition of Stephen's dream of Parnell on his sickbed and the Christmas dinner controversy, Irish politics and the betrayal of Parnell become the chapter's organizing forces. Pivotal to its structure and symbolism is the synchronization of historical and fictional time which follows from a precise dating of Stephen's dream in relation to Christmas and the Christmas dinner. The final disposition and fusion of the narrative materials in chapter I, however, was the result not of one, but of several acts of revision. All available evidence—including the remarkable fact that it was a corrective revision only in the fair-copy manuscript itself which ultimately established the precise temporal relationship of the events on which its symbolism depends—suggests that chapter I acquired its final shape in stages, and that Joyce's awareness of its potential for meaning grew over an extended period of composition.[21] Nor would the internal textual evidence of the chapter's growth seem inconsistent with an assumption that Ettore Schmitz's criticism added incentive to the revising of it. Schmitz could hardly have denied "strength" to a chapter I opening as the present one does, and including the Christmas dinner scene.

Therefore, the act of revision by which the Christmas episode was transferred from chapter II to chapter I appears to have been undertaken after February 1909. A still later dating is suggested by the Trieste notebook. Among its materials, which in their majority are projections for chapter V of *A Portrait*, and for *Ulysses*, there are just a few entries which indicate that both the Christmas dinner scene and the novel's second chapter were still on Joyce's mind in 1909–10. Under the heading "Pappie," and after an entry which can be dated to Christmas 1909,[22] we find these further entries:

He calls a prince of the church a tub of guts. . . .
He offers the pope's nose at table. . . .
He calls Canon Keon frosty face and Cardinal Logue a tub of guts.
Had they been laymen he would condone their rancid fat.[23]

At some time after Christmas 1909, then, the dialogue of the Christmas dinner scene must have been revised sufficiently to put these quotations from John Stanislaus Joyce into the mouth of Simon Dedalus. Three further entries in the notebook—one under "Pappie," and two under "*Dedalus* (Stephen)"—point to chapter II. The names of Pappie's college friends[24] provide material for the Cork episode; and I take the entries for Stephen Dedalus which read, "The applause following the fall of the curtain fired his blood more than the scene on the stage" and "He felt himself alone in the theatre," to refer, respectively, to the Whitsuntide play, and to the scene in the anatomy theatre in Cork.[25] Taken together, this evidence suggests a late revision of chapters I and II, possibly sometime in 1910, or, indeed, in the course of assembling the novel after its near destruction in 1911.

II

The last of Joyce's *Dubliners* stories, "The Dead," has been widely interpreted as signaling a new departure in his art, leading to achievements such as the first chapter of *A Portrait*. The two have commonly been viewed in close temporal sequence, since it is known that *A Portrait* was begun in September 1907, immediately after the composition of "The Dead" (*JJ* 274). From the account here given of the state of the final manuscript and of the stages of composition and revision to be reckoned with in the novel's initial chapters, it follows, however, that only chapter IV can be safely assumed to have existed before 1911 as it survives in the completed novel. Chapters I–III, by contrast, attained their final shape only after that date, and are therefore, in the form in which we possess them, five or more years removed in time from *Dubliners*, and the consummation of its art in "The Dead." Paradoxically, it is chapter V, although presumably the last to be written, which from the vantage point of the finished *Portrait*, and on the evidential basis of the textual documents still extant, reaches back furthest into the novel's textual history and Joyce's artistic development.

Materials from the textual history have been preserved more amply for the fifth chapter than for the earlier ones. They bear witness to the fact that the transformation of the extant *Stephen Hero* fragment (the chapters which Joyce himself called the "University episode" of that novel) into chapter V of *A Portrait* passed through several stages of experiment. Since the first thirteen pages of the chapter in its final form were contained in the *Portrait* manuscript of 1911, it appears that the earliest traceable attempts at rewriting preceded its attempted destruction. They seem to have been aimed at only a slight modification-by-condensation of the *Stephen Hero* materials which, one may assume, would have preserved their essentially additive narrative structure. At the end of chapter XV and midway through chapter XVIII in the *Stephen Hero* manuscript, we find the entries "End of First Episode of V" and "End of Second Episode of V." The final *Portrait* text does not realize the linear revisional plan that these entries point to. What materials have been salvaged from the *Stephen Hero* university episode—e.g., the fire-lighting incident with the dean of studies, the music-room scene with Emma Clery, the episode of the Stephen-Emma-Father Moran triangle, as well as numerous brief descriptive and characterizing phrases earmarked for transfer in the *Stephen Hero* manuscript—now reappear out of their earlier order, changed and integrated into different settings and contexts.[26]

Against the foil of the original *Stephen Hero* incidents and scenes, Joyce searched for a new novelistic technique and new forms of expression through language and style. Increasingly, the narrative was internalized. The hero's mind and consciousness became a prism through which the novel was refracted. Characters were functionalized as correlative to theme. A workshop fragment happens to have survived which paradigmatically reveals the inner logic of the process of artistic reorientation.

The document in question is one (and the only genuine one) of the two "Fragments from a Late *Portrait* Manuscript."[27] An external, purely orthographic indicator, though by its nature a significant one, of the fact that it distinctly postdates *Stephen Hero*, is the revised spelling "Dedalus" (for earlier "Daedalus") of Stephen's family name. It also postdates *Stephen Hero* by its introduction of Doherty, alias Oliver St. John Gogarty. The fictional name appears as early as the Pola notebook entries for *Stephen Hero* of 1904.[28] But when Joyce in the summer of 1905 discontinued the writing of *Stephen Hero,* he had not yet reached the point where he would have brought Gogarty into the narrative—although his friends in Dublin who were granted the privilege of reading the finished chapters were eagerly awaiting that moment.[29] Doherty is not finally cast as a character in *A Portrait,* but reappears as Buck Mulligan in *Ulysses.* The Doherty fragment therefore has justly been viewed as an early vestige of *Ulysses.*[30] But by its situational context, it has a place more immediately within a *Portrait* ambience.

The Doherty episode of the preserved fragment constitutes a section of a kitchen scene between Stephen and his mother. On the manuscript leaf, it is preceded by the last half-sentence from a paragraph which, as A. Walton Litz has observed, appears to be the end of a new rendering of the episode that concluded chapter XIX (in Joyce's numbering) of *Stephen Hero.*[31] The pencil addition to the end of chapter XIX in the *Stephen Hero* manuscript, "If I told them there is no water in the font to symbolise that when Christ has washed us in blood we have no need of other aspersions," is reflected in the fragmentary phrase "shed his blood for all men they have no need of other aspersion." The kitchen scene to which the Doherty episode itself is genetically linked followed, after some pages, in chapter XX (in Joyce's numbering) of *Stephen Hero.* Vestigially, therefore, the manuscript fragment gives evidence of an attempt at linear rewriting of *Stephen Hero* by a foreshortening of its episodic sequence.

Yet technically and stylistically, at the same time, the fragment exemplifies a breakthrough toward the narrative mode of the final *Portrait.* It begins in the middle of Stephen's mental reflection on his own mixed feelings toward Doherty's habits of mocking and blasphemous self-dramatization, and it breaks off as mother and son, confronting one another over the dregs of a finished breakfast in the midst of general disorder in the kitchen, embark upon a dialogue which would appear to be heading toward a new version of the conversation, in *Stephen*

Hero, about Stephen's neglect to make his Easter duty. There, as they talk, Stephen is made to reveal his inner state at length, while his mother is only gradually brought to a realization and awareness of the fact that he has lost his faith. After four wordy pages, the dialogue ends:

Mrs Daedalus began to cry. Stephen, having eaten and drunk all within his province, rose and went towards the door:
—It's all the fault of those books and the company you keep. Out at all hours of the night instead of in your home, the proper place for you. I'll burn every one of them. I won't have them in the house to corrupt anyone else.
Stephen halted at the door and turned towards his mother who had now broken out into tears:
—If you were a genuine Roman Catholic, mother, you would burn me as well as the books.
—I knew no good would come of your going to that place. You are ruining yourself body and soul. Now your faith is gone!
—Mother, said Stephen from the threshold, I don't see what you're crying for. I'm young, healthy, happy. What is the crying for? . . . It's too silly . . .[32]

From this conclusion, Joyce in the fragment distills the new beginning of an exchange of words:

—It is all over those books you read. I knew you would lose your faith. I'll burn every one of them—
—If you had not lost ~~the~~ your faith—said Stephen—you would burn me along with the books—

Within the fragment as it stands, however, this beginning (there is no telling where it would have led, since Joyce himself does not seem to have seen his way to following it up; the fragment ends at the top of its last manuscript page) is only the conclusion of a thoroughly internalized scene. It is primarily Doherty, and not his mother, who is Stephen's antagonist, and he is present not in person, but in Stephen's thoughts. It is in Stephen's mind that his coarse and boisterous blasphemies are called up, the "troop of swinish images . . . which went trampling through his memory." The particulars of Doherty's self-dramatization "on the steps of his house the night before," as remembered by Stephen, all function for Joyce as the artistically objective correlative of Stephen's` rejection` of church rituals and Christian beliefs. Together with the subsequent description of the dirt and disorder in the kitchen they serve to create the mood of Stephen's dejection and weariness—totally different from the defiant "Mother . . . I'm young, healthy, happy. What is the crying for? . . . It's too silly" of *Stephen Hero*—out of which the dialogue grows, and then breaks off.

The technique in the act of rewriting is one of inversion in several respects. From being displayed in external dialogue, the theme of the episode is presented as a projection in narrative images (centered on the antagonist) of the protagonist's mind and memory. The facts and attitudes which emerged only gradually in the fully externalized scenic narration by dialogue, are now anticipated by the economy of poetic indirection. The fragment of conversation which remains begins on the note, and, in foreshortening, on the very words with which its model ended. Mood and atmosphere are enhanced and incidentally altered; the effect of condensation is great on all levels of thought, language, and character presentation. The overall gain in intensity is enormous. Constituting as it does a point of intersection between the earlier episodic pattern of *Stephen Hero* and the new evolving narrative principles and techniques, the "late *Portrait* fragment" thus reveals the significance of Joyce's intermediary *Portrait* experiments.

What presumably remained problematic, however, was to adhere to the device of presenting as a scene at all the crucial moment in the process of Stephen's separation from home, fatherland, and religion. As a scene, it may have been felt to give still too much personal and emotional bias to an essentially intellectual conflict and decision. In the fragment, of course, it depends, additionally, on the introduction into the larger narrative context of the new and essentially insincere character

Doherty. The experiment of using him as a correlative and a mocking projection of Stephen's serious rejection of Christian values was abandoned. This meant that the scene between Stephen and his mother could not take even the shape into which it was tentatively revised. In the final text of *A Portrait*, by further radical narrative condensation, the confrontation of mother and son over the question of the Easter duty was deleted altogether, entering the novel only by way of report in Stephen's final conversation with Cranly.

The elimination of the kitchen scene has broader implications, for it appears that the narrative progression of chapter V as ultimately achieved is determined no longer by scenes, but by conversations and reflections. This seems to be the result of the later revisional experiments of which, now, the notation of the text in the pages of the Dublin fair-copy manuscript itself bears witness. The final chapter of the novel divides into four sections. They are no longer "episodes" in the manner of the Christmas dinner scene, or the Cork episode, or Stephen's flight to the seashore at the end of chapter IV. "Movements" may perhaps be an apter term for them. The second and fourth movements, essentially static, are given to the composition of the villanelle and to Stephen's diary excerpts. It is only in the more dynamic first and third movements that, by a complex sequence of thematically interlocking conversations, the narrative is effectively carried forward.

As with the novel as a whole, so with chapter V in particular, the Dublin manuscript helps to distinguish phases of inscription which permit inferences about the order of composition of its parts. Of fols. 112 ff., for example (beginning "What birds were they?" [224]), Chester G. Anderson has suggested, from observations on variations in Joyce's handwriting, that they may have been among the first to reach the form they have in the Dublin holograph.[33] This is incorrect insofar as chapter IV is inscriptionally clearly the earliest part of the fair-copy manuscript. Nevertheless, Anderson's guess conforms with an impression, gained from further comparison, that the particular variation in Joyce's handwriting observable in fols. 112–20 (through the entire passage that ends "and passed in through the clicking turnstile" [224–26]) recurs also in fols. 39–100 of chapter III, that is, throughout the two hell sermons (116–35). At the bottom of fol. 39, the new hand sets in with the paragraph beginning "The chapel was flooded by the dull scarlet light" (116). The change of hand on the same page clearly puts the inscription of fols. 1–39 before that of fols. 39–100. Thereafter, the second obvious inscriptional discontinuity in chapter III after fol. 100, together with the paleographic likeness of the hell sermon section with fols. 112–20 of chapter V, suggests—in addition to strengthening the earlier argument for a later inclusion of the final transitional section of chapter III—that Joyce at this point proceeded directly from the third chapter to faircopying the nine-page opening of the fifth chapter's third movement. This, as will be remembered, is a passage which richly orchestrates the novel's symbolism. In tone and imagery, it is particularly close to the latter half of chapter IV. Since the hell sermons to which in the inscription of the Dublin holograph it is paleographically linked represent text essentially salvaged from the *Portrait* manuscript of 1911, the text of fols. 112–20 in chapter V, too, may be of pre-1911 origin.

The remainder of the third movement in chapter V may then not only have been inscribed later, as the change in the style of the hand after "and passed in through the clicking turnstile" on fol. 120 indicates; it may also have been written appreciably later. When the textual continuation was ready to be faircopied and Joyce returned to the middle of fol. 120 to join it on where he had left off writing, the beginning of the last preceding paragraph read: "A sudden brief hiss was heard and he knew that the electric lamps had been switched on in the readers' rooms." This was revised to "A sudden brief hiss *fell from the windows above him*," to correspond to the parallel phrase which occurs within the subsequent text on fol. 131: "and a soft hiss fell again from a window above."[34] The manner of the revision, undertaken interlinearly on the manuscript page, is reminiscent of the similar revisions observed in chapter IV and may well support a view that, here as there, Joyce was only after a passage of time returning to text earlier inscribed.

A manuscript section in chapter V clearly set off as an insert from its surroundings is that of the villanelle movement. Its sixteen manuscript pages are (but for the last one) inscribed with a different ink and a different slope of the hand on different paper. The verso of fol. 95, which ends the chapter's first section, is smudged and has yellowed. Similarly, fol. 112, the first page of the third movement, shows traces of having been outer- and uppermost in a bundle. From this evidence it would appear that, for an appreciable time, sections one and three of the chapter existed separately and apart, and that the villanelle movement was later inserted between them. Further observation shows that the last of the sixteen manuscript pages of the villanelle movement is again on paper similar or identical to that used for the rest of the chapter (although this in fact is a mixed batch). Moreover, the leaf (fol. 111) is also heavily smudged on its verso and bears the mark of a huge paper clip. But for the two lines of running prose at the top, it contains only the complete text of the villanelle as concluding the movement. A closer inspection of the manner of inscription on the preceding leaf reveals that the words in its last two lines are spaced out uncommonly widely and are not brought out as far to the right edge of the paper as the text on the rest of the page. The article "the" which is the first word on fol. 111 could easily have been accommodated at the bottom of fol. 110. Therefore, fol. 110 was inscribed after fol. 111, or, in other words, fol. 111 appears to be the last leaf of the villanelle section from an earlier inscriptional (and probably textual) state.

That this section in its final state was inserted in its present position in the Dublin manuscript only after the preceding ninety-five pages of text as written were finally faircopied—and appreciably later at that, as witnessed by the smudged appearance of fol. 95v—is clear from the fact that it opens, with the paleographic break described, in the lower third of fol. 95. That the final transcription of the villanelle movement also postdates the writing of fols. 112–20 is rendered similarly probable by the other physical evidence referred to: the different paper of the insert, and the smudging of fol. 112 itself. But whether the second movement in its original conception is later than the other parts of chapter V is less easy to determine. On the contrary, considering the marks of wear and tear on fol. 111v, it is not even out of the question that the villanelle section in an earlier unrevised state also belonged to the pages of the rescued 1911 manuscript which Joyce "could never have rewritten." But this, from the evidence, cannot be demonstrated. What the inscriptional stratification in chapter V of the Dublin manuscript shows, however, is that Joyce did what he later claimed to have done, assembling the chapter by piecing together sections of manuscript. The chapter was by no means inscribed in the fair-copy manuscript in the regular order of the final text (as the other four chapters apparently were in themselves, though they were not written out in the regular order of the chapters), nor was it probably composed in that order.

On the whole, the indication is that the final shape and structure of chapter V of *A Portrait of the Artist as a Young Man* evolved gradually as Joyce was working on the diverse materials which in the end he succeeded in unifying in this final chapter of the novel.[35] In it, the villanelle interlude on the one hand, the dream movement in the chapter's almost musical structure where Stephen, aesthete and rebellious student, is metamorphosed into a conscious artist who takes upon himself solitude and exile in the search for self-fulfillment,[36] and, on the other hand, the rich orchestration of the novel's imagery and symbolism in the opening pages of the chapter's third movement, are seen from the evidence of their inscription in the fair-copy manuscript to have early roots in the chapter's conceptual genesis. The narrative framework which structurally supports these poetically highly imaginative passages is anchored in the sequences of conversations in the first and third movements and their relation to one another. Their relationship, which, as indicated, appears to reflect Joyce's final experiments at shaping the chapter, may also be seen in terms of a history of the text.

It is movements one and three in chapter V that reuse the largest quantity of *Stephen Hero* materials; and of the two, the first takes the greater share. This section is also that part of the chapter where greatest emphasis is on establishing and maintaining narrative progression in action and in time. That such narrative progression is structured by a sequence of conversations, and no longer by episodes, becomes clear precisely from the fact that *A Portrait* salvages (though often with significant modification) dialogue from *Stephen Hero*, while abandoning the loose episodic framework to which it was there tied. The altercation developing from the fire-lighting by the dean of studies, or the exposition of Stephen's aesthetic theories, are outstanding examples. The close adaptation of a dialogue in dog Latin from *Stephen Hero* to comment upon the issue of signing or not signing the declaration for universal peace in *A Portrait* points to the revisional principle. The corresponding dialogue in *Stephen Hero* counterpoints the reading and reception of Stephen's paper on "Art and Life," an incident which does not recur in *A Portrait*. Significantly enough, this is the only instance where *Stephen Hero* materials have been reused in *A Portrait* totally divorced from their earlier context. The original unity of episode and dialogue has been dissociated.

It is the achievement of the opening movement of chapter V to develop Stephen's attitudes to church, university, and Jesuits; to show how he scorns the emotional and unreflected idealism which motivates alike the declaration for universal peace and the arguments for Irish nationalism; and to set forth his aesthetic theories all in a sequence of encounters with persons he talks to in the course of half a day's wandering through Dublin, from half-past ten in the morning in his mother's kitchen to sometime in the mid-afternoon on the steps of the National Library. This wandering movement, at the same time, is a narrative representation of Stephen's leaving his home and family and finding the theoretical basis for his art. The first section of the chapter takes him halfway into exile.

The third movement, by contrast, while of course gravitating toward Stephen's final encounter and conversation with Cranly, reflects upon and heightens imaginatively and symbolically the attitudes and the positions he has secured in movements one and two. It will be noted that the third movement begins in place and time where the first ended, on the steps of the National Library in the late hours of an afternoon. Its action consists simply of Stephen's seeking out Cranly and separating him from the group of fellow students in order to walk alone with him and talk to him. The device is so similar to Stephen's sequestering one by one the dean of studies, Cranly, Davin, and Lynch earlier in the chapter as to suggest that at some stage in the genesis of chapter V there existed a provisional and experimental plan for tying all the conversations on the issues he faces, and his going away from home into exile, to the narrative sequence of Stephen's wanderings through Dublin in the course of one day. It would have been in embryo the plan realized in *Ulysses*.

But the renouncing of church and faith in the final conversation with Cranly could then not have been linked to Stephen's falling out with his mother over his refusal to make his Easter duty. For that, Stephen would have had to be brought back home once more in the course of the day, which would have broken the chapter's continuous outward movement. Perhaps a sequence was temporarily considered which would have brought all conversations into one day without sacrificing this directional principle. The unfinished revision of the Easter duty conversation in the "Fragment from a Late *Portrait* Manuscript," by the reference to Doherty's "standing on the steps of his house the night before," [37] would seem to be set in the morning. Perhaps it should be seen as a workshop alternative to the kitchen scene at the beginning of the chapter, which by the evidence of the continuous authorial page numbering in chapters IV–V was in the 1911 manuscript and, therefore, possibly predates the fragment. It would, however, have very heavily weighted the opening of the chapter which, as it stands, begins so casually; and the different thematic order of the ensuing conversations it would have demanded may well have proved too difficult to bring into balance.

Within the four-part composition of chapter V several structural principles are at work, of which the organization of the thematic and narrative progression in the first and third movements by means of a logical sequence of conversations is the dominant one. Each exchange requires an intellectual counter-position, and Stephen's dialogue partners are accordingly functionalized as Doherty is in the "late *Portrait* fragment," though not as strenuously internalized. Of the structural patterns that may be inferred as workshop experiments, namely the attempt at concentrating the chapter's action into one day, and the sustaining of a continuous outward direction of Stephen's movements, neither was completely abandoned, or wholly sacrificed to the other. Although the villanelle movement stands between the first and third sections, thereby indeterminately lengthening the chapter's time span, the third movement still continues in time (late afternoon) and place (steps of the National Library) where the first ends. Simultaneously, by a subtle avoidance of definite place, the illusion at least is maintained of a continuous movement away from home and into exile. The narrative is so devised that once Stephen leaves his home by the kitchen door in the morning of the day on which the chapter opens, he is never visualized as returning there again.[38] Care is taken not to localize his awakening to compose the villanelle in a bedroom of the family house. The Easter duty conversation, which would have taken him back to the kitchen, is eliminated from the narrative where, by analogy to *Stephen Hero*, and according to the report of it to Cranly, it should have had its place. Nor is the discussion with his mother about the "B.V.M." in the diary entry of March 24 given a precise setting in Stephen's home. Both physically and spiritually, in the end, his departure into exile is represented as an unbroken outward movement sweeping through the entire fifth chapter.

A few but quite specific textual observations finally help to establish the relative chronology of the chapter's four movements. The initial thirteen manuscript pages (of 1911) bring Stephen out of his mother's kitchen and start him on his wanderings through Dublin. The entire first section of the chapter draws copiously on *Stephen Hero*. Once the structural plan of a sequence of conversations had been decided upon, the remainder of the first movement would have followed materially and logically from the chapter's beginning. The third movement, in the integral shape of its final version, is distinctly later than the first, and as it stands in the Dublin holograph it may postdate the original conception of the villanelle movement. Significantly, it is only in the text of the third movement that Stephen is given the attribute of his ashplant.[39] Also, the Gogarty figure who commonly goes by the name of Goggins is here once called Doherty (245.32), which indicates that the experimental phase in the composition of chapter V to which the "Fragment from a Late *Portrait* Manuscript" bears witness preceded the writing of the third movement (or parts of it). There is no bibliographical, inscriptional, or textual indication of when the finale of the chapter, the diary section, was planned or written. Though ending the manuscript, it may not have been last in composition. It was the villanelle movement in its final revised version which was last inserted in its predetermined position, to complete the fair-copy manuscript, and the entire novel.

III

In its four-part structure, the fifth chapter of *A Portrait of the Artist as a Young Man* is the exact symmetrical counterpart to the first. The childhood overture and the two Clongowes episodes, separated by the Christmas dinner scene, are the mirror image of the two movements of Stephen's wanderings through Dublin, separated by the villanelle episode, and the diary finale. In both chapters, bibliographical and textual evidence reveals that the final organization of their parts was established by intercalation of a contrasting episode into a homogeneous stretch of narrative. Genetically, the novel's beginning and its end appear closely interdependent.

It seems that it was a decision to abandon the sequential or cyclic[40] narrative by episodes as used in *Stephen Hero* in favor of a chiastic center design that broke the impasse in which Joyce found himself over *A Portrait* (and which may have contributed to the desperate action of the attempted burning of the intermediary manuscript in 1911). The textual history of chapter V documents this momentous change in the compositional concept, and there is much reason to believe that from the fifth chapter it retroactively affected the entire work. Discounting the overture and the finale, which functionally relate as much to the entire novel as they do to their respective chapters, the first and last chapters are each themselves chiastically centered on the Christmas dinner scene and on the composition of the villanelle. Since both chapters II and I were recopied after 1911, the Christmas dinner scene would seem only then to have found its place in the first chapter. Moreover, from the style of the hand in chapter I of the Dublin holograph, it appears that it was inscribed late, later certainly than chapters IV and II, and in all likelihood later also than fols. 1–100 of chapter III, and the bulk of chapter V. This would seem to strengthen the assumption of a compositional dependence of chapter I on the form which emerged for chapter V.

Of the three middle chapters, chapters II and IV are in themselves still basically narrated in a linear sequence of episodes. So is chapter III, although here the sequential progression is stayed by the unifying and centralizing effect of a concentration on the single event of the religious retreat. But the chiastic disposition of the novel's beginning and end alters the functional relationships in the sections of the work which they encompass. Chapters II and IV take on a centripetal and a centrifugal direction, and the religious retreat becomes, literally and structurally, the dead center of the novel. If it has been correct to infer an earlier state of chapter III where four, five, or even six sermons were given verbatim, and therefore of necessity in an overtly sequential manner, then the revision, which essentially left only the two hell sermons as rendered in the preacher's own words, was undertaken to emphasize the chapter's midpoint position in the chiastic structure of the book. Within chapter III, divided by Joyce's familiar asterisks into three parts, the beginning in Nighttown and the close in Church Street chapel stand in obvious symmetrical contrast. From the close of chapter II, the Nighttown opening leads naturally into the hell sermon center. The long search for a satisfactory chapter conclusion to lead out of it, indicated by the late inclusion of the final twenty-nine manuscript pages, may reflect Joyce's awareness of how essential for the work's inner balance it was to give the narrative exactly the proper momentum at the onset of its centrifugal movement.

IV

To sum up: from Stanislaus Joyce's testimony we know that James Joyce began to write *A Portrait of the Artist as a Young Man* in September 1907. By 7 April 1908, he had finished three chapters. These, we must assume, were first drafts of the novel's first half which do not as such survive. During the remainder of 1908 no more than partial drafts of chapter IV appear to have been written. In February of 1909, Ettore Schmitz's praise and criticism of the three completed chapters, plus an additional stretch of narrative which may have been the early part of chapter IV, gave Joyce encouragement to continue with the novel. The only certain knowledge we have of his work between 1909 and sometime in 1911 is that he completed chapter IV and entered upon the composition of chapter V. All of chapter IV and the first thirteen manuscript leaves of chapter V survive intact in the Dublin holograph from the *Portrait* manuscript which was nearly destroyed in 1911.

If an inference from the dearth of surviving textual materials for chapters I–IV of *A Portrait* is possible, these chapters were by 1911, or even perhaps as early as sometime in 1909, considered essentially completed. The "Trieste notebook"—which, contrary to earlier dating attempts, appears not to have been started before 1909[41]—contains materials used almost exclusively in chapter V of *A Portrait,* and in *Ulysses.* Perhaps it is in truth a "Dublin notebook," dating from the months of Joyce's visit to Dublin in 1909, where, while he was separated from his manuscript, his memory of persons and incidents would have been refreshed and enriched. In addition, it is just possible, though it cannot be proved, that the text of the "late *Portrait* fragment" also belongs to the 1909–11 phase of work on *A Portrait.* Since, moreover, it also points beyond *A Portrait* to *Ulysses,* and since the notebook and the fragment together are our only workshop evidence of the otherwise externally to be inferred intimate connection between the completion of *A Portrait* and the planning of *Ulysses,* the impossibility of a precise dating of these documents and the textual materials they present is much to be regretted.

By Joyce's own dating in retrospect, the incident of the near destruction of the *Portrait* manuscript occurred in the latter half of 1911. This was a true moment of crisis in the novel's prepublication history. The "charred remains of the MS" remained tied up in an old sheet for some months,[42] and thus it was in 1912 that the writing of the novel entered its culminating phase. According to the mark of division set by the manuscript pages that were transferred physically into the final Dublin holograph, Joyce's post-1911 labors were threefold. He composed all of chapter V, or approximately the last third of the book, in its final form. From it, he devised an essentially new structural plan for the entire book, and, consequently, he revised and recopied chapters I–III. The operations were interrelated and interdependent, and the creative achievement, one may well believe, was on a scale that would have required the best part of two years' work. In 1913, when the title page of the Dublin holograph was dated, the end appears to have been well in sight. On Easter Day 1913, Joyce himself envisaged finishing his novel by the end of the year.[43] He may, however, as so often, have underestimated the time he would need to complete it. He signed the last manuscript page "Dublin 1904 Trieste 1914," and the sections of text which from bibliographical evidence were last included in the manuscript, such as the end of chapter III and the revised villanelle episode, may not have reached their final form much before they were required as copy for the Trieste typist in, presumably, the summer of 1914. But it is a conclusion from the preceding textual and critical approach that, in essence, the novel attained the shape and structure in which we now possess it during 1912 and 1913. Despite all vicissitudes and misfortunes of his day-to-day life,[44] these were two years of concentrated creativity for James Joyce, as he was forging and welding together *A Portrait of the Artist as a Young Man*.

APPENDIX

Stephen Hero

The rejection of "A Portrait of the Artist" by the editors of *Dana* in January 1904 gave Joyce the incentive to write *Stephen Hero*. Outlining his plan for the novel to his brother on the evening of his twenty-second birthday, 2 February 1904, he wrote the first chapter in eight days (*JJ*, 153). The plan called for sixty-three chapters (*Letters*, 2, 83). For the first seven chapters, lyrical in tone (*JJ*, 153) and dealing with Stephen's early childhood, no plans or sketches have survived, except the draft for an addition to chapter I on fol. 9v of the notebook which contains "A Portrait of the Artist." The blank leaves in this copybook were in February–March 1904 filled with notes and plans for chapters VIII to XI and subsequent and general matter. The materials are reprinted in the order of the copybook's page sequence in *Workshop* (pp. 68–74). Bibliographic and paleographic analysis cannot establish beyond doubt the order in which they were entered, but a possible sequence may be suggested as follows: (1) fol. 9v: draft of addition to chapter I; (2) fol. 11: notebook-type entries; (3) fol. 11v: list of characters (names partly real, partly fictional), and plan for chapter VIII in a corner; (4) fol. 10v: plan for chapters IX and X; (5) fol. 8v: plan for chapter XI; (6) fol. 10 (copybook turned): notebook-type entries for "University College."

By the end of March, eleven chapters were written (*The Complete Dublin Diary of Stanislaus Joyce*, ed. George H. Healey [Ithaca: Cornell University Press, 1971], pp. 19–20). By 8 October, when Joyce left Ireland, he had progressed no further than halfway into chapter XII which he completed between October 11 and 19 in Zurich (*Letters*, 2, 67). In Pola, between the end of November and Christmas 1904, Joyce added chapters XIII and XIV, and he sent chapters XII–XIV to his brother Stanislaus in Dublin on 13 January 1905 (*Letters*, 2, 76). Throughout his letters to Stanislaus between 20 October 1904, and 12 July 1905, Joyce kept him informed of the novel's progress. In the last days of December 1904, he embarked upon what he called the "University episode." He estimated it would run to eleven chapters. It took him about twenty-six weeks to write them, or on an average two and a half weeks per chapter. The University episode, chapters XV to XXV, was sent to Stanislaus at the end of June or the beginning of July 1905 (inferred from *Letters*, 2, 91, 93). This marked the end of the work. Joyce did not thereafter return to *Stephen Hero*.

Two fragments of the text of *Stephen Hero* survive, 30 pages of a narrative episode that tells about Stephen's summer visit to Mullingar, and all, except a very few pages at the beginning and end, of the eleven chapters of the University episode. Between the short fragment (pages at Yale and Cornell together consecutively numbered 477–506) and the long one, beginning with page 519, there is a lacuna of only 13 manuscript leaves into which the opening of chapter XV must have fallen. The fragmentary Mullingar episode was consequently part of chapter XIV, written in December 1904. The leaves of the eleven-chapter main fragment of *Stephen Hero* have original numbers from 519 to 902. Due to repeated misnumbering of pages and an occasional missing leaf, the imputed numerical total of 383 pages (see *SH*, "Introduction," p. 9) is found to be reduced to an actual total of 361 leaves. From Joyce's own statement (*Letters*, 2, 132) we know that he wrote 914 pages of his novel. Twelve leaves are therefore missing at the end of the manuscript.

Confusion about several aspects of *Stephen Hero* arises from the 1944 and all subsequent editions of the fragmentarily surviving text. The assumption, given currency by Sylvia Beach and apparently backed by Gorman's biography of 1939 (see *SH*, "Introduction," pp. 7-8), that it was the *Stephen Hero* manuscript which was thrown into the fire and partly rescued, is mistaken. More seriously, Theodore Spencer's edition numbers the chapters of the main fragment from XV to XXVI. A look at the original manuscript at Harvard reveals that Joyce numbered his last chapter "XXV." The editorial error arises in chapter XVIII. Halfway through the manuscript chapter XVIII, at the bottom of page 610, appears the note "End of Second Episode of V" in a large scrawl of red crayon. The text it obliterates is added in the margin of the subsequent leaf. This leaf is headed "Chapter XVIII" (*sic*) in blue crayon. Lacking the knowledge of Joyce's working habits which scholars only in recent years have gained, Theodore Spencer failed to recognize that the crayon markings in the *Stephen Hero* manuscript, related as they are to the composition of *A Portrait*, were made around 1909-11 and do not in any sense constitute a revision of *Stephen Hero*. Moreover, he either misread the blue crayon entry "Chapter XVIII," or believed Joyce to be in error about it. All it presumably means, however, is that Joyce for some reason took the *Stephen Hero* manuscript apart at this point and reminded himself that the pages removed still belonged to chapter XVIII. Theodore Spencer unfortunately assumed a new chapter division and, introducing "XIX," he proceeded to renumber all subsequent chapters. Users of the *Stephen Hero* editions must therefore be warned that chapters XVIII and "XIX" are one chapter, chapter XVIII, and that chapters "XX" to "XXVI" should correctly be numbered XIX to XXV. Only with this correction can the editions be matched against Joyce's comments about the novel in his letters.

Only the original chapter divisions, too, will reveal essential features of the plan and structure of *Stephen Hero*. Of this, no more than the following can here be indicated: the reference to seven chapters on Stephen's early childhood and to the over-all projected length of sixty-three chapters suggests a progression by seven-chapter units. The assumption is strengthened by Joyce's explanation to Stanislaus that "the effect of the prose piece 'The spell of arms' is to mark the precise point between boyhood (pueritia) and adolescence (adulescentia)—17 years" (*Letters*, 2, 79). The last half-sentence of this passage (which survives independently as an epiphany) heads the first extant page of *Stephen Hero*, belonging, as was seen, to chapter XIV. Chapter XXI (in Joyce's numbering) is recognizable as another chapter of transition. It treats of a transitional period, the summer between Stephen's first and second university years. It abounds in images and situations of incoming and outgoing, and it ends in "the shadow of decay, the decay of leaves and flowers, the decay of hope" with the imminent death of Isabel, threateningly envisaged in the adaptation of another epiphany (cf. *SH*, p. 163, and *Workshop*, p. 29). Since, moreover, a man's inner development and the stages of his outward career through life do not coincide, additional structures may be seen to be superimposed upon the cyclical sequence of seven-chapter units. The University episode appears in itself pivotally centered on chapter XX, sixth of eleven chapters, in which Stephen renounces church and faith. A return to Joyce's original disposition of the *Stephen Hero* narrative opens avenues for interpretation even in the fragmentarily surviving text.

NOTES

1. "A Portrait of the Artist" has been reprinted, with many oversights and errors, in "*A Portrait of the Artist as a Young Man*": *Text, Criticism, and Notes*, ed. Chester G. Anderson, Viking Critical Library (New York: Viking Press, 1968), pp. 257-68. In a more reliable text, it appears in Robert Scholes and Richard M. Kain, eds., *The Workshop of Daedalus: James Joyce and the Raw Materials for "A Portrait of the Artist as a Young Man"* (Evanston: Northwestern University Press, 1965), pp. 60-68. In a dozen substantive instances alone (not listing some twenty departures from manuscript punctuation and orthography) the Viking Critical Library text differs from the manuscript in the Lockwood Memorial Library at Buffalo, Spielberg, II. A. (See Peter Spielberg, ed., *James Joyce's Manuscripts and Letters at the University of Buffalo* [Albany, N.Y.: State University of New York Press, 1962].) In two places the

Viking and the *Workshop* texts concur in misreading Joycean key words in the manuscript:

VCL 259.07	*for* correspondent	*read* correspondents
259.08	the fantastic	this fantastic
261.10	illuminated	illumined (also *Workshop* 63.18)
261.11	signature	signatures
261.18	simple	single
261.22	Fatuity	fatuity
262.03	reasons	reason
263.20	arranged	arrayed (also *Workshop* 65.26)
263.24	the	that
263.27	self devourer	the self-devourer
264.05	more	mere
264.08	Apple Trees	the Apple Trees

2. See the Appendix to this essay.

3. Richard Ellmann, *James Joyce* (New York: Oxford University Press, 1959), pp. 274, 325, subsequently cited as *JJ*.

4. The Dublin manuscript has not been subjected previously to stringent bibliographical analysis, nor is the present context the place to provide a full description of it. Only such observations from an examination of the manuscript will be introduced as appear relevant to the views I wish to develop. Thanks to the courtesy of the National Library of Ireland I had the opportunity of investigating the *Portrait* manuscript during the week of the Fourth International James Joyce Symposium in June 1973, although this meant removing from its case for hours at a time the prize item of the Joyce exhibition which had been especially assembled to mark the occasion of the Symposium.

5. The one missing leaf is the first of the "Fragments from a Late *Portrait* Manuscript," (*Workshop*, p. 107), now at the British Museum. This is strongly suggested by the text as reprinted, and is, moreover, bibliographically ascertainable by the size and quality of the paper; by the color of the ink; by the threading hole in the wide margin in the upper left quarter of the leaf, apparently matching the position of such holes in all the chapter's other leaves; and by the penciled numbering in the upper left-hand corner which supplies a missing number "83" in the sequence of the leaves in the Dublin holograph. The confirmation of a second manuscript lacuna by letter from the National Library to Chester G. Anderson, referred to in his "The Text of James Joyce's *A Portrait* . . . ," *Neuphilologische Mitteilungen* 65 (1964): 165–66, n. 5, cannot have been based on a careful examination. There is no further lacuna in the manuscript.

6. The actual numbers are 239–41, 243–313. But, with no lacuna in the text, this is apparently a simple error in the numbering, as Harriet Weaver noted when she checked the manuscript: "evidently a mistake for 242. H.S.W."

7. Present in the Harvard manuscript and the twenty-five leaves at Yale, but previously described only for the five leaves at Cornell, in Robert E. Scholes, ed., *The Cornell Joyce Collection: A Catalogue* (Ithaca: Cornell University Press, 1961), no. 36.

8. *Letters of James Joyce*, vol. 2, ed. Richard Ellmann (New York: Viking Press, 1966), p. 226 f.

9. *Letters of James Joyce*, vol. 1, ed. Stuart Gilbert (1957; New York: Viking Press, 1966), p. 136.

10. On this point, Anderson ("The Text," pp. 182–84) and *JJ*, 365 basically agree. I follow these authorities in "Zur Textgeschichte und Textkritik des *Portrait*," in Wilhelm Füger, ed., *James Joyces Portrait: Das "Jugendbildnis" im Lichte neuerer deutscher Forschung* (Munich, 1972), p. 22; and also—though with a cautionary footnote after first looking into the fair-copy manuscript—in "Towards a Critical Text of James Joyce's *A Portrait of the Artist as a Young Man*," *Studies in Bibliography* 27 (1974): 28.

11. All page references are to the 1964 Viking text as reprinted in the edition cited above, note 1. But the text, unless otherwise indicated, is that of the Dublin manuscript. Italics indicating revisions are mine.

12. *Workshop*, p. 69.

13. *Letters*, 2, 226.

14. In a different context, and without knowledge of the manuscript conditions, I have speculated before "that the latter half of Chapter III, portraying as it does Stephen's intensely painful self-torture, gave particular pains in the writing and was textually fluid for longer than any other section of the novel" ("Towards a Critical Text," p. 38). This hunch now seems to be borne out.

15. See Gabler, "Towards a Critical Text," p. 47.

16. *Letters*, 2, 227.

17. Quantitatively, however, it is highly unlikely that the earlier text was augmented by a full 50 percent, as the addition of 124 pages to the original 238 might suggest. As compared to the inscription of chapter IV, the columns of text in the freshly inscribed chapters are distinctly narrower, especially so throughout chapter I. This factor alone would account for many more pages in the new manuscript portion.

18. *Letters*, 2, 90.

19. As noted in Anderson, "The Text," p. 170n.

20. See especially Hugh Kenner, *Dublin's Joyce* (London: Chatto and Windus, 1955), pp. 114–16; and, recently, Therese Fischer, *Bewusstseinsdarstellung im Werk von James Joyce* (Frankfurt, 1973), pp. 69 ff.

21. The above is a summary of some of the findings of "The Christmas Dinner Scene, Parnell's Death, and the Genesis of *A Portrait of the Artist as a Young Man*" which grew out of the present essay and has appeared in the *James Joyce Quarterly* 13 (Fall 1975): 27–38.

22. "He gave me money to wire to Nora on Christmas Eve." *Workshop*, p. 103.

23. *Workshop*, p. 104.

24. Ibid.

25. *Workshop*, p. 96. Neither entry is provided with a reference to the *Portrait* text, but see 85 and 89–90.

26. In his 1944 edition of *Stephen Hero* (New York: New Directions), Theodore Spencer judged Joyce's red and blue crayon markings in the manuscript to be cancellations. See his "Editorial Note," p. 18. In the light of our increased knowledge today of Joyce's working habits, they would appear rather to be the traces he left as he was going through the manuscript, gathering incidents and phrases that could be reused. Although a large number of the passages so marked do not in fact reappear in *A Portrait*, and quite a few other unmarked ones do, there is still sufficient correspondence between markings and reappearances to warrant a departure from Spencer's interpretation of the use of the colored crayons in favor of an analogy with Joyce's later working habits.

27. *Workshop*, pp. 107–08; and see above, note 5.

28. *Workshop*, p. 85.

29. *Letters*, 2, 103.

30. A. Walton Litz, *The Art of James Joyce* (London: Oxford University Press, 1964), Appendix B, pp. 132–35.

31. *The Art of James Joyce*, p. 137. See the Appendix to this article for a discussion of chapter numbering in the *Stephen Hero* manuscript.

32. *Stephen Hero* (New York: New Directions 1944; 1963), p. 135.

33. "The Text," p. 179n.

34. 232.27; and cf. the manuscript reading of 232.32: "And therefore the air was silent save for one brief hiss that fell." See Gabler, "Towards a Critical Text," pp. 35–36, for a discussion of a later revision further unifying these corresponding phrases.

35. "Stephen's growth proceeds in waves, in accretions of flesh, in particularization of needs and desires, around and around but always ultimately forward," says Richard Ellmann, and points to the correspondence in Joyce's compositional method, which was "to work and rework the original elements in the process of gestation" (*JJ*, 307).

36. Robert Scholes, "Stephen Dedalus, Poet or Esthete?" *PMLA* 89 (1964): 484–89. The critical evaluation of the villanelle episode is continuing: see Charles Rossman, "Stephen Dedalus' Villanelle," *James Joyce Quarterly* 12 (1975): 281–93.

37. *Workshop*, p. 107.

38. The sacramental overtones of the seemingly casual opening are indeed significant—it is his Last Breakfast that Stephen is celebrating.

39. Four times, at 224.04, 225.06, 232.25 and 237.13.

40. See the Appendix.

41. Bibliographically and paleographically, the notebook (Scholes, *Cornell Joyce Collection*, no. 25) gives the appearance of having been arranged, and begun with a run of its first entries through most of the alphabetical headings, at one time. Consequently, the dateable entry under "Pappie" (see above, note 22) takes on significance for the dating of the whole notebook.

42. *Letters*, 1, 136.

43. *Letters*, 1, 73.

44. *JJ*, chapters 20 and 21 *passim*.

A *Portrait* and
the *Bildungsroman*
Tradition

BREON MITCHELL

I

WHEN JOYCE FIRST BEGAN work on *A Portrait*, the *Bildungsroman* already had a long and established tradition, beginning with the "priceless pages" of Goethe's *Wilhelm Meister*. Thus Joyce could, by implication, play off the development of his young hero against a succession of literary figures from the past. In calling his novel *A Portrait of the Artist as a Young Man*, Joyce simultaneously related it to yet another tradition— the static portraiture of the visual arts. Yet when an artist like Rembrandt painted a self-portrait, he froze the moment at which, looking into a mirror, he paused before applying the brush to the canvas. Joyce opposed to this frozen mirror of art the notion of organic growth and change in time:

The features of infancy are not commonly reproduced in the adolescent portrait for, so capricious are we, that we cannot or will not conceive the past in any other than its iron, memorial aspect. Yet the past assuredly implies a fluid succession of presents, the development of an entity of which our actual present is a phase only.[1]

This statement, which opens Joyce's 1904 essay "A Portrait of the Artist," points toward the central concept of the *Bildungsroman*, or novel of development.

The *Bildungsroman* first appeared in eighteenth-century Germany and has continued to reappear in almost every national literature of the Western world.[2] Goethe's *Wilhelm Meister* (1795-96) established a model for this new form of the novel and encouraged others to try their hand at it. The influence of *Wilhelm Meister* has been both profound and pervasive.[3] It is safe to say that no major German novel about a young man's development has been written without a backward glance toward Goethe. And to an important degree his influence may be felt in the major novels of development in France, England, and America as well.

The notion of the *Bildungsroman* is a simple one: the author treats the life of a young man through the important years of his spiritual development, usually from boyhood through adolescence. He is shown as being formed and changed by interaction with his milieu, and with the world. Experience, as opposed to formal education, is considered central to development. The young man must encounter life, and be formed in that encounter. The *Bildungsroman* is inevitably open-ended: it prepares the hero for maturity and life but does not go on to depict that life; in place of experiencing his destiny the hero is made ready to confront it. There is no guarantee of his success, but there is usually good reason to hope for it. The hero of the *Bildungsroman* also has his characteristic traits. He is normally good-hearted, naïve, and innocent. Often he is completely separated from society by birth or fortune, and the story of his development is the story of his preparation to enter into that society. The *Bildungsroman* thus has as an important concomitant interest the relationship of the individual to society, the values and norms of that society, and the ease or difficulty with which a good man can enter into it.

The basic concerns of the *Bildungsroman* have their effect on the structure and style of the novel as well. The novel is held together as a work of art not by the story (as in a conventional novel) but by our interest in the development of the main character. The action tends to be episodic rather than arranged into a tightly woven plot. The form of the novel is itself "open," rather than, for example, the "closed" circular structure of *Finnegans Wake.* Since it is closely concerned with internal development, the *Bildungsroman* also shows a typical texture of narrative techniques suited to such an interest, including inner monologue, narrated monologue, quoted thought, internal analysis, and use of the first person.

In light of even this brief description of the traditional *Bildungsroman,* it is obvious that Joyce's *Portrait of the Artist as a Young Man* is in many ways almost surprisingly conventional, in the literal sense of that term. This is in itself worth pointing out, for Joyce is an author of such inventiveness and originality that points of contact with traditional literary forms are worth holding on to. *Ulysses* strikes many readers as *sui generis;* the *Portrait,* however, functions as a pivot between convention and innovation within the European literary context. The tradition of the *Bildungsroman* offers both an approach to certain major facets of *A Portrait* and a sounding board against which Joyce's important contributions to modern literature may be tested.

II

Although the term *Bildungsroman* is usually translated as "novel of development," it will be worthwhile to begin by defining the concept of *Bildung* more carefully. Almost every character in a modern novel undergoes some change in the course of the work. But *Bildung* is a particular form of development—one in which the various aspects of a young man's experience are united to produce a well-rounded individual who is both knowledgeable and wise. Formal education is only one part of this process, and by no means the most important one. The rise of the *Bildungsroman* in eighteenth-century Germany was closely tied to a lively interest in how best to prepare a young man to take his meaningful and rightful place in society. The word *Bild* in *Bildung* had originally referred to a model (in the sense of modern German *Vorbild*) in terms of which the young man was to be molded. The first such model was Christ, and *Bildung* was the process of formation in his spiritual image. By the end of the eighteenth century, *Bildung* had taken on a wider, more cosmopolitan, meaning. Formal education, it was felt, must be supplemented by a wide range of experiences. The *Bildungsreise*, a journey upon which the young man would visit the important museums and historical sites of Europe, added to his book learning indispensable first-hand knowledge of other countries and peoples. During these years of travel (the *Wanderjahre*) he would attain the polish of a man of the world. Upon his return home he would be prepared to settle down (and no doubt marry), taking his preordained place within the social order. His *Bildung* would be complete.

In *Wilhelm Meister* Goethe went beyond this notion of *Bildung* to suggest that the interaction with life was likely to be a painful one if it were deeply experienced. The events which contribute to the formation of Wilhelm's personality are concrete and fully lived. They include disappointments and personal sufferings not limited to the intellectual and cultural plane. His life with a theater troup and his relationship with women were considered by many of Goethe's contemporaries as shockingly free and amoral. Yet such experiences formed important components of his development. *Bildung* thus attained its broadest and most profound sense: the sum of lived experience which makes up the whole man, and makes him whole.

We should keep in mind, however, that Goethe's novel is the story of a young man who mistakes his vocation. Wilhelm's original goal is the creation of a national German theater. At the close of the novel he has renounced the life of art and, under the guidance of the mysterious Society of the Tower, is about to embark upon a journey which will lead to a life of practical service within the community of man. Because *Wilhelm Meister* was sharply attacked on moral grounds it quickly became the rallying point for a new generation of romantic poets in Germany. The novel seemed to insist on the primacy of life over social conventions, and this was a welcome breath of fresh air to young writers. But they soon realized it was a two-edged sword, for it also insisted on the primacy of life over art and struck at the heart of the romantic notion of artistic mission. This fact is unlikely to have escaped Joyce, and *A Portrait* provides, among other things, a reaffirmation of the concept of artistic vocation.[4]

When Stanislaus suggested the title *Stephen Hero* for his brother's novel, he may well have had the name Wilhelm Meister (i.e., Master) in mind.[5] The ironic distancing achieved through the names is similar; Wilhelm aims toward theatrical greatness and mastery of life, Stephen grapples with the heroic attitude of rebellion. In both cases the author invites the reader to reflect upon the distance between self-image and reality. In settling at last upon the name Stephen Dedalus, and returning to the more or less neutral title *A Portrait of the Artist,* Joyce at least partially tempered his irony. By adding the words "as a young man," he achieved a compensatory distancing—but with a different effect. The self-portrait of 1904 was contemporaneous with the final stage of development depicted, as is a self-portrait in the visual arts. Ten years later Joyce was able to write from a new perspective, looking back with increased maturity upon the struggles of the artist as a young man in the process of formation. In so doing he brought his novel even more clearly into the tradition of the *Bildungsroman,* which is characteristically written from a perspective of achieved stability and maturity. This is evident not only in the fact that the author implies that he knows what the process of *Bildung* is all about (that is, that he himself has gone through the formation, or one very similar to it) but also in the mature quality of the work of art itself. The author may reflect the stages of growth of his central figure in the very words he employs, but he himself will always stand above and behind such a style. To become the artist-god of creation he must have himself undergone the apprenticeship to life he wishes to depict. He can disappear behind this life only after he has lived it.

III

The opening pages of *A Portrait* dip further back into childhood than do most traditional novels of development, and the seemingly random impressions of the small child point to the central themes of the novel to come: art (storytelling), family, politics, incipient love, punishment, and apology, even the foreshadowing of the physical in the initially pleasant unpleasantness of bed-wetting. Almost every major theme is introduced in miniature.

Like Stephen's first step in the aesthetic apprehension of a work of art, the child must begin by separating himself from the rest of reality. Initially the lines of distinction are blurred— he *is* baby tuckoo. On the flyleaf of his geography book at Clongowes he attempts to locate himself physically in space: "He read the flyleaf from the bottom to the top till he came to his own name. That was he: and he read down the page again. What was after the universe? Nothing. But was there anything round the universe to show where it stopped before the nothing place began? . . . It made him very tired to think that way" (16). Gaining a sense of himself is of course one of Stephen's major preoccupations throughout the novel. With his father in Cork, he is later to recite a variant of the same theme in a vain attempt to understand who and where he is: "I am Stephen Dedalus. I am walking beside my father whose name is Simon Dedalus. We are in Cork, in Ireland. Cork is a city" (92). His task is made more difficult by the fact that he is constantly changing. Already by the second chapter of the novel he thinks of his childhood as "dead or lost" (96). He is not yet sixteen years old. Such sensitivity to the very process of growth and change he is experiencing distinguishes Stephen from most of his literary predecessors. He is acutely aware of the rapid disappearance of his past self from moment to moment. Recalling his first premonition of death while in the infirmary at Clongowes he muses: "He had not died but had faded out like a film in the sun. He had been lost or had wandered out of existence for he no longer existed. . . . It was strange to see his small body appear again for a moment" (93).

His final decision to reject the life of the church is marked by a passage which might almost serve as an epigraph for the traditional *Bildungsroman:* "He was destined to learn his own wisdom apart from others or to learn the wisdom of others himself wandering among the snares of the world" (162).

Like the typical *Bildungsroman* hero, Stephen begins as a good-hearted and naïve little boy, unable to understand why his older classmates laugh when he says he kisses his mother good night. The correct answer to their questions is beyond him, for he has yet to learn that there is no answer. Later, at Belvedere, the sin of sacrilege and the mysterious sexual offenses hinted at by his schoolmates stand for yet another realm of life beyond his grasp. He feels set apart from the others and dimly perceives that he differs from them in important ways. In this latter respect Stephen resembles the typical *Bildungsroman* hero as well. Traditionally the hero is cut off from society by birth or fortune, and Stephen is certainly dogged throughout the novel by his humiliating sense of grinding poverty and squalor: "The life of his body, illclad, illfed, louseeaten, made him close his eyelids in a sudden spasm of despair" (234). But the feeling of otherness which possesses him goes far beyond economic conditions: "Stephen watched the three glasses being raised from the counter as his father and his two cronies drank to the memory of their past. An abyss of fortune or of temperament sundered him from them. His mind seemed older than theirs: it shone coldly on their strifes and happiness and regrets like a moon upon a younger earth" (95). It is this same sense of spiritual isolation which has left him a spectator since early childhood. The gap that separates him from others cannot be closed by wealth, as he soon learns when his prize money has been quickly spent:

How foolish his aim had been! He had tried to build a breakwater of order and elegance against the sordid tide of life. . . . Useless. . . .

He saw clearly too his own futile isolation. He had not gone one step nearer the lives he had sought to approach nor bridged the restless shame and rancour that divided him from mother and brother and sister. (98)

It is this unbridgeable spiritual distance which, in the twentieth-century *Bildungsroman*, replaces the more literal exclusion of the hero from society in earlier examples.[6]

The changes Stephen undergoes in the course of the novel, and the choices he is forced to make, arise out of the texture of his everyday life. In the very first chapter he already knows that the tears in his father's eyes must somehow be weighed against Dante's fervent cry "God and religion before everything! ... God and religion before the world!" (39). Ultimately, he will seek to escape both politics and religion, but for the moment he is a lost and deeply puzzled little boy: "Who was right then?" As he grows older it is the interaction with the world around him which contributes to the formation of his character. His fall into a life of youthful degeneration seems temporarily redeemed by his moral decision to repent and confess. But this too is simply a stage in his spiritual growth, and his rejection of the religious life carries with it a clear commitment to a wider realm of experience:

The voice of the director urging upon him the proud claims of the church and the mystery and power of the priestly office repeated itself idly in his memory. His soul was not there to hear and greet it and he knew now that the exhortation he had listened to had already fallen into an idle formal tale. He would never swing the thurible before the tabernacle as priest. His destiny was to be elusive of social or religious orders. (162)

For the moment it seems to Stephen as if life, in all its untidiness, has triumphed: "He smiled to think that it was this disorder, the misrule and confusion of his father's house and the stagnation of vegetable life, which was to win the day in his soul" (162). The final choice of a new and higher ordering of life has yet to be made.

When Stephen at last recognizes the true shape of his destiny, he feels that his soul has "arisen from the grave of boyhood, spurning her graveclothes" (170). "This was the call of life to his soul not the dull gross voice of the world of duties and despair, not the inhuman voice that had called him to the pale service of the altar" (169). "He would create proudly out of the freedom and power of his soul, as the great artificer whose name he bore, a living thing, new and soaring and beautiful, impalpable, imperishable" (170). The final chapter of *A Portrait* provides the necessary counterweight to these flights of rapture. Poverty and the disorder of life have not miraculously vanished. At the university Stephen must struggle with one last decision—to escape the world he knows, completely.

Not only the content, but also the style and structure of *A Portrait* are in part determined by the particular demands of the *Bildungsroman*. Since interest is focused on Stephen's spiritual progression, the novel tends to be episodic; it is clear that the basic division of the work into five chapters reflects this progression and that each chapter presents us with a distinct stage in Stephen's development. Because that development is far from a smooth path to maturity, it should not surprise us that the narrative line of *A Portrait* has its ups and downs as well. The upbeats come at the end of each of the five sections. Nevertheless, the upswing of emotion and release which occurs in the final pages of each chapter is always balanced by a corresponding deflation in the initial pages of the next.

Thus Stephen's triumph at Clongowes in the first section is followed in the second by his move to Belvedere and his discovery of the true face of the encounter through his father's conversation with the rector. The tears of joy and sexual relief with which the second section closes are transformed into bitter remorse in the third. The power of confession and communion which makes life seem so beautiful and peaceful at the end of the third section soon evaporates in the fourth, leaving only a sensation of spiritual dryness. The profane joy and rapture Stephen experiences on the beach at the close of the fourth section is given its inverse mirror image at the beginning of the fifth in the dark pool of the jar and the squalid life which still surrounds him. The open-ended novel, were this rhythm to continue, would point toward yet another spiritual deflation following his departure from Ireland. And indeed many readers feel a fall is in the offing. Nevertheless, we must concede that the rhythm of *A Portrait* is not the simple movement of a pendulum. There is a progression toward maturity and self-knowledge, toward the acceptance of both life and error. If we are not convinced that Stephen has, by the end of the novel, achieved a full measure of wisdom, we must at least admit that the path he has traced is close enough to that of the invisible author hovering behind the work to admit the possibility of his ultimate success. Stephen's *Wanderjahre* still lie before him, but the basic choices have been made, and the important elements of his *Bildung* are all in place.

IV

It is clear that *A Portrait of the Artist as a Young Man* closely parallels the basic form and content of the traditional *Bildungsroman*. I have also suggested that Joyce was consciously working within this tradition. But he did not simply take over a set of conventions. He used the *Bildungsroman* model to attack implicitly the notion of *Bildung* while at the same time enlarging upon the narrative possibilities inherent in the form. To begin with the latter point: Joyce was anxious to show the "fluid succession of presents" which served as the only accurate mirror of the changing personality. But the traditional narrative perspective of the *Bildungsroman*, the mature man reflecting upon the past, did not seem to allow for any but the "iron, memorial" aspect of time remembered. What was needed was a narrative technique which could accommodate itself to change in the central figure while maintaining distance. This would involve a flow of narration which became increasingly complex with the increasing complexity of the mind of the protagonist. The result is apparent from the opening pages of *A Portrait* to the final entries in Stephen's diary. The imitative texture involved offers a series of portraits in which we "see"

Stephen through a narrative style which emphasizes, in its choice of vocabulary and manner of expression, the stage of verbal sophistication he has attained.

The primary narrative technique utilized to this end is narrated monologue (*erlebte Rede*).[7] Stephen's thoughts are given in the third person, past tense, but they still retain the flavor of his actual speech. This technique, which allows the author to filter the thoughts of his characters while depicting a characteristic manner of expression, contributes to what I have termed the "imitative texture" of the work. Narrated monologue is a perfect vehicle for the purposes of the *Bildungsroman* since the continual presence of the author, recalling the development from a point outside the process itself, is implicit in the technique. Joyce enlarges upon this traditional approach to one form of narration by allowing the flavor of his protagonist's thought to "spill over," as it were, into the narration of events themselves. A typical example of this effect is:

The bell rang for night prayers and he filed out of the studyhall after the others and down the staircase and along the corridors to the chapel. The corridors werè darkly lit and the chapel was darkly lit. Soon all would be dark and sleeping. There was·cold night air in the chapel and the marbles were the colour the sea was at night. (17)

These are not actual thoughts passing through Stephen's mind. But his actions, his state of mind, and the description of his surroundings, are given in prose which tells us a great deal about the level of Stephen's sophistication.

When this effect is combined with straightforward depiction of events, as, for example, in the scene with Stephen and his friends on the beach, the author may play off the particular verbal style of his central figure against reality in an ironic counterpoint:

His soul was soaring in an air beyond the world and the body he knew was purified in a breath and delivered of incertitude and made radiant and commingled with the element of the spirit. An ecstasy of flight made radiant his eyes and wild his breath and tremulous and wild and radiant his windswept limbs.

—One! Two! . . . Look out!
—O, cripes, I'm drownded! (169)

Such general remarks on the narrative style of *A Portrait* have been made before. What has not been sufficiently emphasized is the extent to which Joyce contributed in a very direct sense to solving a particular problem of the genre—that of balancing narrative perspective against narrative depiction. Joyce's unique use of an increasingly complex verbal texture (and the corresponding effect of a shifting perspective) combined with more traditional narrative approaches allowed him to both tell and show his story. Joyce's novel of development becomes a double portrait: it shows the artist in the process of formation; it also shows his growing awareness of language and demonstrates his developing ability to handle the medium in which he is to create. Just as a self-portrait by Rembrandt shows us both what the artist looked like at a certain stage of his life and how well he was able to paint at that age, Joyce's *Portrait* depicts *and* demonstrates Stephen's gradual development toward the priesthood of eternal imagination.

But I have suggested that Joyce's novel also contains an implicit critique of the *Bildungsroman*. We tend to view *A Portrait* today as being centrally concerned with the spiritual growth of a sensitive and creative young man. It is certainly that; but for James Joyce it was an explicit attack upon Ireland as well. As previously mentioned, the novel of development has always had a strong interest in the relationship of the individual to society, the values and norms of that society, and the ease or difficulty with which a good man could enter into it. If we substitute the word "artist" for "good man" in this formulation, we have yet another avenue of approach to *A Portrait*.

In emphasizing the importance of openness to life and experience in the formation of a young man, and in underlining the often painful nature of that apprenticeship, Joyce was simply reiterating the received wisdom of the past century. But in ultimately denying, at least in Ireland, the possibility of a full and unfettered life *within* society, he struck at the heart of the very notion of *Bildung*. Consider that *A Portrait* consists of not one, but two, novels of development—one traditional, and one antitraditional. It is interesting to contemplate the effect that might have been achieved had the novel ended with the third section, with Stephen's repentance and confession. Aside from the factor of length, *A Portrait* would be transformed into a more or less conventional nineteenth-century *Bildungsroman*. All the essential elements are present. The pure-hearted and naïve young man has received his basic education, confronted the harsh realities of life, experienced more than one fall, and learned his lessons. Now he is prepared to confront his destiny (in all likelihood entry into the Jesuit order). The novel would still be open-ended ("How simple and beautiful was life after all! And life lay all before him" [146]), but with the clear implication that the young man had weathered the storms of life and was about to enter the harbor.

The fact that Joyce continued the novel, depicting a growth and development away from the church toward art, would not in itself constitute a departure from the *Bildungsroman* tradition. It is, rather, the notion of the necessity of escape from society, of self-imposed exile as a prerequisite to a fulfilling life, which gives a new twist to this form of the novel. The *Bildungsroman* is, by implication and in fact, programmatic. That is, the author is not simply telling the story of the development of a young man—he is also claiming that this development is in some important respect a normative one. Stephen's choices, for Joyce, are surely the right ones.[8] They do not guarantee his success in life, but they do tell us that, for some young men at least, flight from Ireland is an absolute necessity. We are to believe that Ireland was indeed an old sow that ate her farrow. We are to believe that the church in Ireland did indeed represent a danger on the road to a full and creative life. *A Portrait* does not tell us that silence, exile, and cunning are the necessary weapons of all young artists in all societies, but it does claim this in the particular case of Ireland. Thus, while *A Portrait* retains almost every essential feature of the *Bildungsroman*, it frees its hero from the traditional goal of integration into society.[9]

Part of Joyce's particular genius was the ability to draw upon the literary past and deliver it to the future in an enriched form. *A Portrait* is a case in point. Approaching Joyce's novel from the tradition of the *Bildungsroman* in Europe helps illuminate important elements of the work. But it is a tribute to Joyce's creative powers that his interaction with this tradition enlarged the narrative possibilities inherent in the form and altered our subsequent view of what a novel of development could be.

NOTES

1. "A Portrait of the Artist," in *"A Portrait of the Artist as a Young Man": Text, Criticism, and Notes,* ed. Chester G. Anderson (New York: Viking Press, 1968), pp. 257–58. Hereafter references to *A Portrait* and critical apparatus are cited in the text.

2. For a general history and discussion of the *Bildungsroman* see François Jost, "La Tradition du *Bildungsroman*," *Comparative Literature* 21 (1969): 97–115 (includes a detailed bibliography); Fritz Martini, "Der Bildungsroman: Zur Geschichte des Wortes und der Theorie," *Deutsche Vierteljahrsschrift für Literaturwissenschaft und Geistesgeschichte* 35 (1961): 44–63; and Roy Pascal, "The *Bildungsroman*," in *The German Novel: Studies,* by Roy Pascal (Toronto: University of Toronto Press, 1956), pp. 3–99.

3. For a detailed study of the impact of *Wilhelm Meister* on the English novel prior to Joyce, see Susanne Howe, *Wilhelm Meister and his English Kinsmen: Apprentices to Life* (1930; rpt. New York: AMS Press, 1966). She refers to Joyce's *Portrait* in passing, as part of a group of more recent novels which take up the basic theme of the *Bildungsroman*.

4. Maurice Beebe has ably discussed a central concept of the "artist-novel" in his introduction to *Ivory Towers and Sacred Founts: The Artist as Hero in Fiction from Goethe to Joyce* (New York: New York University Press, 1964), which is reprinted in the Viking Critical Library edition of *Portrait*, pp. 340–57. He concentrates upon "the Divided Self of the artist-man wavering between the Ivory Tower and the Sacred Fount, between the 'holy' or esthetic demands

of his mission as artist and his natural desire as a human being to participate in the life around him" (p. 357). Stephen clearly fits into this pattern, but it is helpful to see him in the broader context of the novel of development as well. The "artist-novel" (*Künstlerroman*) is a *Bildungsroman* with an artist as its central figure. The German term *Entwicklungsroman* refers to a novel of development in which the sense of *Bildung*, as outlined in this essay, is not necessarily present. The distinction between the broader category of the *Entwicklungsroman*, and that of the *Bildungsroman*, is presented in detail in Melitta Gerhard, *Der deutsche Entwicklungsroman bis zu Goethes "Wilhelm Meister"* (Halle: Max Niemeyer Verlag, 1926).

5. Stanislaus' own admiration for Goethe is attested to by his diaries for 1904: "[Henry James's] mind, more than any other mind with which I am acquainted, more than Pater's, shows the influence of Goethe. I admire Goethe and I flatter myself that I have a good understanding of his character though I have read very little of what he has written." (*The Complete Dublin Diary of Stanislaus Joyce*, ed. George Healey [Ithaca: Cornell University Press, 1971], p. 126, entry of 2 October 1904.) Stanislaus' discussion of Henry James's *The Portrait of a Lady* also may indicate a source for the final title of the *Portrait* ("A Portrait of the Artist" was Stanislaus' suggestion as well).

We have little evidence of Joyce's attitude toward Goethe. In 1915 he had scoffed at him as "a boring civil servant" (Richard Ellmann, *James Joyce* [New York: Oxford University Press, 1959], p. 406), and the reference to *Wilhelm Meister,* in the "Scylla and Charybdis" episode of *Ulysses* (New York: Random House, 1961) draws a sneer from Stephen. But the summary is an accurate enough description of both Hamlet and the young artist: "And we have, have we not, those priceless pages of *Wilhelm Meister?* A great poet on a great brother poet. A hesitating soul taking arms against a sea of troubles, torn by conflicting doubts, as one sees in real life. . . . The beautiful ineffectual dreamer who comes to grief against hard facts. One always feels that Goethe's judgments are so true. True in the larger analysis" (p. 184). In *Finnegans Wake* (New York: Viking Press, 1939) Goethe's epic *Hermann und Dorothea* becomes "Worse nor herman dororrhea" (p. 283.28), and Goethe himself usually comes out gouty. But if we are to take this as a negative judgment, Goethe is in very good company: "Daunty, Gouty and Shopkeeper, A.G.", (ibid., p. 539.6; A.G. is *Aktiengesellschaft* or "Inc."). As late as 1939 Joyce was still interested enough in Goethe to read his *Conversations with Eckermann* (Ellmann, *James Joyce*, p. 743).

6. An obvious exception to this general statement are the novels of development written by contemporary black American authors, where the problem of entry into society is indeed based on external factors of birth.

7. See Dorrit Cohn, "Narrated Monologue: Definition of a Fictional Style," *Comparative Literature* 13 (1966): 97–112, for a further discussion of this topic. It is interesting to note that the inner monologue, which plays such an

important role in *Ulysses*, is simply not present in *A Portrait* (the diary entries at the close of the novel represent a long-established narrative means of getting the protagonist's thoughts on paper). Strictly defined, inner monologue presents the character's thoughts in the first person, present tense, with no authorial intervention. This includes the deliberate omission of such guides to the reader as quotation marks around the thoughts, and introductory phrases such as "he said to himself," where the presence of the author is clearly felt. When such signals are included, we may speak of "quoted thought." There are, of course, many further qualitative and stylistic distinctions between quoted thought and inner monologue.

8. It may be objected that Joyce leaves us with an insufferable, egocentric young man who has never really come to grips with life or the problems of human relationships. And one can certainly deny that Joyce intended *A Portrait* to be normative even in the case of a Stephen Dedalus. Stephen is not a "finished" human being by the end of *A Portrait*. When we see him again in *Ulysses* he is still insufferable in many respects, and serves as a counterbalance to the essentially "good man" Bloom. Our opinion on such a matter depends upon our conception of Joyce's intentions, his true distance from Stephen, and his judgments about Stephen's life. My tendency is to agree with Ellmann: "Some readers [have supposed] that Joyce could not bear his own hero. But in both portraits, as well as in the intermediate *Stephen Hero*, there is no lack of sympathy on the author's part; he recognizes, however, that earlier stages of the hero's life were necessarily callow, and makes the callowness clear in order to establish the progression towards the mature man" (*James Joyce*, pp. 149–50).

9. An example of a recent *Bildungsroman* that runs against the grain of tradition in this respect is Günter Grass's *The Tin Drum*, trans. Ralph Manheim (New York: Pantheon, 1961). Grass's protagonist, Oskar, also refuses to enter into, or fulfill the demands of, society. But rather than run away he simply refuses to grow up.

A *Portrait* and
Giambattista Vico:
A Source Study

MARGARET CHURCH **4**

DESPITE THE WORK of the "new criticism," of various
deterministic schools of thought, of psychological criticism, of
studies of craftsmanship, or of social or psychological development, without source study one must ignore revealing literary
relationships such as those between *Crime and Punishment*
and *The Trial*,[1] between *Don Quixote* and *Joseph Andrews* or
Madame Bovary, between *Tristram Shandy* and some of the
novels of Virginia Woolf. A good source study provides one
with material for understanding both the work influenced and
the source. It enables one to place the work influenced in a
literary context, to define it and its goals through such context,
and to decide thereby how it succeeds and how it may fail.[2] In
addition, Jorge Luis Borges has shown how awareness of
source may enlarge understanding of the source itself: "Every
writer," Borges claims, "*creates* his own precursors."[3] In
"Pierre Menard, Author of the *Quixote*" Borges points out that
Menard, in "composing" the *Quixote,* has enriched "the halting
and rudimentary art of reading" through deliberate anachro-
nism and that attributing *Imitatio Christi* to Céline or James
Joyce is "sufficient renovation of its tenuous spiritual indications."[4] Thus he would argue that in attributing the *Scienza
nuova* to James Joyce, one may gain insights into the writings   **77**

of Vico as well as into Joyce's own work.[5] Norman O. Brown
has recently demonstrated this point with concreteness in his
Closing Time, in which he juxtaposes passages from Vico and
Finnegans Wake, creating a three-way dialogue with himself as
moderator and chorus.

Genesis is *Natura*
the nature of nations is their *nascimento*   NS,
                the way they were born   147–48

culture is nature
the nations have a natural law which is their nature   NS, 311
                the way they were born

the Vico Rd is the Nascimiento Rd   FW, 452
                (below Big Sur

the way they were born
the birth trauma
           (Otto Rank
determines their character[6]

Intriguing critical possibilities for reinterpretation of both
source and counterpart exist if one can introduce Borges's
theory of mutual interaction of literary works into the field of
criticism.

Scholes and Kain's *Workshop of Daedalus* suggests, of
course, a veritable lode of material which can be exploited by
the critic in this way in connection with Joyce's *A Portrait.*[7] To
sum up what is by now a classic in the literature surrounding *A
Portrait,* in "The Esthetic Milieu" the authors demonstrate how
Joyce's aesthetic theory is grounded in scholasticism (Aquinas), in romanticism (Shelley), in realism (Flaubert), in aestheticism (Wilde), and in symbolism (Yeats). Stephen's "Villanelle
of the Temptress" is seen as stemming from Pater, from the
typological habit of thought characteristic of St. Augustine,
from Symons's discussion of Gerard de Nerval's belief in
metempsychosis, from Yeats, Boyd, Dawson, Swinburne, and
Francis Thompson. Scholes and Kain contend further that the
concept of the poet as manifested in *A Portrait* derives from

Ovid's Daedalian trinity, from the Italian novelist D'Annunzio, and from Oscar Wilde's view of the artist as individualist. In addition, Pater's imaginary portrait series may be seen to stand behind Joyce's work, as well, possibly, as Browning's dramatic monologues.

Other noteworthy work on influences in *A Portrait* abounds, such as that by David Hayman in his study of its Daedalian imagery, in which he discusses Hellenic pattern and counterparts and states that "Joyce found in Ibsen, Flaubert, and D'Annunzio qualities that inform his use of the Daedalus myth."[8] Hayman's comparative article on *A Portrait* and *L'Education sentimentale* points out that Flaubert in particular, also Jacobsen and D'Annunzio, through their several *Bildungsromane* furnished Joyce with "theories, images, points of style and an occasional sequence of scene" as well as traits which enabled *A Portrait* to become "a new departure in the English novel."[9] Brian Dibble's Brunonian reading of *A Portrait*[10] or George Geckle's article on Stephen Dedalus and Yeats[11] also come to mind as valuable source studies. Evert Sprinchorn writes of more general areas of influence on *A Portrait*, such as Homeric, Ovidian, Christian, or that of the Eleusinian Mysteries, and concludes his essay with a postscript on influences.[12] Joyce Warren's article on "Faulkner's 'Portrait of the Artist' throws light on Joyce's book as the source rather than as the recipient of influence.[13]

Studies of Vico and Joyce have, however, been largely limited to *Finnegans Wake*.[14] It has been my contention that Joyce used Vico in his work much earlier than has usually been acknowledged, and the examination of *A Portrait* in the larger context of a gradually unfolding Viconian pattern traceable in Joyce's entire canon will demonstrate Joyce's significant debt to Vico as well as Vico's significant debt to Joyce.

The years 1911 to 1914 when Joyce was working on the final text of *A Portrait* were years when, according to his pupil, Paolo Cuzzi, "Joyce was also passionately interested in this Neapolitan philosopher," Vico. Cuzzi at this time talked to

Joyce about Freud as well, but Joyce, although he listened carefully, said "that Freud had been anticipated by Vico."[15]

Of all the structural and mechanical systems that Joyce employed in his works, Vico's was perhaps the most comforting and germane to the Joycean temperament. Formal orders, and as many as possible, encompass and control everything he wrote. As A. Walton Litz points out, "these neutral but controlling designs" were Joyce's means of ordering his diverse materials.[16] A number of structures have been found in *A Portrait*, and most of them are ones Joyce may have consciously employed. They coexist, suggesting human development on various levels. Basically the structural studies divide into three categories: (1) the studies of scholars like Grant Redford[17] and Thomas E. Connolly[18] who see the structure of *A Portrait* as governed by the aesthetic principles developed in the final chapter of the novel; (2) the studies of Robert Andreach[19] or Thomas Van Laan[20] who propose a structure determined by the spiritual stages through which Stephen moves; and (3) the argument of Richard Ellmann[21] and Sidney Feshbach[22] for the process of physical gestation as an organizing principle in *A Portrait*. Other more general studies stress imagery[23] or motif[24] as a major means of producing unity in the book.

Vico's influence may be found as early as *Dubliners*, and the Viconian pattern is one that fits in with the natural framework of Joyce's thinking.[25] As William York Tindall asserts, to replace Christianity, Joyce needed a system which would give him a sense of order; according to Tindall cyclical recurrence became Joyce's substitute for metaphysics.[26] Furthermore, the Viconian system—with its parallels in the natural cycle of the four seasons of the year and in the cycle of the development of man through childhood, adolescence, and maturity to death— is one that appealed to Joyce as universal. The possibility of cycles existing within cycles at different levels of interpretation allowed for the complexities and ambiguities which teased and attracted the subtle Joycean mentality. This essay will examine, then, the Viconian structure which perhaps enables us to view *A Portrait* in a new light, especially in its relation to *Ulysses* (which Ellmann tells us Joyce had been preparing himself to write since 1907 and which, according to Ellmann, "extends the method of *A Portrait*")[27] and in relation to the theories of Kenner, Tindall, Robert Ryf,[28] and others concerning the continuity to be found in the Joycean canon. As it is in *Dubliners*, the Viconian pattern in *A Portrait* is worked out on the religious, psychological, and mythical levels.

I

Vico's Divine Age (Joyce's Age of the Parents) may be seen as the basis of chapter 1 as it was the basis for the first three stories in *Dubliners*. The key to the Viconian structural pattern appears as early as page 13 where we read, "That night at Dalkey the train had roared," "roaring and then stopping; roaring again, stopping."[29] Vico Road is, of course, located in Dalkey as we learn in the "Nestor" episode in *Ulysses*. Furthermore, the cyclical pattern of the roaring and stopping of the noise is suggestive of Vico. The gods of Joyce's Divine Age are again, as in *Dubliners*, threatening figures, figures like Stephen's father with his hairy face, the older boys at Clongowes, the quarreling elders at Christmas dinner, and Father Dolan.

On the religious level, God the Father and the priests at the school are warped and angry gods, demanding cruel payment from the consciences of their young charges. Father Arnall and the prefect of studies, Father Dolan, with his pandybat, combine to inflict unjustly shame, agony, and fear on Stephen. And Father Conmee, who at the end of chapter 1 is viewed by Stephen and the other boys as a savior and protector, sees, we later learn, the whole incident of Stephen's beating as amusing. These are the figures of spiritual authority who dominate Stephen's life at school in this Divine Age.

In his psychological relation to the adults at home and to the older boys at school, Stephen fares scarcely better. In his infancy he fears his father and in his childhood is left "terror-stricken" by the violence of the argument over Parnell at Christmas dinner. Dante refers to Parnell as "a bad man" (16), and yet Mr. Casey sees him as "My dead king!" (39). For the boy, therefore, this national figure is an ambiguous leader. The older boys at school provide even less real leadership. Their names, Rody Kickham, Nasty Roche, and Cecil Thunder, connote violence and filth. And Wells, another older boy, shoulders him into the slimy ditch causing him to become ill. Both physical and mental torture are inflicted by these "gods," even though Rody Kickham keeps a pair of greaves in his locker (reminiscent of knightly armor in a heroic age). Meanwhile, stalking the halls of the castle is the ghost of an earlier and nobler time, a real leader, a marshal in a white cloak, who had received his death wound on a battlefield near Prague and who seems to say "*drive away from it* [the castle] *all*" injustices (19). Such leaders exist, however, only in Stephen's fantasies.

The movement into the Age of the Sons, Vico's Heroic Age, is heralded in the last sentence of chapter 1 by the "pick, pack, pock, puck" of the cricket bats "like drops of water in a fountain falling softly in the brimming bowl" (59). This sound has been a punctuating device throughout the entire latter section of the chapter, indicating that time is about to overflow into a new age of human development. The pock of the corks in "Ivy Day in the Committee Room" likewise had punctuated the movement toward the climax when time overflows and Hynes recites his poem on Parnell. In the same way the "Sirens" episode in *Ulysses* is filled with clacks, taps, claps, pops, suggesting a falling apart or breaking up of continuity in the movement of the episode toward the new Age of the Fathers, the "Cyclops." As Joyce uses this sound at the end of chapter 1 of *A Portrait of the Artist*, it may be seen as a Viconian sign of the coming of a new age of adolescence, and of the "heroic."

II

The decline of the Age of the Parents is clearly apparent on the first page of chapter 2 where Uncle Charles is relegated to the outhouse to smoke his villainous black twist. Furthermore, we discover the key to cyclical recurrence on the next page in Stephen's run around the park (a familiar image in *Finnegans Wake*) as Mike Flynn stands timing him near the railway station (reminiscent of the train which roars and stops in chapter 1). Trains recirculate and, therefore, are often Viconian images for Joyce. The Age of the Sons in *A Portrait* is at first one of sentimental idealisms and Bovaristic daydreams (unlike that in *Dubliners* where the heroic is mocked by the crassness of Lenehan and Corley and the innocence and stupidity of Jimmy Doyle and Bob Doran), for this is the adolescence of "the artist." Stephen reads about and identifies with the Count of Monte Cristo and dreams of a Mercedes of his own. He founds a gang of adventurers and imitates Napoleon's dress. He sees himself as a kind of "Childe Stephen" (connoting both heroism and immaturity). When the family moves, he circles the square timidly for a time, but soon regains momentum. The myth and the romance are closely related in this chapter to Stephen's psychological development, and the religious element is pushed temporarily into the background. His Mercedes materializes in E. C., the girl he is with on the tram (the symbol of recirculation), and even his school bears a romantic-sounding name, Belvedere. At his school Stephen takes the chief part in a play, a farcical role like that of Quixote himself, yet all the actions of Stephen as hero are ineffectual and unproductive, and the play leaves him with a sense of wounded pride and fallen hope.

The relationship between son and father continues to deteriorate, for on the trip to Cork Simon declares: "I'm a better man than he is any day of the week" (95), and Stephen is "wearied and dejected by his father's voice" (92). This is what Joyce meant when he told Paolo Cuzzi that Vico anticipates Freud, for in Vico's Heroic Age the younger generation and the older reenact the rivalry inherent in the oedipal dilemma. At the end of chapter 2 Stephen's mock-heroic attempt to usurp the role of the father in the home with thirty-three pounds, his prize money, and to rescue the family, also fails. And his dreams of his Mercedes are, in the last pages, actualized in the arms of a prostitute. Ironically, the heroic age of the artist is finally embodied in Stephen's iniquitous cry of abandonment, "a cry which was but the echo of an obscene scrawl which he had read on the oozing wall of a urinal" (100).

III

The Age of the People (the Human Age) is seen in chapter 3 of *A Portrait* (as it had been in *Dubliners*, in the story "Grace") in terms of "religious" communion with one's fellowmen. The new age is introduced by the December dusk which tumbles "clownishly after its dull day" (102). Like Mr. Kernan, Stephen is enjoined to a retreat and to confession. The torments ensuing on disobedience are made clear to him. Alone he moves toward religious community, attempts to reach outside himself and to attach himself to a larger social segment. An old woman with a "reeking withered right hand" (141) directs him to his confessional as the warped characters in "Grace" had directed Mr. Kernan. Stephen feels that he has entered into another life, the body of our Lord and the community of saints. And yet the dreams of religious community found in chapter 3 turn out to be no more conclusive than the sentimental daydreams which had haunted Stephen in his Heroic Age.

IV

For a short time, however, Stephen finds communion and symmetry in the church until he recognizes, in chapter 4, in a revelation paralleling Vico's *Recorso*, that his destiny is to learn apart from others. "He would fall. He had not yet fallen but he would fall silently . . . falling, falling but not yet fallen, still

unfallen, but about to fall" (162). Then he crosses the bridge
over the stream of the Tolka. The imagery recalls "The Dead,"
the *Recorso* of *Dubliners*, with its sense of falling and the
falling snow. Stephen's sudden and stark recognition is one of
death, emptiness, and restriction (symbolized by the window
cord) in the life of the priesthood. Like Gabriel Conroy's, this
life now seemed "grave and ordered and passionless" (160).
The emphasis in the first part of the chapter is upon sundering
ties, first with his mother as he moves toward the university
and "a new adventure," then in the crossing of bridges (two
times in six pages, 162-67), indicating his entry into new worlds
and the changing direction of his existence. The final epiphany,
his name Dedalus as prophecy, prefigures a new father figure
in the mythical Daedalus, a replacement for Simon, and a new
direction in the turning tide and the cranelike girl who will
replace Mercedes. This new Daedalus symbolizes the artist as
does the crane which is capable of flight. The tide begins to
flow in, and Stephen feels "the vast cyclic movement of the
earth" (172) revolving toward a new Divine Age or Age of the
Fathers attendant upon this *Recorso*. Joyce's material quite
naturally falls into the Viconian pattern partly because Vico's
plan is primordial and archetypal of a lived life. In "To live, to
err, to fall, to triumph" (172), Vico's entire schema is submerged.

V

Perhaps one reason that critics have overlooked Vico in *A
Portrait* is that it contains five chapters, rather than four. But in
a book about a young man in search of a father, two rounds of
the Age of the Fathers are appropriate. Nevertheless, the
second cycle, despite the high hopes of the artificer in the
preceding *Recorso*, is as sterile and restrictive in its own way as
the priesthood toward which the first cycle had moved. The
new cycle begins with the gods of the university, the fathers
who teach literature, art, and philosophy and under whose

authority Stephen now finds himself. Hugh Kenner suggests
that this fifth chapter is perhaps "a suspended chord,"[30] and it
may indeed be a chord linking *A Portrait* with the "Telemachia," the first three episodes of *Ulysses*. This may be the Age
of the Fathers to the new Age of the Sons found in the
"Telemachus" episode. The Divine Age of the university leads,
however, to a Heroic Age of abstraction, theory, and teleologi-
cal systems. Viewing Joyce's entire canon, then, in the light of
Vico, we can see close parallels between *Dubliners* and *A
Portrait* as well as the final chapter of *A Portrait* as a background for the opening of *Ulysses*. The middle section of
Ulysses may also be modeled on a Viconian pattern, and the
"Nostos," then, leads into the giant *Recorso* of *Finnegans
Wake*, just as the fifth chapter of *A Portrait* leads into *Ulysses*.

The new gods in chapter 5 are figures like the Dean and
other professors, Stephen's literary models, Aristotle and Aquinas. And yet the Dean teaches without joy and with his literal
and matter-of-fact mind serves the marketplace rather than the
creative arts. The fires which he lights are made from coals and
twisted papers. Stephen mocks these gods of the marketplace
as he imagines them "ambling and stumbling, tumbling and
capering, kilting their gowns for leap frog" (192). They exhibit
a stupid and dogged failure to understand the meaning and
purpose of the arts. Nor can Stephen countenance the false
gods of the other students like the tsar in whose name a petition
for peace is being circulated. Furthermore, the gods of aesthetics, Aristotle and Aquinas, lead Stephen into complex and
abstract theory which is easily drowned out by even a dray
loaded with old iron. Rhythm, Stephen finds, "is the first
formal esthetic relation of part to part in any esthetic whole"
(205), reminding us of the rhythm of part to part imposed by
Joyce's reliance on Vico. The rhythm of structure is also
implied in Aquinas's *Consonantia* which Stephen apprehends
in theory. Yet in this world of abstractions, the artist is
eventually, in Stephen's own words, "refined out of existence"
(215).

Toward the end of chapter 5 we are again moving toward a new Heroic Age, the Age of Telemachus. The bird imagery once again suggests the possibility of escape, not only from the fathering principles of nationality, religion, and language, but also from the whole elaborate ideology of the fathering university as is implied in the passage from Swedenborg, who sees that birds have not perverted the order of times and seasons by intellect. The cyclical pattern of Vico is also suggested by Swedenborg's reference to birds going and coming and building unlasting homes (224–25). The conclusion to this Age of the Fathers becomes, then, *Non serviam* and flight as Stephen listens to the call of ships and appeals once more to the mythical artificer, Daedalus. However, the gods of the university have been abandoned in no real sense, for the knife blade of Stephen's intellect is the basis for his new nickname Kinch in *Ulysses,* and the "ineluctable modality of the visible" and other metaphysical concerns are the main subjects of Stephen's thoughts and conversation throughout the "Telemachia." Whereas the first cycle had led to a spiritual stasis, this second cycle leads to an intellectual stasis, "an esthetic emotion . . . raised above desire and loathing" (205) as Stephen had defined it earlier. Even with the girl at the end he turns on his "spiritual-heroic refrigerating apparatus" (252).

We leave Stephen, then, in the last pages of *A Portrait* as "a young man" on the verge of departing from his second Age of the Fathers. Joyce has promised us no more. He is a young man lacking the understanding and compassion to refrain from quarreling with his mother on the score of religion, lacking insight into his own motivations (Cranly tells him, "your mind is supersaturated with the religion in which you say you disbelieve" [240]), and dependent on the empty forms of an aesthetic and metaphysical system. And yet he does not fear his exile and goes into it with high hope, recognizing perhaps in his diary that in hoofs hurrying in the night one hears the eternal patterns of all journeys through the ages of the divine, the heroic, and the human.

For Joyce is saying in *A Portrait,* through Vico, that the Divine Age, the Age of the Fathers, may influence the development of the entire cycle so that in the end (the fifth chapter) new gods must be sought to replace the meaningless, empty, or shoddy ones who produce only barren repetition of experience. Repetition of experience must lead to mastery of experience, not to return for the sake of return. Freud has made the same point. It is to this end that Stephen has sought in chapter 5 for the original father, "the old artificer," the Daedalus who had fashioned both labyrinth and wings, both nets and the means of freedom from those nets. But the tragedy represented in *A Portrait* is that Stephen has found fatherhood neither in the sacred fount of the church nor in the ivory tower of the university.[31]

NOTES

1. See Margaret Church, "*Crime and Punishment* and Kafka's *The Trial,*" *Literature and Psychology* 19 (Fall 1969): 47–55.

2. See J. T. Shaw, "Literary Indebtedness and Comparative Literary Studies," in *Comparative Literature: Method and Perspective,*" ed. Newton P. Stallknecht and Horst Frenz, rev. ed. (Carbondale: Southern Illinois University Press, 1971), pp. 84–97.

3. Jorge Luis Borges, "Kafka and His Precursors," in his *Labyrinths: Selected Stories and Other Writings,* ed. Donald A. Yates and James E. Irby (New York: New Directions, 1964), p. 201.

4. Borges, p. 44.

5. Giambattista Vico (1668–1744), Italian philosopher of law and cultural history, author of *Scienza nuova* which appeared in 1725. An abridged translation is available: *The New Science of Giambattista Vico,* trans. Thomas Goddard Bergin and Max Harold Fisch (Garden City, N.Y.: Doubleday, 1961).

6. *Closing Time* (New York: Random House, 1973), p. 25.

7. Robert Scholes and Richard M. Kain, eds., *The Workshop of Daedalus: James Joyce and the Raw Materials for "A Portrait of the Artist as a Young Man"* (Evanston: Northwestern University Press, 1965).

8. "Daedalian Imagery in *A Portrait,*" in *Heriditas: Seven Essays on the Modern Experience of the Classical,* ed. Frederick Will (Austin: University of Texas Press, 1964), p. 33.

9. "*A Portrait of the Artist as a Young Man* and *L'Education sentimentale:* The Structural Affinities," *Orbis Litterarum* 19 (1964): 161.

10. "A Brunonian Reading of Joyce's *Portrait of the Artist as a Young Man*," *James Joyce Quarterly* 4 (Summer 1967): 280–85.

11. "Stephen Dedalus and W. B. Yeats: The Making of the Villanelle," *Modern Fiction Studies* 15 (Spring 1969): 87–96.

12. "A Portrait of the Artist as Achilles," in *Approaches to the Twentieth-Century Novel*, ed. John Unterecker (New York: Crowell, 1965), pp. 9–50.

13. "Faulkner's 'Portrait of the Artist,'" *Mississippi Quarterly* 19 (Summer 1966): 121–31.

14. See Margaret Church, *Time and Reality: Studies in Contemporary Fiction* (Chapel Hill: University of North Carolina Press, 1963), pp. 53–66.

15. Richard Ellmann, *James Joyce* (New York: Oxford University Press, 1959), p. 351.

16. A. Walton Litz, *The Art of James Joyce* (New York: Oxford University Press, 1964), pp. 38–39.

17. "The Role of Structure in Joyce's *Portrait*," *Modern Fiction Studies* 4 (Spring 1958): 21–30.

18. "Kinesis and Stasis: Structural Rhythm in Joyce's *Portrait of the Artist as a Young Man*," *University Review* 3 (1966): 21–30.

19. *Studies in Structure: The Stages of Spiritual Life in Four Modern Authors* (New York: Fordham University Press, 1964).

20. "The Meditative Structure of Joyce's *Portrait*," *James Joyce Quarterly* 1 (Spring 1964): 3–13.

21. Ellmann, *James Joyce*, pp. 306–09.

22. "A Slow and Dark Birth: A Study of the Organization of *A Portrait of the Artist as a Young Man*," *James Joyce Quarterly* 4 (Summer 1967): 289–300.

23. William York Tindall, *The Literary Symbol* (New York: Columbia University Press, 1955), pp. 78–86.

24. Lee T. Lemon, "*A Portrait of the Artist as a Young Man*," *Modern Fiction Studies* 12 (Winter 1966–67): 441–52.

25. See Margaret Church, "*Dubliners* and Vico," *James Joyce Quarterly* 8 (Winter 1968): 150–56.

26. *James Joyce: His Way of Interpreting the Modern World* (New York: Scribner's, 1950), p. 65.

27. Ellmann, *James Joyce*, p. 367.

28. *A New Approach to Joyce: "A Portrait of the Artist" as a Guidebook* (Berkeley and Los Angeles: University of California Press, 1962). Ryf sees *A Portrait* as a guidebook to Joyce's later work.

29. James Joyce, *A Portrait of the Artist as a Young Man* (New York: Viking Press, 1964), p. 13. Future references to this edition will appear in the text.

30. *Dublin's Joyce* (London: Chatto and Windus, 1955), p. 121.

31. Maurice Beebe, whose book *Ivory Towers and Sacred Founts: The Artist as Hero in Fiction from Goethe to Joyce* (New York: New York University Press, 1964) I have in mind here, first suggested to me the possibility of Vico's influence on *A Portrait*.

Epiphanies of Dublin

RICHARD M. KAIN

5

"DUBLIN WAS a new and complex sensation" (66). And, in the words of *Stephen Hero:* "As he walked thus through the ways of the city he had his ears and eyes ever prompt to receive impressions" (*SH*, 30). Awareness of the city must have been as formative an influence on the eleven-year-old Joyce in 1893 as it was for his fictional surrogate.[1]

Before coming to Dublin Stephen had indulged in romantic dreams, his imagination afire from *The Count of Monte Cristo.* He had identified himself with "that dark avenger," against a background of "the bright picture of Marseilles, of sunny trellisses" (62). The lovely figure of the heroine Mercedes had haunted him, but characteristic of his defiance was his admiration for the count's "sadly proud gesture of refusal" (63). He had longed for "that magic moment" in which he would be "transfigured," when "*weakness* and *timidity* and *inexperience* would fall from him." (The key words, italicized by me in these two paragraphs, become motifs throughout the novel, and, indeed, become important themes in much of Joyce's work.) In his imagined quest, overtones of love, religion, and art are blended: "He wanted to meet in the *real* world the unsubstantial *image* which his *soul* so constantly beheld. He did not know where to seek it or how: but a premonition which led him on told him that this *image* would, without any overt act of his, *encounter* him" (65). Stephen is always conscious of the contrast between the reality he sees and the ideal he seeks. The search is passive, that of a humble acolyte awaiting a sign. Through the mystery of words he had been afforded "glimpses of the *real* world," and he had begun "to make ready for the great part which he felt awaited him the nature of which he only dimly apprehended" (62).

At crucial points in his development there are verbal antic- ipations of the ringing words which announce the final trium- phant acceptance of mission. Memories of Mercedes accom- pany the onset of sexual desire, which, in fact, does eventuate ironically in his first experience with the prostitute. He recalls "the holy *encounter* he had then imagined at which *weakness* and *timidity* and *inexperience* were to fall from him" (99). Thus the very words of an opening episode in the second chapter are modulated at the end of the chapter. Again, at Belvedere College in the dim evening light of the schoolroom as he worked on an equation, the trail of figures suggests first "the vast cycle of starry life" and then "his own *soul going forth* to *experience*, unfolding itself sin by sin" (103). In response to the director's question of whether he has a vocation for the priesthood, another variation on the theme is sounded: "In vague sacrificial or sacramental acts alone his will seemed drawn to *go forth* to *encounter reality*" (159). At the shore, just before his sight of the wading girl, his name seemed prophetic, "a symbol of the artist *forging* anew in his workshop out of the sluggish matter of the earth a new soaring impalpable imper- ishable being" (169). Daydream, sexual desire, the sense of sin, refusal of the priesthood, and vision of earthly beauty culmi- nate in the well-known manifesto: "I *go* to *encounter* for the millionth time the *reality* of *experience* and to *forge* in the smithy of my *soul* the uncreated conscience of my race" (252–53).

The steps of this modern pilgrim's progress are delineated by significant episodes and by a musical development of

verbal echoes. After his first initiation to the city, Stephen
wanders to the docks and there experiences the conflict
between romantic ideal and sordid reality. On the one hand
the scum of the river, the noisy drays, and the unkempt
policeman, and, on the other, life's "vastness and strangeness"
evoked by the destinations of the merchandise being loaded on
the ships (66). In this passage can be found the seeds of many
stories in *Dubliners*. The attraction of the exotic, of foreign
lands and of arcane knowledge, plays an important role in
"The Sisters," "An Encounter," "Araby," "Eveline," and "After
the Race." The theme is reduced to banality in Little Chandler's admiration for the pseudosophistication of Ignatius
Gallaher ("A Little Cloud"), and to pathos in the sentimentality
of Maria's singing "I Dreamt that I Dwelt in Marble Halls"
("Clay"). The implicit irony in each of these situations is
intensified by the recitation of doggerel verse at the end of "Ivy
Day in the Committee Room."

Though young Stephen's interest in sounds, in words, and in
poetry had been apparent since childhood, as depicted so
sensitively in the first chapter of *A Portrait*, his early experience
in Dublin becomes a prologue to a sequence of insights—the
visit to the quays and to the "jovial array of shops lit up and
adorned for Christmas" (67). Immediately follows a series of
epiphanies. It is useful to distinguish between insights and
epiphanies, the first being embedded in the narrative and
supplied with comment by the narrator. We are told that
Stephen's visits to the quays left him with "vague dissatisfac-
tion" and that despite the Christmas festivity "his mood of
embittered silence did not leave him" (67). The epiphanies are
complete sketches, devoid of interpretation, each of these
opening with the words "He was sitting." They are introduced
by an avowal of impersonality: "He chronicled with patience
what he saw, detaching himself from it and testing its mortify-
ing flavour in secret" (67). The second episode is the fifth in the
series of forty extant Epiphanies.[2] So much controversy has
marked the discussion of the epiphany that one hesitates to use

the term. There is much to commend Sidney Feshbach's clarification in using the word epiphany to mean the general concept, "epiphany," within quotation marks, for the process of apprehension, and Epiphany, capitalized, for the Joyce texts. Mr. Feshbach provides an illuminating treatment of the concept throughout the Joycean *oeuvre*. He notes the three episodes, but does not link them with Stephen's arrival in Dublin.[3]

Dublin plays a somewhat minor role in *A Portrait* compared with the geographical matrix of *Ulysses*, though touches throughout suggest the atmosphere—the shops in Blackrock and the track in the park near the station (60–61), rides with the milkman and walks in the country (63), the road where the boys taunt Stephen about his admiration for Byron (80–82), the "foul laneways" of Nighttown (100), Church Street chapel, scene of Stephen's confession (141), "the jesuit house in Gardiner Street" (161), the strand with the wading girl (165–73), and neighborhoods of home, school, and university. Viewed through Stephen's awareness, the environment is more important as a setting or source of epiphany than as a scene for action. Yet so pervasive is the atmosphere that readers hardly realize how few are the specific locations and how sparse the descriptive detail.[4] Often a phrase will suffice. For the Bank of Ireland: "He and his father went up the steps and along the colonnade where the highland sentry was parading" (96). Trinity College is "the grey block of Trinity on his left, set heavily in the city's ignorance like a dull stone set in a cumbrous ring" (180).

Through Joyce's art, substance becomes essence. The tram episode, in its various renderings, is an illustration, as well as an example of Joyce's economy in his use of material. It is first found as an Epiphany, then in *Stephen Hero*, and finally, three times in *A Portrait*. Here is the Epiphany:

The children who have stayed latest are getting on their things to go home for the party is over. This is the last tram. The lank brown horses know it and shake their bells to the clear night, in admonition.

The conductor talks with the driver; both nod often in the green light of the lamp. There is nobody near. We seem to listen, I on the upper step and she on the lower. She comes up to my step many times and goes down again, between our phrases, and once or twice remains beside me, forgetting to go down, and then goes down. . . . Let be; let be. . . . And now she does not urge her vanities—her fine dress and sash and long black stockings—for now (wisdom of children) we seem to know that this end will please us better than any end we have laboured for.[5]

This childhood experience is recalled by both participants in *Stephen Hero,* when the scene is reenacted, with fuller use of detail; the tension between them is emphasized, as their adolescent hearts relive that earlier moment of innocence:

One rainy night when the streets were too bad for walking she took the Rathmines tram at the Pillar and as she held down her hand to him from the step, thanking him for his kindness and wishing him good-night, that ≪episode of their childhood seemed to magnetise≫ the minds of both at the same instant. The change of circumstances had reversed their positions, giving her the upper hand. He took her hand caressingly, caressing one after another the three lines on the ≪back of her kid glove and numbering her knuckles,≫ caressing also his own past towards which this inconsistent hater of [antiquity] inheritances was always lenient. They smiled at each other; and again in the centre of her amiableness he discerned a [centre] point of illwill and he suspected that by her code of honour she was obliged to insist on the forbearance of the male and to despise him for forbearing. (*SH,* 67–68)

Observe the self-conscious description of Stephen as an "inconsistent hater," first of antiquity, then, more vaguely in revision, of inheritances. The slashed passages also indicate, at whatever time they were made, that Joyce's writing was already becoming more suspended, more aware of the unstated.

In *A Portrait* this episode becomes a motif. Its first appearance has the atmosphere of the poetic Epiphany. Emma's shawl is noted, and "sprays of her fresh warm breath" fly "gaily above her cowled head," while "her shoes tapped blithely on the glassy road." The horses, the driver and the conductor are carried over from the Epiphany, with discarded tram tickets giving further substance. Stephen's attitude is reduced to a simple joy:

> She had thrown a shawl about her and, as they went together towards the tram, sprays of her fresh warm breath flew gaily above her cowled head and her shoes tapped blithely on the glassy road.
>
> It was the last tram. The lank brown horses knew it and shook their bells to the clear night in admonition. The conductor talked with the driver, both nodding often in the green light of the lamp. On the empty seats of the tram were scattered a few coloured tickets. No sound of footsteps came up or down the road. No sound broke the peace of the night save when the lank brown horses rubbed their noses together and shook their bells.
>
> They seemed to listen, he on the upper step and she on the lower. She came up to his step many times and went down to hers again between their phrases and once or twice stood close beside him for some moments on the upper step, forgetting to go down, and then went down. His heart danced upon her movements like a cork upon a tide. (69)

When the incident was versified by Stephen, in callow imitation of Byron, "all these elements which he deemed common and insignificant fell out of the scene" (70). In writing, "there remained no trace of the tram itself nor of the trammen nor of the horses: nor did he and she appear vividly. The verses told only of the night and the balmy breeze and the maiden lustre of the moon" (70). Two years later Stephen could regard his poem as a sign of immaturity. After all, it had followed the romantic convention, even in its title, "To E—— C——." His attitude of blasé wisdom fails to conceal pangs of regret for the loss of past illusions:

> All day he had thought of nothing but their leavetaking on the steps of the tram at Harold's Cross, the stream of moody emotions it had made to course through him, and the poem he had written about it. All day he had imagined a new meeting with her for he knew that she was to come to the play. The old restless moodiness had again filled his

breast as it had done on the night of the party but had not found an outlet in verse. The growth and knowledge of two years of boyhood stood between then and now, forbidding such an outlet. (77)

Eight more years pass, and Stephen, now a student at the university, once more returns to verse, though in a mood of disillusionment. As recollected then, much of the same phrasing is used, an intentional echo, but the self-consciously literary "blithely" is omitted, as well as the romantic quiet of the night and the dancing heart. The episode becomes more tightly woven, and is expressed in more evocative and precise language, perhaps an indication of imaginative development from the lyric form to the epic or dramatic:

He had written verses for her again after ten years. Ten years before she had worn her shawl cowlwise about her head, sending sprays of her warm breath into the night air, tapping her foot upon the glassy road. It was the last tram; the lank brown horses knew it and shook their bells to the clear night in admonition. The conductor talked with the driver, both nodding often in the green light of the lamp. They stood on the steps of the tram, he on the upper, she on the lower. She came up to his step many times between their phrases and went down again and once or twice remained beside him forgetting to go down and then went down. (222)

The memory concludes with weary ejaculations: "Let be! Let be!" Once more Stephen has to repress his innate romanticism. The villanelle he has almost completed seems more futile than his childlike admiration: "Ten years from that wisdom of children to his folly. If he sent her the verses? They would be read out at breakfast amid the tapping of eggshells. Folly indeed!" (222).

History is not so much a nightmare to the young Stephen as it is a vague dream, a faded tapestry, a litany of failure for the older generation, steeped in alcoholic sentiment, and, for ardent but immature youth, an absurd pastime of learning Irish, signing petitions, or trying to follow the manual of military drill. One may risk overinterpretation here, as in so much of Joyce criticism, but there seems to be a definite development of maturity in Stephen's historical awareness. As a child at Clongowes Wood he had been thrilled by the romantic legends of the castle, the dashing exploit of the patriot Hamilton Rowan in eluding the English, and the ghost of the marshal in the Austrian army which supposedly appeared on the staircase at the time of his death at the Battle of Prague in 1757. The castle itself, lighted at night, "was like something in a book" (10), like Leicester Abbey, which had degenerated into a sentence in the spelling book, just as the Wars of the Roses had become team labels for class competition. His father's faded pride in his granduncle's presentation to the Liberator, Daniel O'Connell, fifty years before, is similar to his nostalgia at the bank, once the Parliament building: "— God help us! he said piously, to think of the men of those times, Stephen, Hely Hutchinson and Flood and Henry Grattan and Charles Kendal Bushe, and the noblemen we have now, leaders of the Irish people at home and abroad. Why, by God, they wouldn't be seen dead in a tenacre field with them" (97). The father's lament is made ludicrous by a parody of sentimental song, as he continues, "No, Stephen, old chap, I'm sorry to say that they are only as I roved out one fine May morning in the merry month of sweet July." [6]

There is no need to recount here the traumatic experience of the death of Parnell, as sensed by Stephen in the Clongowes infirmary, or the famous Christmas dinner scene, ruined by political animosity, bitter anticlericalism, and pathos. During the week of the retreat, history as a record of the past becomes an epiphany of buried heroes and buried hopes:

The English lesson began with the hearing of the history. Royal persons, favourites, intriguers, bishops, passed like mute phantoms behind their veil of names. All had died: all had been judged. What did it profit a man to gain the whole world if he lost his soul? At last he had understood: and human life lay around him, a plain of peace whereon antlike men laboured in brotherhood, their dead sleeping under quiet mounds. (125-26)

A final vision of Dublin as a disheartening symbol precedes the inner call to flight: "Like a scene on some vague arras, old as man's weariness, the image of the seventh city of christendom was visible to him across the timeless air, no older nor more weary nor less patient of subjection than in the days of the thingmote" (167). One of the many ironies in regard to Joyce's Dublin is that the phrase, "seventh city of christendom," has often been taken as honorific. Indeed, it does sound so, and its source long puzzled the present writer, who inquired of historians and scholars, Irish and American, to no avail. At last, an undergraduate student of one of my colleagues came up with a plausible source. In Revelation 3:15 the seventh of the early Christian churches is enjoined, "I know thy works, that thou art neither cold nor hot: I would thou wert cold or hot." The following verse characterizes the attitude of Stephen, if not that of Joyce: "So then because thou art lukewarm, and neither cold nor hot, I will spue thee out of my mouth."

The city had long since been a "dull phenomenon" (78), and in keeping with Stephen's passionate interest in language even its name had taken on a dispirited quality: "The letters of the name of Dublin lay heavily upon his mind, pushing one another surlily hither and thither with slow boorish insistence" (111).

Escape is symbolized by floating clouds, nebulous music, a summons: "A voice from beyond the world was calling" (167). An ironic anticlimax follows immediately, as the yells of friends pierce this revery. Even their banter is meaningful, however. "Come along, Dedalus!" they shout, "Stephanos Dedalos! Bous Stephanoumenos! Bous Stephaneforos!" (168). The Greek phrases, so easily taken as ridicule—"Crown bearer," "Ox garlanded," "Ox garland-bearing"—associate the name Stephen with the first Christian martyr as well as with pagan sacrifice. Exile resembles death, and the names Daedalus and Icarus allude not only to the craft of an artificer but to a fatal flight.

The boisterous taunts of schoolfellows are an instance of the controlling image of voices in *A Portrait*. It could be said that Dublin is heard rather than seen in the novel; certainly a directory of places would be slight compared to hundreds in *Ulysses*. Voice is, of course, but one in a host of epiphanies, for every incident, itself an epiphany or cluster of epiphanies, is carefully selected, integrated, and modulated. At the Whitsuntide play Heron cries "Admit!" as he teases Dedalus about Emma. It is "the familiar word of admonition" (78), thought of which recalls Mr. Tate's charge of heresy in Stephen's English theme and a hazing by students when Stephen defends Byron. These experiences lead to reflection on the commands he must resist: "He had heard about him the constant voices of his father and of his masters, urging him to be a gentleman above all things and urging him to be a good catholic above all things" (83). In the gymnasium he had been told "to be strong and manly and healthy," and with the rising nationalism, "yet another voice had bidden him be true to his country" (84). He anticipated, too, that "a worldly voice would bid him raise up his father's fallen state," while the school code "urged him to be a decent fellow, to shield others from blame or to beg them off and to do his best to get free days for the school." We need hardly be told by Joyce that these conflicting voices were "hollowsounding" (84).

Most unforgettable of voices is that of Father Arnall in his sermons on the Four Last Things, but most touching of all is the account of the Dedalus children singing in their lodgings, temporary as always:

He was listening with pain of spirit to the overtone of weariness behind their frail fresh innocent voices. Even before they set out on life's journey they seemed weary already of the way.

He heard the choir of voices in the kitchen echoed and multiplied through an endless reverberation of the choirs of endless generations of children: and heard in all the echoes an echo also of the recurring note of weariness and pain. All seemed weary of life even before entering upon it. And he remembered that Newman had heard this note also in the broken lines of Virgil, *giving utterance, like the voice of Nature herself, to that pain and weariness yet hope of better things which has been the experience of her children in every time.* (163-64, italics in text)

Weariness is another motif—in Stephen's memories of Shelley's "To the Moon," in his view of Dublin from the North Bull, his recollection of Ben Jonson's song, and in his villanelle (96, 103, 167, 176, 217).

Voices are mimicked and accents noted. Stephen's father imitates "the mincing nasal tone" of Father Conmee (72), and Stephen himself has a try at it, encouraged by Heron: "—Go on, Dedalus, he urged, you can take him off rippingly" (76). Heron mocks Emma's questioning about Stephen's part in the play. Stephen observes a false courtesy and a note of superiority in the "hard jingling tone" of the British convert, the dean of studies (187). The "sharp Ulster voice" of MacAlister is mentioned (193), and Cranly's accent is found lacking in quality: "Cranly's speech, unlike that of Davin, had neither rare phrases of Elizabethan English nor quaintly turned versions of Irish idioms. Its drawl was an echo of the quays of Dublin given back by a bleak decaying seaport, its energy an echo of the sacred eloquence of Dublin given back flatly by a Wicklow pulpit" (195). Prostitutes solicit, a mad nun screeches, Stephen's father curses, a monkeylike dwarf in the library purrs, and the director speaks "gravely and cordially" (154) in interviewing Stephen about entering the priesthood, with "a voice bidding him approach, offering him secret knowledge and secret power" (159). The words "grave" and "gravely" toll through this passage like a knell. At one point Stephen is so overwhelmed by his sense of guilt as to have a hallucination of mysterious creatures outside his bedroom door, waiting, watching, and uttering enigmatic phrases (136).

Stephen's insights are occasionally marked by humor, sometimes by pity, but most often by disgust. The old "Uncle" Charles is an object of rather patronizing amusement, as when he is consigned to the outhouse to smoke his foul-smelling tobacco and rationalizes that "it will be more salubrious" (60), and when Stephen reflects that his granduncle's prayers might be for divine grace or perhaps "that God might send him back a part of the big fortune he had squandered in Cork" (62), a

kind of supernatural bankruptcy settlement. At times Simon
Dedalus is regarded with ironic pity. In his constant efforts to
keep up appearances, he is a kind of fallen Falstaff, especially
in Cork, when his imagined accomplishments are contrasted
with the purpose of the trip, the sale of his property. The "fine
decent fellows" he had mingled with in his youth are now but
"scattered and dead revellers." To Simon, however, they have
a place in his private Pantheon:

Everyone of us could do something. One fellow had a good voice,
another fellow was a good actor, another could sing a good comic
song, another was a good oarsman or a good racketplayer, another
could tell a good story and so on. (91)

And so they "kept the ball rolling" and "were none the worse"
for it—the perennial waste of talent among stage Irishmen. "—
We're as old as we feel, Johnny, said Mr Dedalus," voicing the
tired cliché, and continuing, "And just finish what you have
there, and we'll have another" (95), a characteristic juxtaposition of sentiment and alcohol. Irony is intensified as the
reminiscing Dedalus states, "I hope he'll be as good a man as
his father." The cliché about age—"as old as we feel"—is
paradoxically exemplified in Stephen's reaction; he indeed
feels old, though only a boy: "His mind seemed older than
theirs: it shone coldly on their strifes and happiness and regrets
like a moon upon a younger earth. No life or youth stirred in
him as it had stirred in them" (95-96).

His father's easy code of values finds expression in his
admiration for the Jesuits: "Those are the fellows that can get
you a position" (71). One position, it turns out, was a clerkship
in the Guinness brewery! They not only have influence but
they are "fed up, by God, like game-cocks," and, to push the
point further, Simon goes on to relate how Stephen's unjust,
humiliating, cruel punishment at Clongowes had become a
joking matter between the rector and Father Dolan. His own
insensitivity becomes indistinguishable from that of the Jesuits:

We had a famous laugh together over it. Ha! Ha! Ha!
Mr Dedalus turned to his wife and interjected in his natural voice:

—Shows you the spirit in which they take the boys there. O, a jesuit for your life, for diplomacy! (72)

Epiphany is defined in *Stephen Hero* as "a sudden spiritual manifestation, whether in the vulgarity of speech or of gesture or in a memorable phase of the mind itself" (*SH*, 211). There is no doubt as to which category—vulgar or noble—Mr. Dedalus and the Jesuits belong. Their identity is reinforced at the Whitsuntide play when Stephen recalled another of his father's phrases, "that you could always tell a jesuit by the style of his clothes," and "at the same moment he thought he saw a likeness between his father's mind and that of this smiling welldressed priest" (84).

In revolt against the hypocrisies around him, Stephen welcomes epiphanies of disgust. After the play he strides away alone "amid the tumult of suddenrisen vapours of wounded pride and fallen hope and baffled desire" (86). At the morgue he read the sign of the alley "*Lotts*" and felt relief at "the rank heavy air." Here, at least, is reality: "—That is horse piss and rotted straw, he thought. It is a good odour to breathe. It will calm my heart" (86).

For American readers at least it will be of interest to describe the educational institutions in *A Portrait*, and to trace Stephen's wanderings through Dublin.

Clongowes Wood College, the most fashionable boarding school in Ireland, is about twenty miles southwest of Dublin. Despite its name, it, like Belvedere College, is preparatory. The original castle was destroyed in the Cromwellian invasions. It was rebuilt by the Browne family late in the seventeenth century and sold to the Jesuits in 1814. Situated on extensive grounds and approached by a handsome avenue of trees, the imposing block of the castle had been extended before Joyce's time by a long corridor which connected the other buildings. According to a prospectus of 1886, the college is located "in the pleasantest part of Kildare . . . in the midst of beautiful and well-wooded grounds of 500 acres in extent." Cricket, tennis, football, bathing, "and all outdoor games" are mentioned. "To prevent bullying, and for the better formation of character," we are told, there are three age groups, each with its own playing fields, indoor recreational facilities, "and for each division there is a separate readingroom well-stocked with books suitable to the age and tastes of the boys."[7]

Though the prospectus states that "boys are received from the age of seven," when James Augustine Joyce entered in the fall of 1888 he claimed to be "half-past six." There is one extant photograph of a small child seated alone on the ground directly in front of the Reverend W. Power, S.J., with five older boys on benches on each side, the rest standing, a group of thirty-five students altogether.[8] The isolation is symbolic of Stephen's timidity so sensitively portrayed in the novel's first chapter. Joyce used some real names. R. Kickham, C. Roche, C. Wells, and M. Saurin are in the photograph.[9] The article describes the death from rheumatic fever of Stanislaus Little, who died in 1890 at the age of sixteen. Joyce was then in residence; the novel predates Little's death as having occurred before Stephen's time: "He might die before his mother came. Then he would have a dead mass in the chapel like the way the fellows had told him it was when Little had died" (24). Were Stephen to die, he thinks, "he would be buried in the little graveyard of the community off the main avenue," and the bully Wells "would be sorry then."

The atmosphere at Clongowes is cold, damp, and dim. The football grounds are chill, and the small boy skirts the rough play of the teams. We read of "the white look of the lavatory" (11), the damp refectory, the "cold night smell in the chapel" (18), the curtained cubicles in the dormitory, and the swimming bath with "the warm turfcoloured bogwater, the warm moist air, the noise of plunges, the smell of the towels" (22). The infirmary is noted only for the wan light and early dusk seen through the window. The prefect's "nocoloured eyes" (50) symbolize his cruel and unjust punishment of Stephen, who, stung with shame and indignation, walks hesitantly up the stairs to "the narrow dark corridor" (55), passing shadowy portraits and the rooms of the community to knock on the rector's door. A photograph of this corridor appears in Richard Ellmann's biography of Joyce.

Belvedere is less fully described. We see only the small courtyard where the Whitsuntide play is performed and the chapel which, here used as dressing room and a setting for light humor, is the scene of the retreat, then "flooded by the dull scarlet light that filtered through the lowered blinds," with one shaft of light "like a spear" striking the brass candlesticks on the altar (116). The beauty of the Georgian mansion is not recognized, but, oddly enough, finds its way into the meditations of Father Conmee in *Ulysses*. Conmee, twice rector for Joyce, at Clongowes Wood and at Belvedere, in memory "smiled at smiling noble faces in a beeswaxed drawing room, ceiled with full fruit clusters" (*U, 223*)—the stucco work in the first floor Diana, Apollo, and Venus rooms, done by Michael Stapleton about 1785.[10]

Had Joyce been more visually aware he might have "walked and moved in times of yore" (*U, 223*) with Conmee both at Belvedere and at University College, where the muses grace the ground floor of Clanwilliam House and an allegory of the elements is found in the handsome first floor saloon. We may suggest that the author's weak eyesight might have precluded him from a source of joy, and perhaps of irony, at the contrast between gracious rococo mythology and the dull pedantry of the educational process. Stephen enters "the sombre college" (184), aware only "of a corruption other than that of Buck Egan and Burnchapel Whaley" (184), eighteenth-century roisterers, the latter having lived in Clanwilliam House, No. 85, and having built the adjoining No. 86, St. Stephen's Green, the center of Joyce's University College. Another source of symbolism was overlooked by Joyce in failing to note the recumbent lion over the entrance of No. 86. Having once lived at "Leoville" with another lion, Joyce could have also linked Leopold Bloom and the sign of the zodiac, perhaps could have found a wry pleasure in observing that the beast at No. 86 is not what it appears, being a lead imitation of stone.

We enter a dark corridor and see the "chilly grey light that struggled through the dusty windows" of the physics theatre (184). It is here that Stephen engages in his discussion with the dean of studies on lighting fires, on distinctions between the beautiful and the good according to Aquinas, on Epictetus, and on the word *tundish*. *Stephen Hero* gives more detail about this pseudo-Gothic classroom with benches rising toward the pointed windows in the apse (*SH*, 100). An instance of Joyce's art of compression is his reduction of several pages describing the faculty in *Stephen Hero* to a fantasy in *A Portrait* provoked by the "limp priestly vestments that hung upon the walls" which seem "to sway and caper in a sabbath of misrule" in reaction to a joke by a classmate:

The forms of the community emerged from the gustblown vestments, the dean of studies, the portly florid bursar with his cap of grey hair, the president, the little priest with feathery hair who wrote devout verses, the squat peasant form of the professor of economics, the tall form of the young professor of mental science discussing on the landing a case of conscience with a class like a giraffe cropping high leafage among a herd of antelopes, the grave troubled prefect of the sodality, the plump roundheaded professor of Italian with his rogue's eyes. (192)[11]

Stephen's mocking disrespect visualizes the professors "ambling and stumbling, tumbling and capering, kilting their gowns for leap frog, holding one another back, shaken with deep fast laughter, smacking one another behind and laughing at their rude malice."

We catch glimpses of college life as background to student discussions. A crowd at the entrance promotes a testimonial to the tsar; in the inner hall the dean of studies is poised on the staircase, attempting to escape an eager student while another earnest conversation takes place nearby. Cranly, Temple, and Stephen leave by way of "the weedy garden" to the rear, where they meet the president on the path, to the accompaniment of "the thuds of the players' hands and the wet smacks of the ball" from the handball alley (200).

University College Dublin had an unusual group of students among Joyce's contemporaries, none of them treated with respect by the arrogant Stephen Dedalus. Some were destined to become scholars (Felix Hackett, Arthur Clery, Seumas Clandillon, Constantine Curran), others to play roles in the Free State government (Hugh Kennedy, Eugene Sheehy, John O'Sullivan), and some, equally promising, to become victims of the First World War or the Anglo-Irish War (Thomas Kettle, Francis Sheehy-Skeffington, George Clancy). Dismissed in *Stephen Hero* as "a day-school full of terrorised boys" (*SH*, 232), the university, if scarcely a seat of learning, did manage to achieve by accident more than it had planned. Kevin Sullivan indicates the superficiality of college requirements. The annual examinations had passing grades of 30 percent, while 70 percent earned first class honors. Sullivan comments that "these standards, in terms of percentages, are hardly impressive. They are even less impressive when one examines the kind and quantity of work to which they were applied." [12] Joyce's first year English examination, for a passing grade, included only a few units: grammar, an essay, *Ivanhoe*, the first book of *Paradise Lost*, and "Lycidas." The course might be adequate for a high-school junior. An honors examination added some Dryden, *Richard II*, and *The Tempest*. Sullivan makes the wry remark: "But Joyce never took honors in English at University College, nor is there any evidence that he ever tried for them. It is not hard to see why." [13]

As we all know, education is not a matter of entrance examinations or grades, though ambitious parents continue to think in such terms. The evidence given, not merely by Joyce, but by the recollections of his contemporaries, is that of an intense, sometimes quarrelsome band of debaters on issues religious, literary, political, and philosophical. If Stephen is constantly presented as a genius among worldlings, in fact Joyce was *primus inter pares*. [14]

Chapter 5 of *A Portrait* has been criticized as fragmentary, but a rhythmic pattern of episodes can be discerned. The shabby house of the family opens and closes the narrative and is the scene of Stephen's villanelle in the middle. There are three walks, again spaced toward the beginning, in the middle, and near the end. In the first, Stephen meditates alone, his mind turning to literary allusion and philosophic speculation. After the class at college, he expounds his aesthetic theories to Lynch as they stroll eastward to the canal and return along Merrion Square, thence into Leinster Lawn to the National Library. Two scenes at the library are interrupted by an interlude in which Stephen composes a villanelle to Emma. The verse-writing passage may, in fact, be intended as an inserted reverie or a flashback, for it is framed by bird images. As he sees Emma on the steps Stephen reflects, "And if he had judged her sharply?" His questions continue with a suggestion of her innocence: "If her life were a simple rosary of hours, her life simple and strange as a bird's life ... ?" (216). After the villanelle episode we find Stephen again—or still—on the same library steps, watching the birds for augury.

The scene of the girls at the National Library reminds me of Renoir's *Les Parapluies*, which depicts the same uncertainty about a shower:

Their trim boots prattled as they stood on the steps of the colonnade, talking quietly and gaily, glancing at the clouds, holding their umbrellas at cunning angles against the few last raindrops, closing them again, holding their skirts demurely. (216)

Epiphany 25, written about 1904, contains two almost identical sentences, as well as "a white rosary of hours," an early wording of "a simple rosary of hours" in *A Portrait:*

In the colonnade are the girls, an April company. They are leaving shelter, with many a doubting glance, with the prattle of trim boots and the pretty rescue of petticoats, under umbrellas, a light armoury, upheld at cunning angles. They are returning to the convent—demure corridors and simple dormitories, a white rosary of hours.[15]

The Renoir painting is one of the disputed Hugh Lane legacy, part of which under present agreement commutes every five years between the Tate Gallery in London and the Dublin

Municipal Gallery. Could Joyce have known the painting? It was exhibited in Dublin by Hugh Lane in November 1904, a month after Joyce's departure, and bought by Lane in the following year. Joyce might have seen a reproduction of the painting at that time.

The second library scene—or a resumption of the first—contains the augury of the birds and another glimpse of Emma. It is followed by a walk with Cranly in which Stephen admits apostasy. The intensity of discussion precludes many indications of place (the general direction is southward of St. Stephen's Green).

The chapter's plan emerges: the family house at beginning, middle, and end; three peripatetic discussions, one on literature, a second on aesthetics, the last on religion; scenes at the university and at the library. The artistic control in the chapter contrasts markedly with the loose organization of *Stephen Hero*. *A Portrait* gives highlights of four college years in several episodes, while in the earlier manuscript two years occupy the twelve extant chapters, each of which contains many separate units. Chapter XVI, for instance, the first complete chapter, opens with Stephen's devotion to aesthetics, then his role as "an enigmatic figure in the midst of his shivering society" (*SH*, 35), discussions with his brother, verse writing, solitary walks through Dublin, characterizations of classmates, discovery of Ibsen, and, finally, evenings of charades at the Daniel residence. It is conceivable that Joyce discarded the manuscript and attempted to destroy it because it was to him, as to Rimbaud, mere "literature." We read in *Stephen Hero:* "The term 'literature' now seemed to him a term of contempt and he used it to designate the vast middle region which lies . . . between poetry and the chaos of unremembered writing. Its merit lay in its portrayal of externals" (*SH*, 78).

The passage in *A Portrait*, in which Stephen crosses the city on his way to the university, reflecting on Hauptmann, Newman, Ibsen, Cavalcanti, and Jonson, has proved a jousting ground for critics. Romantic it is, and sentimentally phrased, a purple passage undoubtedly, and probably intentionally so. The Dublin milieu provides another frame of irony, for the episode is preceded by the screech of a mad nun (175)[16] and followed by an encounter with an eccentric consumptive (177). The association of Hauptmann's heroines with the "rain laden trees" has the authentic fin de siècle accent: "the memory of their pale sorrows and the fragrance falling from the wet branches mingled in a mood of quiet joy" (176). The description of "the cloistral silverveined prose of Newman" represents an incisive taste, though its relevance to "the sloblands of Fairview" is dubious. The association of Ibsen with "Baird's stonecutting works" is more appropriate, infusing "a spirit of wayward boyish beauty" (176). Ibsen was one of Stephen Hero's idols, as he was of the young Joyce. An image of the fearless artist, Ibsen is described in *Stephen Hero:* "[Ibsen with his profound self-approval, Ibsen with his haughty, disillusioned courage, Ibsen with his minute and wilful energy.] a mind of sincere and boylike bravery, of disillusioned pride . . ." (*SH*, 41). Romantic, sentimental, at once ironic and sincere, this epiphany of Dublin anticipates the ruminations in *Ulysses* and illustrates the classic temper as defined in *Stephen Hero*.

Though extraneous to the final version of *A Portrait*, and hence not acceptable as evidence to strict textual critics, Stephen Hero's distinction between the romantic and the classic is applicable to the progress from Stephen's adolescent dreams of Mercedes to the mature acceptance of sordid reality which we find in *Ulysses*. The romantic outlook is characterized as "an insecure, unsatisfied, impatient temper which sees no fit abode here for its ideals and chooses therefore to behold them under insensible figures," which are given "to wild adventures, lacking the gravity of solid bodies." In contrast the classic temper, "ever mindful of limitations, chooses rather to bend upon these present things and so to work upon them and fashion them that the quick intelligence may go beyond them to their meaning which is still unuttered" (*SH*, 78).

NOTES

1. This essay will not discuss the critical commonplace of distinguishing between Joyce and Stephen, nor with the reading of *A Portrait* as subtly ironic. A fictional persona is assumed, as well as a mode of ambiguity. Citations in the text are to *A Portrait of the Artist as a Young Man* (New York: Viking Press, 1964); *Stephen Hero* (New York: New Directions, 1944; 1963); *Ulysses* (New York: Random House, 1961).

2. Robert Scholes and Richard M. Kain, eds., *The Workshop of Daedalus: James Joyce and the Raw Materials for "A Portrait of the Artist as a Young Man"* (Evanston: Northwestern University Press, 1965), p. 15.

3. "Hunting Epiphany-Hunters," *PMLA* 137 (March 1972): 304-06.

4. Clive Hart and Leo Knuth, *A Topographical Guide to James Joyce's "Ulysses"* (Colchester: A Wake Newslitter Press, 1975), list thirty-eight names of Dublin places and establishments in *A Portrait*, approximately half the number they find in *Dubliners*.

5. *The Workshop of Daedalus*, p. 13.

6. The street ballad is identified by Don Gifford and Robert Seidman in *Notes for Joyce* (New York: E. P. Dutton, 1967) as "The Bonny Labouring Boy." It begins: "As I roved out one fine May morning, / All in the blooming spring. . . ."

7. The prospectus is quoted by Kevin Sullivan in *Joyce Among the Jesuits* (New York: Columbia University Press, 1958), pp. 231-33, and reprinted in part in *The Workshop of Daedalus*, p. 131.

8. George A. Little, "James Joyce and Little's Death," *The Irish Rosary* 16 (July–August 1962): 213-18. The photograph is on p. 215.

9. Kevin Sullivan in *Joyce Among the Jesuits*, pp. 13–59, gives the most complete account of Clongowes Wood in Joyce's day. He notes that twelve of the sixteen boys mentioned are given their real names, fictitious names being given to undesirable characters such as Moonan, Athy, Boyle, and Corrigan (p. 48). Sullivan overlooks at least five. The other characters, in order of appearance, are Rodolph Kickham (1888-93), Christopher Roche (1888-92), John Cantwell (1888-89), Cecil Thunder (1889-94), John Lawton (1890-96), Charles Wells (1888-90), Michael Saurin (1887-93), Aloysius Fleming (1891-94), Patrick Rath (1886-91), James Magee (1889-92), "the Spaniard who was allowed to smoke cigars and the little Portugese" (13), that is, Jose Arana y Lupardo (1890-92) and Francisco da Silva Ruas (1891-93), "Kickham's brother" (40) Alexander (1886-90), "a fellow out of the second in grammar" (40), Dominick Kelly (1886-90), Thomas Furlong (1889-94) and Anthony MacSwiney (1889-91). Cf. list in T. Corcoran, S.J., *The Clongowes Record 1814-1932* (Dublin, n.d.), pp. 165-221. It is noteworthy that Joyce used more names from his brief stay at Clongowes Wood College than he did for his Belvedere College years.

10. Rooms at Belvedere College and at University College are authoritatively discussed and illustrated in C. P. Curran, *Dublin Decorative Plasterwork of the Seventeenth and Eighteenth Centuries* (London: Alec Tiranti, 1967), pp. 33, 80–84, 86, 87, and plates IV and 128–38 for Belvedere; pp. 25, 30, 32, 33, 35, 38, 39, 48, 49, 57, and plates 82–85 for No. 85, St. Stephen's Green; pp. 37, 38, 59–61, 63, 87, and plates 86–89 for No. 86 St. Stephen's Green.

11. Sketches of faculty members are scattered through *A Page of Irish History: Story of University College Dublin 1883–1909*, compiled by Fathers of the Society of Jesus (Dublin and Cork: Talbot Press, 1930); *Struggle with Fortune: A Centenary Miscellany*, ed. Michael Tierney (Dublin: Browne and Nolan, n.d.); and *Centenary History of the Literary and Historical Society 1855–1955*, ed. James Meenan (Tralee: Kerryman Press, n.d.).

The dean of studies (Joyce's "Father Butt") was the Reverend Joseph Darlington, S.J. (not John, as in Ellmann); the president, the Reverend William Delany, S.J.; "the little priest with feathery hair," the Reverend Matthew Russell, S.J.; the professor of economics, the Reverend Thomas H. Finlay, S.J.; and the tall young professor of mental science, Professor William Magennis.

12. Sullivan, *Joyce Among the Jesuits*, p. 158.

13. Ibid., p. 159.

14. In view of the scarcity of *A Page of Irish History*, it may be of interest to quote here two seldom noticed references to Joyce: "During his student days James Joyce was not taken seriously. It was understood that he had a weird sort of talent but no one in the College seems to have guessed that he was destined to achieve world-wide celebrity" (286n.). The second, in an essay by Arthur Clery, refers to *A Portrait*. After mentioning the "high moral standard" of the students, Clery observes that "readers of Mr. James Joyce will get a different impression, but this is the actual fact. Among the students of the college about this time were—P. H. Pearse, T. M. Kettle, F. Sheehy-Skeffington. Joyce is true as far as he goes, but confining himself to one small knot of medical students he gives a wrong impression of the whole" (586n.).

15. *The Workshop of Daedalus*, p. 35.

16. Hart and Knuth, *A Topographical Guide*, identify the St. Vincent's Lunatic Asylum, under the care of the Sisters of Charity, 3 Convent Avenue, Fairview.

Consciousness and Society in A Portrait of the Artist

JAMES NAREMORE

6

ALTHOUGH *A Portrait of the Artist as a Young Man* is centered exclusively in Stephen Dedalus's mind, it preserves at every moment that dialectic between individual subjectivity and social reality which enables us to identify a character. Stephen tries to isolate himself in a private world, but the novel makes us feel the pressure of a public world outside, never giving way to the wishes, fantasies, and unrealized possibilities which Georg Lukács has called "abstract potentiality."[1] Lukács, who regarded Joyce as a decadent and solipsistic writer, was surely incorrect: Joyce's protagonist lives in a world of abstractions, but the novel does not; in fact, one of Joyce's chief strengths as a writer is that he always shows us how consciousness is determined by a social existence.

From his earliest experiments with the interior monologue, Joyce was aware that the private self could not be isolated from the larger, objective world. In "The Dead," for example, as Gabriel Conroy listens to Mary Jane Morkan run through her tedious Academy piece, he allows his mind to wander. An apparently inconsequential sight—Aunt Julia's picture of the two murdered princes—sends him off into a reverie, and he finds himself ineluctably drawn to thoughts of his childhood, his mother, and his marriage. But his thinking is presented *113* neither as a *recherche du temps perdu* nor as the sort of mystical falling away into darkness that one finds occasionally in the novels of Virginia Wolf. In Joyce's work, the inner monologue never represents a satisfactory escape from an unpleasant reality, even though his characters often try to use fancy or imagination to liberate themselves. Thus, the more Gabriel tries to drift away, the more his thoughts serve as a commentary on his present circumstances, showing how his character has been molded by his family and his social life.

It is this "social" aspect of Joyce's literary experimentation that I wish to discuss. My primary aim is to show some of the ways that Stephen Dedalus's ideas, language, and art have been affected by his economic status and his Catholic upbringing. At the same time, however, I have been aware that James Joyce was born into the same class and culture as Stephen; I therefore propose to conclude with some tentative speculations about the relationship between the innovative form of Joyce's novel and the author's own social existence. In this way we will see that Joyce's work belongs in a tradition of literary realism, but a realism of a special, modernist type which tries in subtle ways to escape what Stephen later calls the "nightmare of history."

I

Most readers of *A Portrait* are aware that Simon Dedalus's fall from prosperity coincides directly with Stephen's growing alienation from family and country, but comparatively little has been written about the subject. Perhaps one reason for our lack of attention is that the money problems of the Dedalus household are presented indirectly, from the point of view of a child who can barely understand why he is becoming poor. Then, too, as Stephen grows older he maintains a certain bohemian contempt for materialism; his very name implies saintliness, while his father is equated with Simon Magus. The implied author of the narrative remains silent, ever the aloof,

Flaubertian ironist. Nevertheless, the financial disasters of the elder Dedalus can be shown to have a crucial effect on Stephen's consciousness, just as the identical family crisis must have affected the consciousness of James Joyce.

The economic situation of the Dedalus family is clarified if we step somewhat outside the novel and consider a few simple facts about Joyce's own background. In his later life, Joyce described his father's occupation as "a bankrupt." According to Yeats, whose disdain for the Catholic middle classes is well known, John Joyce was essentially a minor canvasser for Parnell, like one of the seedy, white-collar types we meet in "Ivy Day in the Committee Room." A somewhat fuller description is contained in Stephen's famous remarks on Simon, which do not add lustre to the picture: "A medical student, an oarsman, a tenor, an amateur actor, a shouting politician, a small landlord, a small investor," etc., etc.[2] Yet the bitterness here scarcely conceals the fact that Stephen, like Joyce, was born into what his friend Cranly calls "the lap of luxury" (241). We know that the Joyce forebears were modest men of property in Cork; they claimed to have descended from the noble families of Galway (Joyce's father carried a coat of arms wherever he moved), and they were distantly related to several nationalist leaders, including Daniel O'Connell. Joyce's grandfather was also sometimes a bankrupt, but he held down the cosy government job of inspector of hackney coaches and was able to maintain a family in the fashionable suburb of Sunday's Well. When Joyce's father was twenty-one, he inherited the Cork properties, which produced an income of £315 a year, plus an additional bequest of £1000 from his grandfather, John O'Connell. By the time he was settled down with a family of his own, he had tied his fortunes to Parnell's rising star.[3] He started life as a member of the comfortable Irish Catholic bourgeoisie; he regarded himself as a gentleman, and he had social ambitions for himself and his son.

The identical fatherly ambitions can be seen everywhere in the early chapters of *A Portrait*, and they have a good deal to do with the developing psychology of Stephen Dedalus, who grows up convinced of his special place in the society. At the age of six he is sent to Clongowes Wood to acquire the best class of schooling. "Christian brothers be damned!" Simon later says. "Is it with Paddy Stink and Mickey Mud? No, let him stick to the jesuits in God's name, since he began with them. They'll be of service to him in later years. Those are the fellows that can get you a position" (71). Almost immediately at Clongowes, Stephen encounters the characteristic snobbery of the place:

—What is your name?
Stephen had answered:
—Stephen Dedalus.
Then Nasty Roche had said:
—What kind of a name is that?
And when Stephen had not been able to answer Nasty Roche had asked:
—What is your father?
Stephen had answered:
—A gentleman.
Then Nasty Roche had asked:
—Is he a magistrate? (8-9)

Despite such bullying, or partly because of it, Stephen identifies with his father's hero, the aristocratic Parnell, and with the fabled nationalists and churchmen who are memorialized everywhere around him.[4] On the playground, he looks up at the castle and thinks of the patriot Hamilton Rowan; in the classroom, he wears the white rose of York, and leads his faction into battle against Jack Lawton's group of Lancastrians. His developing pride in what he takes to be his heritage will remain to haunt him in the final part of the book, when the repellent Temple, obsessed with heredity and the noble families of Ireland, bestows such fawning admiration. "I know all the history of your family," Temple says. "Do you know what Giraldus Cambrensis says about your family?" (230).

In the first chapter, when Stephen returns home for the holidays, he is surrounded by warmth and prosperity. He undergoes an initiation rite; dressed in a stiff Eton collar, he is brought down to the family circle like his father before him. In this setting, Mr. Dedalus becomes a symbol not just of masculinity but of high social status and security. Every inch the *paterfamilias*, he stands before a roaring fire, backed by a pier glass and a large mantel piece, twirling his moustache and spreading his coattails in satisfaction; he ceremoniously pours whiskey from a decanter for the household pet, Mr. Casey; and later, when the family servants have brought the meal, he lifts a "heavy cover pearled round the edge with glistening drops" to reveal a plump turkey. Stephen thinks immediately of the circumstances under which the bird was purchased:

He knew that his father had paid a guinea for it in Dunn's of D'Olier Street and that the man had prodded it often at the breastbone to show how good it was: and he remembered the man's voice when he had said:
—Take that one, sir. That's the real Ally Daly. (29)

In virtually every detail, the Christmas dinner functions to emphasize Stephen's conception of his father as a prosperous "gentleman" who presides over a large family and wields influence in the affairs of the country. Even the antagonism between the Ribbonman Casey and Dante Riordan grows out of the great national split, and the climactic moments of the episode, with Casey sobbing out for his "dead king" and Stephen gazing in terror at his father's tears, are designed to convey the boy's feelings of tragic nobility.

Stephen's disillusionment coincides with his father's money crisis, which in turn is indirectly linked to the fall of Parnell. Thus, by the end of chapter 2, Stephen is almost completely unsettled when Heron remarks, "O by the way . . . I saw your governor." He quails, noting that "any allusion to his father by a fellow or a master put his calm to rout in a moment" (76). By chapter 5, the family fortunes have undergone a complete reversal, and Stephen is intensely, almost obsessively aware of what he calls the "disorder" of his life. Instead of a Christmas dinner, he eats a solitary breakfast while staring at a set of greasy pawn tickets. Everything in the household seems filthy and makeshift: a battered alarm clock lying on its side tells the time; baths are administered in the kitchen sink and the bather has to dry with a pair of damp overalls. The children, who were discreetly tucked away at the beginning of the novel, are now everywhere underfoot, their voices chanting confusedly about who should prepare a place for Stephen to wash. The house is large enough to have an upstairs (an indication that the family still clings to its station), and from somewhere above we hear Simon's whistle, followed by a shout: "Is your lazy bitch of a brother gone out yet?" Stephen's only response to this brilliant oath is to comment archly on its lower-class confusion of genders (175).

As Stephen's economic situation forces him more and more into association with the common world of Dublin streets, as he becomes increasingly disillusioned with the shabby hypocrisies of his father, he suffers a psychic pain. This pain sets in as early as the second chapter, when he begins to understand "in a vague way" that money troubles will keep him from returning to Clongowes in the fall: "For some time he had felt the slight changes in his house; and these changes in what he had deemed unchangeable were so many shocks to his boyish conception" (64). The "boyish conception," however, is never really abandoned. He tells us at the close that he longs for a beauty which "has not yet come into the world" (251), but his longing has a clear basis in the gentlemanly prosperity of his childhood. From the beginning he has been depicted as a sensitive plant; the youngest child at Clongowes, he instinctively and understandably draws back from the rough, dirty atmosphere of the schoolyard, just as he will later understandably shrink from too close a contact with gritty Irish poverty. Throughout the novel he continues to seek out "nobility," using the only means left open to him—childhood fantasy, religion, and aestheticism.

Even before the money crisis arrives, Stephen has grown fond of imagining himself in the role of the Count of Monte Cristo; but these idealized fantasies are not enough to compensate for his first experiences with Dublin, which leave him feeling uneasy and oppressed. The family's move from the "comfort and revery" of suburban Blackrock is precipitous and confusing. Dublin is a "new and complex sensation," associated with the growing senility of Uncle Charles and the "bare, cheerless house" where the family portraits stand aimlessly about (66). The city streets are filled with anonymous crowds and "illdressed bearded policemen"; the water along the quays is dotted with multitudes of corks, bobbing in a "thick yellow scum"; "amid this new bustling life he might have fancied himself in another Marseilles," Stephen feels, "but he missed the bright sky and the sunwarmed trellises of the wineshops" (66). Somewhat later, after he has cashed his essay and exhibition prize, he is able to impose a kind of order on the new house; he sends the family to the theater, arranges the bookshelves, begins to overhaul his room, and takes great pleasure in setting up an elaborate loan bank. Soon, however, the money disappears; disorder returns, and the flurry of activity closes with the epiphany of a half-finished bedroom and a pot of pink enamel paint.

To the older Stephen, Dublin becomes a place of terrible squalor and confusion, completely different in his imagination from Paris, where he hopes to find refuge. He continually seeks to evade what he at one point calls "consciousness of place" (141), and one avenue for such an escape is the church, a powerful force of tradition and order which he recognizes, even after he has left it, as a "symbol behind which are massed twenty centuries of authority and veneration" (243). In chapter 3, for example, he makes his way to confession through the drab back streets of Dublin. In the midst of his overwhelming sexual guilt and his feelings of insignificance in the eyes of God, he becomes dimly aware of his surroundings:

The squalid scene composed itself around him; the common accents, the burning gasjets in the shops, odours of fish and spirits and wet sawdust, moving men and women. An old woman was about to cross the street, an oilcan in her hand. He bent down and asked her was there a chapel near.

—A chapel, sir? Yes sir. Church Street chapel. (141)

Inside the church, however, the atmosphere is quite different. As he kneels among the poor celebrants of the mass, the young scholar is overcome with beatific peace: "The board on which he knelt was narrow and worn and those who knelt near him were humble followers of Jesus. Jesus, too, had been born in poverty and had worked in the shop of a carpenter, cutting boards and planing them, and had first spoken of the kingdom of God to poor fishermen, teaching all men to be meek and humble of heart" (141). Clearly Stephen does not associate the humble carpenters and poor fishermen of Jesus' ministry with the odors of fish and wet sawdust he has just experienced outside the church. The images of pretty, patient poverty in his fantasies have become a comfortable substitute for the real thing.

For a while Stephen believes the church will spare him the torments of hell, leading him upward to a prosperous, aestheticized heaven: "At times his sense of such immediate repercussion was so lively that he seemed to feel his soul in devotion pressing like fingers the keyboard of a great cash register and to see the amount of his purchase start forth immediately in heaven, not as a number but as a frail column of incense or as a slender flower" (148). In such moments, the young simoniac is already beginning to use the language of a Decadent poet. Indeed his feelings are brought on by a "pressure" which has something in common with the "dark pressure" of the prostitute's lips in an earlier scene.

As he grows older, however, Stephen cannot preserve such illusions. His immediate fear of punishment subsides, and he begins to conceive of heaven as "an eternity of bliss in the company of the dean of studies" (240). In chapter 4 he acknowledges his false humility and his affection for the pomp and aristocratic ceremony of the priesthood: "If ever he had seen himself celebrant it was as in the pictures of the mass in his child's massbook, in a church without worshippers . . . at a bare altar and served by an acolyte scarcely more boyish than himself" (159). But the religion of beauty to which he now turns functions in much the same way as the church, as we can see from the way Joyce counterpoints his aesthetic musings with the chaotic sights and sounds of the city. A dray filled with iron comes round the corner of Sir Patrick Dun's hospital, drowning Stephen's remarks on "esthetic apprehension" with the "harsh roar of jangled and rattling metal" (209). Stephen argues on behalf of a serene, godlike artist, detached from his creation, paring his fingernails; but the image reminds us of the effeminate Tusker Boyle, and of Stephen's desire to keep the clean hands of a gentleman. Significantly, Joyce gives Lynch the final word on Stephen's artistic credo: "-What do you mean, Lynch asked surlily, by prating about beauty and the imagination in this miserable Godforsaken island? No wonder the artist retired within or behind his handiwork after having perpetrated this country" (215).

In other words, Stephen's theories are an elaborate defense mechanism, a withdrawal from life. The disparity between his real circumstances and the nobility he conceives for himself has become too great. Recoiling from his family and his society, he makes himself a member of a bohemian elite, and convinces himself that he has been born in the wrong time and the wrong place. Like Yeats, whose writings he quotes several times in the last chapter, he thinks of himself as an artist-aristocrat, using imagination to free himself from twentieth-century Dublin. He wanders the ugly, commercialized streets of the city, meditating on art in order to ward off reality. Passing the sloblands of Fairview, he thinks about "the cloistral silverveined prose of Newman" (who, we remember, gave us the definition of a gentleman); noticing the provision shops on North Strand Road, he calls up the "dark humour of Guido Cavalcanti"; in front of Baird's stonecutting works in Talbot Place he evokes Ibsen and, ludicrously, "a spirit of wayward boyish beauty"; the "grimy marinedealer's shop beyond the Liffey" causes him to repeat a rather ninetyish line from one of Ben Jonson's songs: "*I was not wearier where I lay.*" As a result he feels that "the spirit of beauty had folded him round like a mantle and that in revery at least he had been acquainted with nobility." In the midst of "common lives," surrounded by what he calls the "squalor and noise and sloth of the city," he walks on "fearlessly and with a light heart" (176–77).

The effect of such attitudes, as S. L. Goldberg has observed, is to "extend the exile of the artist into the exile of art."[5] By the end of *A Portrait of the Artist,* Stephen has not yet resolved the problems which beset him. Unable to come to a recognition of necessity, he uses artistic theory to repudiate his circumstances. His religion of art functions as an instinctive and in one sense quite justified rejection of his personal and national history.

II

But Stephen's attraction to the church and later to the priesthood of art, his implicit distaste for what his father calls "Paddy Stink and Mickey Mud," are more complex matters than a simple longing for the comforts of an upper social class. Stephen, who is always a good student, has been brought up in the repressive atmosphere of puritanical Irish Catholicism, which teaches that there is a clear distinction between soul and body ("soul" remains one of the most important words in his vocabulary, even after he has ostensibly left the church). Throughout his later life he will suffer from the effects of this false duality. He is fascinated with his own bodily functions— the smell of urine on oilcloth, for example—but he is taught that expressions such as "he'd give you a toe in the rump" are not "nice" things to say, and that rough boys like Nasty Roche are "stinks" (8–9). He is educated by priests in a boys' school where sexual feelings are expressed in forbidden games, and he develops an ambivalence toward dirt, excrement, and sexuality itself. Given such a background, the growing poverty of the Dedalus family exerts a profound psychological threat for Stephen. Contact with the poor means contact with dirt, and dirt evokes a powerful anxiety.

In chapter 2, for example, Stephen goes for a ride with the

milkman, and is delighted to have the chill night air blow away his memory of the cowyard, quieting his repugnance at the "cowhairs and hayseeds" on the driver's coat. He is pleased chiefly by the comfortable houses he sees along the roads of Blackrock: "Whenever the car drew up before a house he waited to catch a glimpse of a wellscrubbed kitchen or of a softlylighted hall and to see how the servant would hold the jug and how she would close the door." It might be possible to enjoy such a job as the milkman's, he thinks, "if he had warm gloves and a fat bag of gingernuts in his pocket to eat from" (64). But the actual contact with the "moocow" he first learned about in nursery stories is another matter; throughout his later life he unconsciously associates milk and cows with an uncivilized, debased world which he is trying to transform or escape. To Stephen, Ireland itself becomes an old sow that eats her farrow; the antithesis of Art he conceives as a man hacking in fury at a block of wood, accidentally forming the image of a cow; and the "true" artistic emotions evoked by the Venus of Praxiteles he imagines as having nothing to do with her breasts and thighs, her ability to bear "burly offspring" or give "good milk to her children."

A similar process can be seen in the development of Stephen's ideas about the Irish peasantry. Early in the book, in a passage so filled with joy that it breaks into rhyme, he fantasizes about returning home from Clongowes to the cheers of farming people along the way: "They passed the farmhouse of the Jolly Farmer. Cheer after cheer after cheer. Through Clane they drove, cheering and cheered. The peasant women stood at the halfdoors, the men stood here and there. The lovely smell there was in the wintry air: the smell of Clane: rain and wintry air and turf and smouldering corduroy" (20). But later in the novel, as Stephen loses his secure distance from the poor classes and sheds some of his boyhood naïveté, the smells of corduroy and turf give way to dung and horsepiss; the figure of the peasant, once a pretty picture on the roadside, becomes a far more complex symbol of ignorance and betrayal, taking on characteristics of the old harridan Mr. Casey spits at in the train station. In the last chapter, for example, the "womanhood" of Ireland becomes associated in Stephen's mind with the women at Clane, whom he begins to imagine as slightly sinister but amoral souls, possessing the secret of the Irish "race." He equates E. C. with one of these threatening, vampirelike women, and when he becomes jealous of her flirtations with a young priest, he blatantly expresses his class pride: "His anger against her found vent in coarse railing at her paramour . . . a priested peasant, with a brother a policeman in Dublin and a brother a potboy in Moycullen. To him she would unveil her soul's shy nakedness, to one who was but schooled in the discharging of a formal rite rather than to him, a priest of eternal imagination" (221).

Stephen's social snobbery is therefore distantly related to his attitudes about sex. In fact, his fear of sinking into common Dublin life is intensified because the family money troubles coincide directly with his adolescence, a period when, he later remembers, "in what dread he stood of the mystery of his own body" (168). For Stephen both the church and art become means not only to acquire "nobility," but to enter a realm of pure spirit, shedding the repellant flesh forever.

As an adolescent Stephen associates sexuality with evil, and evil, in turn, he expresses in excremental imagery. His first sexual encounter is with a prostitute, whom he equates with the "obscene scrawl which he had read on the oozing wall of a urinal" (100). When he suffers the torments of sexual guilt, he has a vision of his own personal hell, which, like many religious authorities before him, he conceives not as a fiery pit but as a dung heap:

A field of stiff weeds and thistles and tufted nettlebunches. Thick among the tufts of rank stiff growth lay battered cannisters and clots and coils of solid excrement. A faint marshlight struggled upwards from all the ordure through the bristling greygreen weeds. An evil smell, faint and foul as the light, curled upwards sluggishly out of the cannisters and from the stale crusted dung. (137)

Terrified that he will be doomed to this hell, he regards his penis with horror:

But does that part of the body understand or what? The serpent, the most subtle beast of the field. It must understand when it desires in one instant and then prolongs its own desire instant after instant, sinfully. It feels and understands and desires. What a horrible thing! Who made it to be like that, a bestial part of the body able to understand bestially and desire bestially? Was that then he or an inhuman thing moved by a lower soul than his soul? His soul sickened at the thought of a torpid snaky life feeding itself out of the tender marrow of his life and fattening upon the slime of lust. O why was that so? O why? (139–40)

Stephen hopes to save himself by entering the church, but Joyce makes it clear that the religious experience is not really an escape from sexuality, only a repression and displacement of sexual desires. Stephen does everything possible to suppress the temptations of the flesh, dedicating his life to a ceaseless round of prayer and mortification. He fasts; he walks the streets with downcast eyes; he sits in the most uncomfortable positions, refusing even to scratch when he itches; he will not allow himself to sing and he deliberately subjects himself to unpleasant noises; still fascinated with urine, he seeks out a "stale fishy stink" in order to offend his sense of smell. But as he walks down the street staring at the pavements, he fingers a set of rosary beads in his pocket, in a surrogate masturbation. He imagines the beads are "flowers" (one inevitably thinks of Bloom's "flower" in the bath), and yet flowers of a "vague unearthly texture," without odor or name (148). Fastidious as ever, he finds it extremely difficult to "merge his life with the common tide of other lives," and he is attracted to exotic religious texts, such as the "neglected book written by saint Alphonsus Liguori," which he describes in erotic, Paterian language:

A faded world of fervent love and virginal responses seemed to be evoked for his soul by the reading of its pages in which the imagery of the canticles was interwoven with the communicant's prayers. An inaudible voice seemed to caress the soul, telling her names and glories, bidding her rise as for espousal and come away, bidding her look forth, a spouse, from Amana and from the mountains of the leopards; and the soul seemed to answer with the same inaudible voice, surrendering herself. (152)

Notice that the eroticism here is presented in traditionally "feminine" terms, the soul pictured as a female "surrendering herself" in passionate espousal to her lover, identified only as an "inaudible voice." The passage is only one of many instances in which Joyce suggests latent homosexuality disguised as priestly idealism, and this threat of homosexuality becomes one of the unstated though clearly implied reasons for Stephen's disillusionment with the Jesuits.

But the priesthood of art, the pure aestheticism which Stephen embraces after he has forsaken the church, functions as yet another means of rejecting the body. Joyce understands, as Stephen does not, that art cannot be disassociated from the human passions which inspire it. Stephen continually tries to make this separation: for example, he spiritualizes the girl he encounters on the beach, making her seem a visionary apparition even while he is aware of being erotically stimulated by the "profane joy" of her upraised skirts (171). Likewise, Stephen's inspiration for his villanelle comes as a result of a wet dream; the temptress in the verse remains a highly sexual creature, masked, like the Virgin Mary before her, in a religious imagery. One reason the poem is so poor is that it is dishonest to the emotions that led to its creation.

Even though he would have himself believe that the proper artistic response to the Venus Praxiteles is a dispassionate stasis, most of Stephen's attempts to write poetry are intimately connected with his sex life. Except for his abortive try at a poem about the betrayal of Parnell, his earliest verses are attempts to express erotic feelings. In chapter 2, for example, he tries to write lines to "E——C——." He wants to recapture the mood of the evening before, when he was feverishly agitated by a flirtation on a tramcar. Joyce has already shown us the previous evening with all the intensity of poetry, brilliantly capturing the welter of the boy's emotions. He makes us sense the tapping of the girl's shoes on a glassy winter road, the tramhorses with their jangling bells, the green light of the tram, the empty seats littered with colored tickets. We feel the boy's overpowering desire to kiss the girl, and his deflated emotions when his courage fails and he is left on a deserted car, staring at the corrugated footboard. But when Stephen himself tries to write about this incident, he leaves out the details, imagining them to be "common and insignificant." At the top of the page he enters the Jesuit motto "A.M.D.G.," and then tries to record an "undefined sorrow":

There remained no trace of the tram itself nor of the trammen nor of the horses: nor did he and she appear vividly. The verses told only of the night and the balmy breeze and the maiden lustre of the moon. . . . After this the letters L.D.S. were written at the bottom of the page and, having hidden the book, he went into his mother's bedroom and gazed at his face for a long time in the mirror of her dressingtable. (70-71)

We can forgive the child for his narcissism and his bad poetry, but the process Joyce describes is symptomatic of a more serious problem that confronts Stephen as he grows older. The circumstances surrounding the composition of the villanelle of the temptress are not much different from the ones we find here. The later poem is very much in vogue with the literary atmosphere of the nineties, but like most of the poems in that style it is rarified nearly out of existence. Even in his later, "artist" phase Stephen is continuing to react against what he regards as the "common and insignificant" reality, continuing to pare his fingernails above what he no doubt feels are the base and dirty aspects of his life. He hopes to escape into the free, pure air of art; but until he recognizes that no life is completely isolate, until he learns to accept and properly criticize his actual experience, he cannot be a poet or even a mature individual.

III

Imagining that he can deny his past, Stephen adopts a new father, an "artificer" more in keeping with his noble image of himself, and proposes to exchange Dublin for Paris. And yet even the form of the novel tends to underscore his naïveté, showing that his experience in Ireland has influenced all his responses to the world, down to his very speech. Joyce makes us aware of this fact by presenting the story through a sort of pastiche of Stephen's consciousness, a series of "styles" designed to present the *quidditas* of the character. This impersonal technique not only gives the novel its powerful immediacy, it reveals Joyce's deep understanding of the historical, geographical, and psychological determinants of language.

Stephen himself has nearly the same gift, as we can see from the way he is attuned to the speech of all the Irish social orders. He fantasizes about the "sleek lives" of the Anglo-Irish patricians, who "knew the names of certain French dishes and gave orders to jarvies in highpitched provincial voices which pierced through their skintight accents" (238). He listens to the aged captain in the National Library and remarks on his "genteel accent, low and moist, marred by errors," wondering if this speech implies "noble" blood thinned by an "incestuous love" (228). He is sensitive to the fact that the dean of studies does not recognize *tundish* and pronounces *home, Christ, ale, master* with an English inflection. He notes that Cranly's drawl comes from "the quays of Dublin," and his eloquence from a "Wicklow pulpit" (195). Typically, he patronizes the "peasant" Davin, who calls him "Stevie": "The homely version of his christian name on the lips of his friend had touched Stephen pleasantly when first heard" (180). "Stephen had turned his smiling eyes towards his friend's face, flattered by his confidence and won over to sympathy by the speaker's simple accent" (181–82).

Stephen's own rather prissy, formal way of speaking is, as he himself tells us, a carefully acquired habit, an attempt to disentangle himself from his environment and the "nets" which have been flung at him. But the tie between language and social reality cannot be so easily severed. It is possible for Stephen to affect a formal speech, but this only marks his desire to achieve a superior status. It is therefore important that we not mistake the often florid language of the book for the voice of Joyce or his persona. Otherwise we are likely to miss the full implications of passages like this one from the second chapter:

He became the ally of a boy named Aubrey Mills and founded with him a gang of adventurers in the avenue. Aubrey carried a whistle dangling from his buttonhole and a bicycle lamp attached to his belt while the others had short sticks thrust daggerwise through theirs. Stephen, who had read of Napoleon's plain style of dress, chose to remain unadorned and thereby heightened for himself the pleasure of taking counsel with his lieutenant before giving orders. (63)

Out of context, this reads like conventional exposition, and if we encountered it in the ordinary novel we could deduce certain attributes of the narrator's personality. In *A Portrait,* however, the prose takes on the function of characterization. The slight disparity we feel in this passage between language and content, the rather "adult" terms used to describe children's games ("ally," "adventurers in the avenue," "unadorned," "taking counsel with his lieutenant") is a way of indicating how Stephen sees himself in relation to the other boys. His Napoleonic social ambitions, his romantic tendency to become aloof and superior even while he is enjoying play, are conveyed not only by what is said but by the very diction in which it is couched.

Likewise, in subsequent sections of the book, the prose reflects Stephen's intellectual or spiritual life, becoming what Hugh Kenner has called a "meticulous pastiche of immaturity."[6] We have, for example, the dense ecclesiastical language at the beginning of chapter 4, when Stephen is immersed in religious duties:

By means of ejaculations and prayers he stored up ungrudgingly for the souls in purgatory centuries of days and quarantines and years; yet the spiritual triumph which he felt in achieving with ease so many fabulous ages of canonical penances did not wholly reward his zeal of prayer since he could never know how much temporal punishment he had remitted by way of suffrage for the agonising souls: and, fearful lest in the midst of the purgatorial fire, which differed from the infernal only in that it was not everlasting, his penance might avail no more than a drop of moisture, he drove his soul daily through an increasing circle of works of supererogation. (147)

This is very different from the baby talk that opens the book, but it is far from being "mature"; in fact it is more obfuscating than ever. Notice that the lengthy period is made up of three complete statements, the first ending with a semicolon and the second with a colon. All three sentences are imbedded with qualifications and fine distinctions, until the reader's head, like Stephen's, begins to spin through "an increasing circle of works of supererogation."

By contrast, consider this language, which occurs just after Stephen has rejected the church and just before he experiences his poetic vision on the beach:

A veiled sunlight lit up faintly the grey sheet of water where the river was embayed. In the distance along the course of the slowflowing Liffey slender masts flecked the sky and, more distant still, the dim fabric of the city lay prone in haze. Like a scene on some vague arras, old as man's weariness, the image of the seventh city of christendom was visible to him across the timeless air, no older nor more weary nor less patient of subjection than in the days of the thingmote. (167)

This, clearly, is the way a young aesthete of the nineties might talk to himself, composing phrases which have a delicate and fatigued music. In his mood of world-weary sensuality, Stephen sees nothing that is not faint, dim, distant, vague, or veiled. Everything is languid and fragile, from the "slowflowing" Liffey to the "slender masts" to the "dim fabric of the city." Notice also that even though Stephen has turned away from Catholicism, he retains the aesthete's nostalgia for an aristocratic, medieval Christianity, suggested here in the "vague arras," the "seventh city of christendom" and the "days of the thingmote."

The later chapters of the book are filled with near-parodies of Pater, the pre-Raphaelites, and the Decadents, but occasionally we can hear another voice, as when Stephen meditates bitterly on the dean of studies in chapter 5:

It seemed as if he used the shifts and lore and cunning of the world, as bidden to do, for the greater glory of God, without joy in their handling or hatred of that in them which was evil but turning them, with a firm gesture of obedience, back upon themselves; and for all this silent service it seemed as if he loved not at all the master and little, if at all, the ends he served. *Similiter atque senis baculus*, he was, as the founder would have had him, like a staff in an old man's hand, to be left in a corner, to be leaned on in the road at nighfall or in stress of weather, to lie with a lady's nosegay on a garden seat, to be raised in menace. (186)

These sentences, in spite of their somewhat anticlerical bitterness, might have come from a skillful preacher. The leisurely syntax, the flair for allusion and analogy, the ear for what used to be called "cadence"—all this probably derives from Cardinal Newman, whom Stephen regards as the greatest writer of prose in English. In fact Newman is mentioned only a page and a half later: "I remember a sentence of Newman's," Stephen says, perhaps unconsciously acknowledging his master.

Therefore, the self-consciously literary style Stephen adopts in the closing chapters, the empurpled Paterian eloquence and the Newmanesque phrasemaking, serves to make him a recognizable type. He is a literary intellectual whose philosophy and poetry are supersaturated with the Catholic influences of his upbringing, and he is highly representative of the English and Anglo-Irish artists of the eighties and nineties. Like those artists he reacts against society by trying to create a priesthood of art. Like them he draws "less pleasure from the reflection of the glowing sensible world . . . than from the contemplation of an inner world of individual emotions mirrored . . . in a lucid supple periodic prose" (166–67). He says at the end of the book that he is going forth to encounter the "reality" of experience so that he may create a "consciousness" for his "race." His rebellion has undeniably heroic aspects; for example, his unwillingness to commit even small hypocrisies out of fear of a "chemical reaction that would be set up in my soul by false homage" (243). In fact, however, his journey to Paris is at least partly an attempt to escape the oppressive reality of a déclassé family and a country which was widely regarded as the social inferior of Europe. He is in no position to give Ireland a new consciousness, because his own consciousness is so completely derived from the minor poets of decadent literature.

IV

Nevertheless, if Joyce implicitly criticizes Stephen's aesthetics, Joyce himself remains an artist who has evolved from a position very like Stephen's. Joyce's politics, for example, although far more complex and progressive than those of Dedalus, resemble the young man in certain ways. As a novelist Joyce is never the apolitical aesthete he is sometimes made out to be. In *Ulysses* he gives support to Griffith's movement, even while he criticizes the anti-Semitism and elements of reaction in other areas of Irish nationalism. And yet for Joyce, as for Stephen, Irish history seems almost to have stopped with the collapse of his father's job prospects. The aristocratic leadership of Parnell had been lost forever, replaced by a more commonplace Fenianism from which both Joyce and Stephen chose to disassociate themselves. History would treat such attitudes ironically. For example, Stephen jokes about his college friends' "rebellion with hurleysticks" (202), but two real-life counterparts of these boys would subsequently die from British gunfire. Like Stephen, Joyce often spoke of his countrymen as faithless betrayers; but to make this attitude intellectually respectable, he had to freeze time, never moving beyond Bloomsday.[7]

We know also that the young Joyce's attitudes about aesthetics in the Pola notebooks are almost identical with some of the ideas found in the fifth chapter of *A Portrait*. Through a process of intensive and courageous self-analysis, Joyce matured into a literary genius, yet if there is any knowledge to be gained from the experience of Stephen Dedalus, it is that a man never completely escapes his past. Joyce could learn to criticize his life, but he could not change his entire consciousness and become another man. He was able, as a mature artist, to record all the unpleasant details of life in dear dirty Dublin, but he remained an uncommitted exile, a literary aristocrat who regarded himself, for a while at least, as the unacknowledged legislator of Ireland. He was able to write about Molly Bloom as an explicitly sexual creature, but not without making her an amoral, essentially ignorant being who is mystified into an archetypal earth mother. He was able to confront the human body more directly than anyone before him, but he had to maintain a thin line of defense against the subject, aestheticizing raw life with the most carefully wrought prose in the history of the English novel. Along with Stephen, Joyce continued to see life in terms of a dualism, a division between matter and spirit which his novels would attempt to reconcile. He chose a severe classicism as his means, rejecting Stephen's romanticism, but his problem remained the same as that of his hero. Like many Irishmen before him, he had been given an "excremental vision," and it is difficult to find a page of his later writings where references to dirt and bodily functions do not coexist with the rarified lyrical temperament we associate with Stephen Dedalus.

Psychologists tell us that we can understand and cope with anxieties, but not that we can do away with them entirely. Joyce had a similar view of human personality, and it is no surprise that he partly retained the defensive aestheticism he criticizes in *A Portrait*. In fact, the aloof, "impersonal" narrative technique of the novel indicates that in still other respects the boy has been father to the man. Pastiche and parody, Joyce's chief technical devices, are relatively undetermined ways of using language; they allow the speaker to detach himself from his own mannerisms so that he may exercise the limited freedom of imitating someone else. Joyce, as much as Stephen, wanted freedom, and he therefore chose to become a sort of literary forger, deliberately composing books out of a mixture of styles, trying to keep his own language as transparent and impersonal as possible. By this means he would cunningly evade the onus of personality; he would achieve an escape Stephen Dedalus could not manage; he would, at last, become like a god, clear in sight and unburdened by nature or the necessity which no doubt weighed so heavily upon his ordinary self. But his escape is only apparent. The ordinary Joyce, mortal after all, has been projected back into the novels in the form of autobiographical characters who live a socially determined existence.

NOTES

1. *Realism in Our Time* (New York: Harper & Row, 1964), p. 26.

2. James Joyce, *A Portrait of the Artist as a Young Man* (New York: Viking Press, 1964), p. 241. All page references in the text are to this edition.

3. Richard Ellmann, *James Joyce* (New York: Oxford University Press, 1959), pp. 11–16.

4. On his first day at Clongowes, Joyce's own father reminded him that John O'Connell, his great-grandfather, had presented an address on those very grounds. The father then gave his son two five-shilling pieces, telling him never to peach on another boy (Ellmann, *James Joyce*, pp. 26–27).

5. *The Classical Temper: A Study of James Joyce's "Ulysses"* (New York: Barnes and Noble, 1961), p. 64.

6. *Dublin's Joyce* (Bloomington: Indiana University Press, 1956), p. 120.

7. Further comments on Joyce's politics can be found in Malcolm Brown's excellent study, *The Politics of Irish Literature* (Seattle: University of Washington Press, 1972), pp. 385–89.

Joyce's "Features of Infanc~

CHESTER G. ANDERSON 7

I

J AMES J OYCE's *A Portrait of the Artist as a Young Man* ends with
a flourish of rhetorical grandeur as Stephen Dedalus,
revolutionary hero of the ineradicable ego, prepares to fly into
exile from Dublin to Paris. The tone of the diary entry is
exclamatory, the mode apostrophic, the motif yet another
rebirth to an heroic foster-father, the rhythm all but Marlovian,
the omnipotent moral aim the salvation of the Irish and the
human race through poetry: "Welcome, O life! I go to encounter for the millionth time the reality of experience and to forge
in the smithy of my soul the uncreated conscience of my
race. . . . Old father, old artificer, stand me now and ever in
good stead."[1] Even if we had forgotten Stephen's castration
fears, his phobias and fetishes, his paranoia, his morbid guilt
feelings and obsessions, his homosexual wishes and strong
desire to be female, his coprophilia and mild masochism, the
rhetoric itself might help us guess that this manic crest will
have its trough. Or we might predict the trough from the
again-and-again recurrence of the "million" encounters, as well
as of the many rebirths that we have witnessed in the preceding pages. The only thing final about this ending is the flourish
itself.

We are not very surprised to find, therefore, when we meet Stephen Dedalus again at the beginning of *Ulysses*, that he is sick, though the intensity and variety of his neuroses make us wonder what their unconscious and infantile sources are. He is wearily and morbidly mourning his mother, who has been dead for nearly a year. He thinks he killed her. He has moved out of the impoverished family home, abandoning his younger brothers and sisters to his father's drunken tyranny. He cannot save them, he feels. He cannot get along with his best friend, feeling persecuted by him and by his science-art of medicine (including "the new Viennese school" of Freud) at the same time that he feels homosexually attracted to him.

He is still rebellious, but his rebellion amounts to ineffectual sarcasm addressed to those around him, to God, and not least to himself. His conscience gnaws at him furiously: he names it, with paranoid accuracy, the "agenbite of inwit." [2] He fears this biting attack so deeply that he has projected it onto nature itself—what Mulligan calls the "scrotumtightening sea" (*U*, 5). Fearing that sea, he has not bathed his louse-covered body since the preceding October. He cannot hold a teaching job. In any case, he is a poor teacher, alternately ·brooding over himself and his unanswerable questions and laughing hysterically at private jokes told to his bewildered charges. He sorely needs a girl friend, but all he can manage are wishes, fantasies, envy of his pupils, and "morose delectation" over a female gypsy cocklepicker and over male Mulligan. He still sees his salvation and the salvation of his race in his writing of poetry, but all he can achieve—Dedalus as forger—is a theft from a translation by Douglas Hyde which he obsessively amends into an ugly fantasy—at once homosexual and incestuous—of being sucked to death by a vampire, while he as vampire sucks and impregnates his mother to death.

Even the Blakean "intellectual imagination," which at the end of the "Nestor" episode seems to Stephen capable of rescuing him from the "nightmare" of personal and racial history, turns to urine and snot by the end of the "Proteus." In

"Circe," to take but one glance forward, it turns to "shite," though Stephen quickly turns it back again. When his mother arises from the grave, her foul breath "*choking* [Stephen] *with fright, remorse and horror,*" her cajoling tone turns to demands for repentance and her protestation of love for him since his uterine days changes to threats:

Beware! (*She raises her blackened, withered right arm slowly towards Stephen's breast with outstretched fingers.*) Beware! God's hand! (*A green crab with malignant red eyes sticks deep its grinning claws in Stephen's heart.*)

STEPHEN

(*Strangled with rage.*) Shite! (*His features grow drawn and grey and old.*)

BLOOM

(*At the window.*) What?

STEPHEN

Ah non, par exemple! The intellectual imagination! With me all or not at all. *Non serviam!* (U, 582)

We have been here before, of course, over and over again. The paradigm of this scene is, as we shall see, the first page and a half of *A Portrait*. What got Stephen into this fix must be one of the questions. What made him an artist must be another. Joyce answered them repeatedly. But, luckily for us, he spoke in parables.

Joyce first sat down to write the story of himself as Stephen Dedalus on 7 January 1904, five months after his mother's death, in a narrative essay called "A Portrait of the Artist." The following summer—the summer during which *Ulysses* takes place—he wrote the first stories of *Dubliners*, signing them "Stephen Daedalus" when they were published in *The Irish Homestead*. The first words he wrote in this beginning of his artistic maturity were these:

The features of infancy are not commonly reproduced in the adolescent portrait for, so capricious are we, that we cannot or will not conceive the past in any other than its iron, memorial aspect. Yet the past assuredly implies a fluid succession of presents, the development of an entity of which our actual present is but a phase only. (257–58)

So close to Sigmund Freud's basic notion that "really, we can never relinquish anything,"[3] these words are our main basis for a psychoanalytic explanation of Joyce's work. In spite of his complex and intricate use of sublimation, projection, repression, and the other defenses of his "ineradicable egoism" (as he called his conscious self in the "Portrait" essay and again in *Stephen Hero*), the repressed would return again and again in new forms, demanding new defenses. Fortunately, many of these defenses, or "growth mechanisms," became, even in childhood, verbal defenses that would pattern themselves ultimately into his four prose masterpieces.

Generally speaking, his artistic work—his "forgery," as he came to call it, looking back on the rhetoric of the end of *A Portrait*—amounted to a repeated reconstitution of the mother whom he had "killed." Why not just a plain "Oedipus complex," a desire to kill his father and marry his mother? We feel comfortable, somehow, with that nowadays. But Stephen's feeling is weird, like feelings we have all forgotten. It suggests a fixation on pre-oedipal, pregenital stages of his development, though of course the more comfortable conflict is there as well. In the earlier stages he had destroyed his mother in manifold ways, beginning in his first year.

According to Melanie Klein, the nuclei of the Oedipus conflict and of superego formation are substantially developed "from the middle of the first year to the third year of the child's life."[4] They begin in what Freud called the "cannibalistic" or oral-sadistic stage, when the child, his sucking libido unsatisfied and unsatisfiable, fantasizes destroying the mother's breast and eating his way through the flesh into her innards to devour the contents—reproductive organs, feces, babies, and the father's penises, some of which he has incorporated orally.[5] The anxiety aroused by these destructive wishes causes the child to fear that he might destroy himself with his omnipotent weapons or by talionic reprisal for his instinctual aggression against the "combined hostile parent." His anxious fear causes the first split of the superego from part of the id and the projection of it onto the combined parent. From this "terrifying superego" of infancy he can protect his immature and fragile ego only by again and again destroying the projected object.

This sadistic and terrifying process—one that Joyce referred to as the "eatupus complex" (*FW*, 128)—grows dynamically through the urethral and anal stages of development in the first and second years. When the same mother who had frustrated his oral desires interferes with his urethral and anal pleasures as well, urine, feces, flatulence, and the musculature as a whole are added to the child's oral weaponry, as well as to the weaponry ranged against him. Only gradually, as his wishes begin to focus on his genital aim, does his primary sadism subside and come under the control of his strengthening ego through repression, sublimation into scoptophilia, epistemophilia and the like, and through the various means of making reparation by restoring the body of the mother or combined parent. Just as the sadistic fantasies in "number, variety and richness are wellnigh inexhaustible" (including not only the "infant of from six to twelve months trying to destroy its mother by every method at the disposal of its sadistic tendencies—with its teeth, nails and excreta and with the whole of its body, transformed in imagination into all kinds of dangerous weapons"—but also "phantasies in which his parents destroy each other by means of their genitals and excrements"), so the means of defense and reparation must be almost infinite. It is only by such reparation that the ego can be reassured that it is whole and not "castrated" or destroyed. And so we get individual human beings and artists in all their complexity.

When Joyce-Stephen grew big enough, and long after he had repressed these infantile wishes and sublimated them into his intense desire to know ("epistemophilia") and to write, he assaulted his Mother Church and Mother Ireland and not least the city that gave him birth, that "weary lover whom no caresses move" (251), as he called her when he first abandoned her. Too bad for May Joyce (but lucky for us and our own cannibalistic desires) she up and did actual die. The restitution demanded by Joyce's terrifying superego-conscience was enormous, more than anyone but a great man could repay. Like a child rebuilding the castle or town with the same blocks that he has just smashed down, Joyce rebuilt Dublin, founded a new and better church as a "priest of eternal imagination" (221), and reconstituted the mother (always an emblem of reconstructing the threatened self) in many ways, again and again.

Most of the "features of infancy" in the portrait of Joyce-Stephen must be inferred retrospectively, of course, from the standpoint of adolescence. Even more might be inferred from *Ulysses* and *Finnegans Wake*, where the mechanisms of defense or growth, as Joyce achieved what Carl Jung called "inconceivable" mental health, became necessarily more complex.[6] But in a brief essay we cannot hope to do more than try to see the features as they are presented in the opening pages of *A Portrait* and in the few facts that we know of Joyce's early life, looking forward to but a few of the main currents in the later stream of events.

We must ignore Joyce's and Stephen's frequent belittling hostility toward Freud. We must say summarily a number of things that may seem outlandish, reductive, unbelievable, and perhaps disgusting to the reader. Worst of all, we must ignore the very arts that made Joyce Joyce—humor, comedy, irony, wit, metaphor, the imitation of action, *Einfühlung*, *Kunstwollen*, sentence structure, and so on. The difference between Freudian definition and explanation and Joycean art is the difference between Freud's definition of the "anal character" and Bloom's identification with the pigeons flying between Trinity College and the Bank of Ireland, thinking, "Must be thrilling from the air" (*U*, 162). Or between Klein's discussion of the pregenital origins of the Oedipus conflict and Joyce's entering the mind of Stephen Dedalus to find: "When you wet the bed first it is warm then it gets cold" (7).

But there is nothing for the discrepancy. It is a part of the irrevocable duality of the mind, itself a result, maybe, of the primary, infantile questioning of the difference between the sexes. If I meet you in Neary's or Kavanagh's, Mulligan's in Poolbeg Street, or the Bailey in Duke Street, we can sit with our jars and recite the portions of Joyce's works that we remember.

II

James Joyce was born to John Joyce and Mary Jane ("May") Murray Joyce (he was thirty-three, she twenty-three) on 2 February 1882, as the first surviving child.[7] His mother was proud, stubborn, but "nice." His father was a heavy but hearty drinker, a spendthrift, a loser in politics and business, an energetic jokester and storyteller who sentimentally praised his past and did not grow to much wisdom. A sister, Margaret Alice ("Poppie"), was born when Joyce was not quite two and a brother, Stanislaus, when he was almost three. Two other brothers and five other sisters had been born by the time Joyce approached the end of his eleventh year.

Joyce was born at 41 Brighton Square, Rathgar, a tiny triangle of green rather than a square. In his second year, some time before 17 December 1884, when Stanislaus was born, the family moved to 23 Castlewood Avenue, Rathmines. It was in Rathgar and nearby Rathmines that the infantile "murder" of the mother took place and was repressed, only to return with such biting violence following her actual death in 1903. In *Finnegans Wake* Joyce clearly "confesses" his fixation on this universal infantile sadism and identifies the scene of the primal crime: "Oh day of rath! Ah, murther of mines!"[8]

We know for certain only one memory of those first two and one-half years—that his father told him the story that opens *A*

Portrait, about the "moocow coming down along the road" that "met a nicens little boy named baby tuckoo."[9] It seems likely that John Joyce's babysitting was occasioned by the birth of Margaret on 18 January 1884, and that the story is a response to Joyce's having asked epistemophilically where babies come from—himself, the little girl who had usurped his mother's breast, and the others with which the mother was surely filled. Before Stanislaus was born Joyce and his father also (judging from the opening page of *A Portrait*) walked to "Betty Byrne's" house and bought lemon platt candy.

That Joyce at this time fantasized anal birth for himself and his siblings can only be inferred. The fantasy is apparently universal in young children, and it is often associated with sweet food.[10] It is prominent in *Finnegans Wake*. As ALP's voice merges with Shem's at the end of the "Shem the Penman" episode, the "turfbrown mummy" tells her sons "old the news of the great big world, sonnies had a scrap" (*FW*, 194). They fought, to be sure, but they were also sons born "as crap."

That the fantasy is present may be indicated by the meaning of *tuckoo*. The widely accepted suggestion that it is a version of cuckoo seems unlikely. Adults who talk babytalk to children do not change *k*-sounds to *t*-sounds. It seems more likely, as well as more appropriate, that it is simply the father's babytalk *oo* added to the common nineteenth-century slang word *tuck*, meaning "food," especially such delicacies as pastries and jam. Joyce uses the word in this sense in both *Ulysses* and *Finnegans Wake* (*U*, 375, 427; *FW*, 196, 225, 406).

That is, one of the things that young Jim-Stephen understands John-Simon to be saying is, in effect: "When you and now your little sister were born you were delicacies good enough to eat. Your mother came down the road [and ate you] and carried you to our house [where she excreted you]." It would seem to be this meaning of *tuckoo* that sponsors the association in the ensuing paragraph: "He was baby tuckoo. The moocow came down the road where Betty Byrne lived: she sold lemon platt." That is, Stephen (Joyce) is comparing himself and secondarily his baby sister as "tuck" with another delicacy, "lemon platt," that comes from the house of another mother, "Betty Byrne." They are "topheetuck" or "sweets fished out of the muck," as Joyce puts it in *Finnegans Wake* (*FW*, 225, 563).

The tuck, the lemon platt, and the cachou that Dante gives Stephen in exchange for tissue paper at the end of the first page of *A Portrait* have multiple, unconscious motivation for Stephen. They represent both the lost oral satisfactions of the mother's breast and the contents of her body, including her milk, her flesh, her mysterious sexual apparatus, her many babies, her feces, and the penises of the father that she has incorporated orally. This is clearest in the instance of the cachous that come from the "bad" or "castrating" mother surrogate, Dante. They come in apparently endless supply from her "press," in which she has incorporated the "two brushes" representing Michael Davitt and Parnell, the back of one of which is destined to be ripped off by Dante's scissors, just as Stephen's father and Mr. Casey are to be "castrated" and reduced to childish tears by the same woman who screams at the Christmas dinner table, "We won! we crushed him to death!" (39), over the dead body of Parnell. Stephen eats the sweets, apparently, in a pleasant way that conceals his repressed, polymorphous-perverse, sadistic assault on them. But he also *is* the sweets and is therefore horribly threatened by his own infantile cannibalism. The anxiety caused by his fear of retaliation breeds what Klein calls the "terrible superego" of infancy. These features of Stephen's infancy, hidden from him now by repression and sublimation, he will come more and more clearly to recognize.

Joyce plainly tells us that the epistemophilic route of Stephen's sublimation relates to Dante's innards in the first example of it after he has arrived at Clongowes. Stephen offers a defensive sublimation: "Dante knew a lot of things. She had taught him where the Mozambique Channel was and what was the longest river in America and what was the name of the highest mountain in the moon" (10–11). He relates it not to the geography of the world but to the geography of the castrating mother: "And when Dante made that noise after dinner and then put up her hand to her mouth: that was heartburn" (11).

The next four lines of *A Portrait*, judging from Stephen's lisping, also take place in Rathmines, before the family moved to Bray, when Stephen-Joyce was five years and three months old:

> *O, the wild rose blossoms*
> *On the little green place.*

He sang that song. That was his song.

> *O, the green wothe botheth.*

Viewed as another attempt to explain his genesis, his song amounts to a defensive rejection of the parents entirely: he simply grew like an Irish rose. The song looks forward to Stephen's fantasies of peasant parents (18, 20), of being a "fosterchild and fosterbrother" (98), and of repeatedly being reborn.

His rebirths are too many to enumerate here. However, there are major examples at the end of each chapter which help form the basic spiral structure of the book. At the end of chapter 1, Stephen descends into hell to complain to Conmee about Dolan's pandying and successfully returns with the magic elixir of justice to his classmates, who make a "cradle of their locked hands" (58) to emblemize the rebirth. More visibly anal is the rebirth at the end of chapter 2, when he comes out of the filthy "maze of dirty and narrow streets" to find the prostitute and be "awakened from a slumber of centuries" (100). Displacing this fantasy upward by the end of chapter 3, he is given a "purified body" and "another life" (146), with the promise of resurrection itself. At the end of chapter 4, his soul arises "from the grave of boyhood, spurning her graveclothes" (170). And so on, as we have seen.

Such fantasies of rebirth, of parentless or virgin births, and of reconstituting the body seem always to provide reassurance that the sadistic attacks on the mother have not succeeded in destroying her and that therefore the talionic revenge against the infant's own body has not been wreaked. But, more important for the development of Stephen as artist, the performance of the song (as later the dance and rhyme) offers reparation. Both in content (the rose as blooming, androgynous reproductive apparatus) and in form (as a creation of rhythm, tune, and words enacted) the song amounts to a sublimation of the sadistic wishes, which can remain repressed.[11]

So, to recapitulate, the matricide was done in Rathmines. In *Finnegans Wake,* Joyce clearly "confesses" his fixation on this universal infantile sadism, identifies the murder of the mother with the talionic terror of destroying the self, and returns to the scene of the crime: "Oh day of rath! Ah, murther of mines!" (*FW,* 340). Or, similarly, when Mutt tries to explain his origins to Jute, he stammers out in oral-urethral-anal rage: "I trumple from rath in mine mines" (*FW,* 16), including his fear of being "crumpled" by it.

It seems likely that the lines beginning at 7.13 of *A Portrait* and continuing to the end of the "overture" section at 8.15 all take place during the year or so following the move of the Joyce-Dedalus family to Bray in 1887. They are made continuous by references from one paragraph to the next. This continuity is most significant between the bed-wetting paragraph and the mother-smell paragraph, for it suggests that Joyce-Stephen was enuretic at least into his fifth year, through the climax of the phallic and oedipal phases of infantile sexual development:

When you wet the bed first it is warm then it gets cold. His mother put on the oilsheet. That had the queer smell.

His mother had a nicer smell than his father.

The first thing that one notices about the passage is the use of the second person pronoun to refer to Stephen and of the present tense to refer to the bed-wetting, the only such usages in the overture. The shift from third person and past tense emphasizes the disturbance that the enuresis causes in the stream of Stephen's consciousness. In psychoanalytic terms the grammatical shifts stress that the bed-wetting is a repetition compulsion rather than a simple memory: that is, it is an acting out again of part of a repressed experience as if it were (as indeed it becomes) a contemporary experience. Generally speaking, this is the method of *A Portrait*—technique as discovery—and it will be discussed briefly below in connection with Stephen's compulsion to play with the flaps of his ears.

It is clear that Stephen's bed-wetting has not been a continuous autoerotic activity since infancy, but that he has been more or less "trained" and has returned at the climax of the phallic-oedipal stages of development to a true enuresis. This is made certain by the fact that it is only after the wetting that his mother puts the oilsheet on the bed.

On the most basic level Stephen is regressing to pregenital sadism in order to attack the mother or "combined hostile parent," who is having oral-urethral-anal fun that excludes the child. Hence, the double ambiguity of "His mother put on the oilsheet. That had the queer smell." The first sentence says both that she put it on the bed and that she put it on herself, as if she were identified with the bed and was the sadistic object. On the other hand, the "queer smell" is contrasted with the "nice" smell of the mother and compared with the worse smell of the father, so that the boy is attacking him as well in a more familiar oedipal assault. As we shall see, this rhetorical ambiguity reflects the ambivalence in the boy. He has anxious conflicts about whether to identify with the father or the mother.

According to psychoanalysts more conventional than Klein, enuresis is one of the most common examples of a "conversion symptom"; that is, the change in physical function which unconsciously and in a distorted form expresses instinctual impulses that had been repressed. Otto Fenichel, for example, citing ten references to the work of other psychoanalysts, says that "an example of a pregenital expression of predominantly genital wishes in a conversion symptom is presented by bedwetting, the most frequent masturbatory equivalent in children."[12] It seems likely that Joyce-Stephen had been forbidden to masturbate and that "the enuresis represents a substitute and equivalent of suppressed masturbation," oedipal urges overlaying and mingling with the more archaic sadistic wishes.

Fenichel is explicit about the oedipal nature of this conversion symptom in a five-year-old: "Like masturbation, enuresis may fulfill the role of an efferent function for various sexual wishes. At the height of the development of the Oedipus complex it is first and foremost a discharge instrument of the Oedipus impulses."[13] Joyce supports this view by identifying the restricting and shaming sheet with the father. But as we have seen, he is very mixed up about it, identifying himself more strongly with the mother than with the father.

Stephen's identification with his mother begins in the first sentence of the book with the neologism *nicens* (the only one in the book) and is continued in no less than sixteen uses of the word *nice* in the first chapter, compared to only five in the rest of the book. He is handling the castration threat by castrating or effeminizing himself. He is also, Klein would argue, regressing to a pregenital "femininity complex" in which his powerful wish, like Bloom's in the "Circe" episode of *Ulysses,* is to have a baby.

Stephen's enuresis does seem more passive and feminine than active and masculine. His identification with the mother and his defensive yearning are for earlier days before the siblings arrived. Fenichel says: "In boys the incontinence usually has the meaning of a female trait; such boys hope to obtain female kinds of pleasure by 'urinating passively.' Further, the passive way of urinating may express a regression to the early passive-receptive ways of pleasure."[14] We will return to this passive conversion—perhaps the most consequential of the features of infancy in Joyce-Stephen—as soon as we have continued to the end of the overture.

In the song of the rose and the hornpipe dance, the young artist was learning ways of sublimating pregenital impulses and organizing them under his capacity for genital activity. That he dances to the tune of his mother's instrument may be of special significance; for the weirdest aspect of Joyce-Stephen's need was to make himself androgynous (though seeming basically female, since he was a man) so that he could be loved by an androgynous woman (though she, being a woman, might seem basically a man: a "phallic woman"). To this, too, we must return.

His life was complicated by the arrival in Bray of "Uncle Charles" (William O'Connell, his father's uncle) and "Dante" (Mrs. "Dante" Hearn Conway, a "spoiled nun"), the one a kind of soft, anal, grandfather type, the other the "castrating" or "terrible" mother we have already seen, on whom the boy could project so many of his childish fantasies.

Nevertheless, Stephen prospered and reached the childhood utopia of genitality, fooling around in his fifth year with Eileen Vance in an attempt to "socialize his libido." It was an attempt with which he would have great difficulty for many years. Like Earwicker's sin in the park in *Finnegans Wake*—maybe it was masturbation, maybe exposure and urination, maybe just looking—what Stephen does to or with Eileen is not clear, though no doubt each reader gets up more or less consciously his own image of the crime. Joyce, of course, "intends" this response from the reader; it is the first rule of his fictional technique. Most of my students think the children "played doctor"—exposed their bodies to one another—though some say that they only kissed one another. I myself think that the crime was "unlawful watching and besetting," like the crime charged against Bloom (*U*, 455), and that the besetting included a contribution from Stephen of urine or feces. Joyce seems to agree with me in *Finnegans Wake,* when he gives to a survivor of Eileen the accusation, "playing house of ivary dower of gould and gift you soil me peepat my prize" (*FW*, 327). But as we are seeing, the scoptophilia and the soiling are intimately related in their psychogenesis.

If the threat of punishment fits the crime, whatever Stephen has been watching or doing is as related to his oedipal desires as his masturbation and resulting enuresis were, for he is threatened with "castration" in the most classic way: by having his eyes pulled out, as Oedipus himself pulled out his with Jocasta's brooch. It is important that the threat comes from Dante, the "bad" mother split from the "nice," rather than from Mr. Vance, who in the corresponding epiphany makes the threat (267–68). There are, of course, strong aesthetic reasons for not bringing Vance into the story in person. But aside from that, the "terrible mother" as castrator fits into the pregenital fixations in Joyce-Stephen's psyche that we have been trying to discern. In *Ulysses*, as we have seen, the mother herself will be represented as the "scrotumtightening sea" and will arise from the grave with the castrating crab in her hand (*U*, 5, 582).

Stephen defends himself against Dante's threat by identifying with the mother and retreating back into the womb (hiding under the table), as well as by composing a brief chiasmic poem out of the threat:

> *Pull out his eyes,*
> *Apologise,*
> *Apologise,*
> *Pull out his eyes.*
>
> *Apologise,*
> *Pull out his eyes,*
> *Pull out his eyes,*
> *Apologise.* (8)

This "word defense," handling the threat with the primitive (anal-urethral) magic or omnipotence of words, is obviously the essential move toward Stephen's becoming an artist—a development from his similar motives in listening to the moocow story, singing the rose song, or dancing to the mother's hornpipe.

What Stephen was looking for when he peeped at Eileen's "prize" was apparently a penis. That she, like his mother, Dante, and his sisters, does not have one is the basic threat. It will increase his enduring need to provide females with a penis and to pretend that he does not have one. Or, more accurately, to fantasize that both he and his love objects are androgynous. The most obvious evidence for this need is in the coprophilia that Joyce expresses in the letters he wrote to Nora Barnacle in 1909, where the feces that Joyce imagines watching or hearing her produce reassure him that she has the penis that he knows is missing.

III

Before considering the letters, however, we should pursue the passive conversion in Stephen's enuresis on the first page of *A Portrait* to his position as artist in the last chapter of the book. There we find him composing his "Villanelle of the Temptress," partly identifying himself with her. He imagines that "in the virgin womb of the imagination the word was made flesh. Gabriel the seraph had come to the virgin's chamber" (217). That Joyce-Stephen is here the Blessed Virgin being impregnated in order to give birth to the poem is beyond doubt. What may be disputed is the continuity between this moment and his enuresis at age five on the first page of the novel.

But the "sweet music," the "dewy wet" soul, and the "waves of light" that pass over the artist's limbs (217) all bespeak the iconographic representation of the Annunciation that Joyce and Ezra Pound joked about.[15] And the representation is itself extensively demonstrated by Ernest Jones to be a fantasy of anal impregnation of the mother by the flatulence or other excretions of the father, displaced upward from anus to ear, from flatulence to the "breath" of the Holy Ghost and the "speech" of Gabriel, from the urine to the "light."[16] Joyce put the joke of all this, transmitted by the "dove" or "pigeon," into each of his prose works, most memorably in Mulligan's "Ballad of the Joking Jesus," which begins:

> *I'm the queerest young fellow that ever you heard.*
> *My mother's a jew, my father's a bird.*

With Joseph the joiner I cannot agree,
So here's to disciples and Calvary.

If anyone thinks that I amn't divine
He'll get no free drinks when I'm making the wine
But have to drink water and wish it were plain
That I make when the wine becomes water again. (*U*, 19)

In *Stephen Hero* Stephen refers to the Holy Ghost as "a spermatozoon with wings added" and to "Jehovah the Second" as "the middle-aged gentleman with the aviary."[17] In *A Portrait* Joyce puts Ernest Jones's analysis in a nutshell when, as Temple speaks on the National Library porch of Stephen's *"Pernobilis et pervetusta familia,"* Goggins farts and Dixon asks, "Did an angel speak?" (230).

That these images, as well as the smoke, vapour, incense, bird, bell, and murmuring lips, the stammering and the writing itself are anal-urethrally oriented is clear. One need not, in fact, understand this as an application of Freud, Klein, Jones, Fenichel, et al. to Joyce. One may simply read him. The "virgin chamber" gives another meaning to the title of *Chamber Music*, a meaning allied to the well-known story that Gogarty, Stanislaus Joyce, and Gorman tell in their several versions. That is, the poems of *Chamber Music* were viewed as holy and virgin births, each "place" where they occurred to Joyce a sacred place, the poems (as later the *Dubliners* stories) "epicleti"—moments of transubstantiation in which the Holy Ghost again descended with his wind-fire-light-water and bird-talk to impregnate the virgin-mother-artist, who can then give birth to the god-child-work.

As far as the poet is concerned, the act of composition is passive and "feminine": "Towards dawn he awoke. O what sweet music! His soul was all dewy wet. Over his limbs in sleep pale cool waves of light had passed. He lay still, as if his soul lay amid cool waters, conscious of faint sweet music" (217). The poem comes to him as he lies passively on a wet bed, simply. And as he completes the inspired composition, his watery speech gives him not only the poem, but also a self-authorized "uterim" from which he can give birth again to himself as man and artist with a minimum of anxiety:

A glow of desire kindled again his soul and fired and fulfilled all his body. Conscious of his desire she was waking from odorous sleep, the temptress of his villanelle. Her eyes, dark and with a look of languor, were opening to his eyes. Her nakedness yielded to him, radiant, warm, odorous and lavishlimbed, enfolded him like a shining cloud, enfolded him like water with a liquid life: and like a cloud of vapour or like waters circumfluent in space the liquid letters of speech, symbols of the element of mystery, flowed forth over his brain. (223)

It is to just this realization of the urethral-anal-feminine-regressive-castration-defense elements of his art, as well as to the enuretic return to bed-wetting on the opening page, that the Shaun side of Joyce's character refers when he says: "Shem Macadamson, you know me and I know you and all your shemeries. Where have you been in the uterim, enjoying yourself all the morning since your last wetbed confession? I advise you to conceal yourself, my little friend" (*FW*, 187–88). In fact, all of the "concealing and revealing" element in Joyce's art (as less consciously in the art of other writers) finds its source in the "shame" attached to the pregenital stages of infantile sexuality, as we have been arguing. Joyce says all this and more when he returns in the "Kevin-Jerry" chapter of *Finnegans Wake* to tell again the story of his birth as child and artist:

Hush! The other, twined on codliverside, has been crying in his sleep, making sharpshape his inscissors on some first choice sweets fished out of the muck. A stake in our mead. What a teething wretch! How his book of craven images! Here are posthumious tears on his intimelle. And he has pipettishly bespilled himself from his foundingpen as illspent from inkinghorn. He is jem job joy pip poo pat (jot um for a sobrat!) Jerry Jehu. (*FW*, 563)

That is, he first began to make the lancet of his art from the cannibalistic stage of the weaning trauma ("making sharp-shape his inscissors") as he had the tuckoo-fantasy of anal birth ("sweets fished out of the muck"). But his real step forward as writer was when he "pipettishly" (a urine word usually reserved in *Finnegans Wake* for sister Issy) "bespilled himself from his foundingpen." This may have been a necessary step backward for him as man-child: "horn"—one of Joyce's favorite words for his penis in the 1909 letters—should be "king" and therefore the urine is "illspent." But "illspent" also includes the *lsp* code for urine used throughout *Finnegans Wake,* so that Joyce is saying that the urine was kept ("pent") from the art of writing until he released it ("spent" it) in his childhood enuresis and opened up the possibilities of founding his pen and giving birth to himself as Jesus ("Jerry Jehu").

IV

If there were space or time, we should here or now go on to discuss the few details about Joyce's early life that we know from sources outside his fictive autobiographies—his repeated playing of a sadistic Satan with his siblings, his fear of being flushed down the toilet by his mother, and so on—to show how they relate to the "features of infancy" that we have discussed. Instead, one eye on realities, we can best place the earflap game in context and trace it to the composition of the villanelle. In that way we can see more clearly the power and pervasiveness of infantile urges. Along the way we can show how the letters Joyce wrote to Nora Barnacle in his twenty-seventh year confirm our analysis.

Stephen first plays with the flaps of his ears in the refectory at Clongowes early in the first chapter of *A Portrait.* It is a regressive moment. On the playground he has suffered the phallic threat of the "rude feet" of the footballers. He is homesick. He recalls kissing his "nice mother" good-bye when his parents brought him to Clongowes. He identifies her with the castle, which, like her, is "nice and warm," and he entertains a primal-scene fantasy about it, recalling that "the butler had shown him the marks of the soldiers' slugs in the wood of the door" (10). Fenichel says that "very often sadistic impulses are tied up with scoptophilia: the individual wants to see something in order to destroy it (or to gain reassurance that the object is not yet destroyed). Often, looking itself is unconsciously thought of as a substitute for destroying ('I did not destroy it; I merely looked at it')."[18] Is it Simon or Stephen who has sent the slugs into the mother's door? If the slugs are the father's penises, can Stephen destroy them by looking at them? A risky fantasy. He tries another, transforming the castle into an abbey and killing off the father in it: "*Wolsey died in Leicester Abbey*" (10).

The Wolsey fantasy is one of several major ways in which he advances from the assault on the mother to the assault on the father, though in it, too, he has attacked the father within the abbey-castle mother, as he had in the risky Rowan fantasy. His most direct assault on the father is in the fantasy of the marshal who receives "his deathwound on the battlefield of Prague" (19) and in the related fantasy of the death of Parnell.

The entertaining of forbidden wishes sends Stephen home in his imagination to the hearthrug in sole possession of the mother. But this is as forbidden as the assault on the beast with two backs. The terrible superego of infancy returns with all of the power of the id from which it had initially split: he regresses beyond the pleasure principle and repeats compulsively the anal-sadistic punishment of having been shouldered into the ditch by Wells, the ditch that in fantasy includes the fecal, phobic, gnawing rat with its beady black eyes which a fellow had once seen "jump plop into the scum." Feminizing himself in a less phobic way, he thinks of the nice phallic mother—her "jewelly slippers" richly containing the fetishistic feet in their "lovely warm smell" (10). Risky again. He brings on, in recompense, a proper earlier sublimation—the epistemophilia about the Mozambique channel and Dante's innards that we have discussed above. He hears Simon Moonan called a "suck" and has an extensive daydream about the word and the sound of the word in relation to his father's pulling the stopper from the hole in the basin of the lavatory in the Wicklow Hotel (11).

Stephen seems torn between the wish to incorporate the father's penis orally and the wish to incorporate the mother's penis anally. He resolves this conflict in a curious way, it would seem, when wishes surviving from his feminine stage of infantile sexuality manage to change Emma into a bird whom he receives into his virgin womb to give birth to the villanelle. But this leads our story.

Having failed in his institutionalized epistemophilia—he is beat out in sums by Jack Lawton—he is depressed by the time he arrives in the refectory (12). He cannot eat the damp bread. Such phobic attitudes toward food are so common in our childhoods that we respond to them powerfully in literary representation. This moment looks forward to the greasy mutton, the ravaged turnover, the crusts of fried bread, and so on later in the novel. The damp bread would seem to emblemize in Stephen's fantasy both the innards of the mother and the penis of the father. He will become talionically sick in his "breadbasket." The Oedipus situation does not have to be argued, but merely quoted: "He longed to be at home and lay his head on his mother's lap" (13).

It is with this complex wish, then, that Stephen first fiddles with the flaps of his ears:

He wanted to cry. He leaned his elbows on the table and shut and opened the flaps of his ears. Then he heard the noise of the refectory every time he opened the flaps of his ears. It made a roar like a train at night. And when he closed the flaps the roar was shut off like a train going into a tunnel. That night at Dalkey the train had roared like that and then, when it went into the tunnel, the roar stopped. He closed his eyes and the train went on, roaring and then stopping; roaring again, stopping. It was nice to hear it roar and stop and then roar out of the tunnel again and then stop. (13)

Wanting full possession of the mother—wishing, even more directly than Hamlet wishes, "to lay his head on his mother's lap"—instead he plays a compulsive game with the flaps of his ears. The game amounts to anal masturbation "displaced upward" to the ears. The fantasized analogy seems to include: fingers : ears :: mother's penis : anus; train : tunnel :: mother's penis : anus; roar : ears :: mother's phallic flatulence : anus. The game is partly memory—"that night at Dalkey," to which we will ultimately return—but the memory is incomplete and inadequate for handling the anxiety caused by the repressed event. Stephen must also act out in symbolic form a repetition of the repressed experience as if it were a contemporary experience. This kind of activity is one of the meanings Freud gave to the "repetition compulsion."[19] It is also one of Joyce's major techniques as a novelist; technique as discovery and undoing.

The next time the earflap game is used by Joyce it is treated more like a simple fantasy. Stephen is in the study hall, epistemophilically meditating the geography of the infinite universe. He has just recalled Dante's having "ripped the green velvet back off the brush that was for Parnell one day with her scissors":

He felt small and weak. When would he be like the fellows in poetry and rhetoric? They had big voices and big boots and they studied trigonometry. That was very far away. First came the vacation and then the next term and then vacation again and then again another term and then again the vacation. It was like a train going in and out of tunnels and that was like the noise of the boys eating in the refectory when you opened and closed the flaps of the ears. Term, vacation; tunnel, out; noise, stop. (17)

The train and the rhythm, without the earflaps, return that night in Stephen's dream:

The train was full of fellows: a long long chocolate train with cream facings. The guards went to and fro opening, closing, locking, unlocking the doors. They were men in dark blue and silver; they had silvery whistles and their keys made a quick music: click, click: click, click.

And the train raced on over the flat lands and past the Hill of Allen. The telegraphpoles were passing, passing. The train went on and on. It knew. (20)

The dream seems to condense a variety of wishes and infantile imaginings—the fathers as uniformed (naked?) guards opening the mothers' apertures with silvery whistles and keys; the edible mother devoured by the child; the child, anxious about the anal intrusion and reprisal of the combined hostile parent, figuring himself as the chocolate ("tuckoo") train to be devoured—presented to the ego as a pleasant dream of sexual rhythm. In the dream his mother kisses him. His father is elevated into a marshal, the same one (unconsciously but obviously) that he had thought of before going to sleep as having "received his deathwound" (19). (The marshal is connected to the guards by his authority and uniform.) The latent content of the dream is pat: Stephen's wish to have exclusive possession of the mother, his father dead, is fulfilled in the dream; while on the manifest level the ego and superego are satisfied by the transformation of the father into a marshal and by the innocence of the kiss.

The only actual train trip Stephen takes during the "action" of *A Portrait* occurs in chapter 2 when he and his father take the night mail to Cork to sell the last ancestral properties and to see the word *Foetus* carved in the dark stained wood of a desk in the anatomy theater of his father's university. Connected verbally to the chocolate dream-train by the "telegraphpoles passing," it seems in many ways its opposite, much as reality opposes dream. It is a sad journey, leading away from home and mother. As the train leaves Kingsbridge station (as in another train Stephen had left that station for Sallins and Clongowes six years before), Stephen recalls "his childish wonder of years before and every event of his first day at Clongowes" (86). But he feels "no wonder now" and does not actually mention a single event—no mother-kiss, no castle with soldiers' slugs, no square ditch, no dead marshal, no disgusting food, no earflaps. He and his father are inside a female train; he uses the pronoun "her" to refer to it. But Stephen's ego in his early adolescence seems in detached control:

He saw the darkening lands slipping past him, the silent telegraphpoles passing his window swiftly every four seconds, the little glimmering stations, manned by a few silent sentries, flung by the mail behind her and twinkling for a moment in darkness like fiery grains flung backwards by a runner. (87)

This sentence is in the "dangling" style often used in *A Portrait*, in which a simple sentence is extended further and further, in what may well be an anal-retentive way, by series, appositives, participles, and so on, all hung from a single verb or noun. The image of the moment in Stephen's growth resonates most precisely with the end of "A Painful Case," where James Duffy (a study in what Freud first named the "anal character") feels himself "an outcast from life's feast" after sentencing Emily Sinico to "ignominy, a death of shame" by suicide under the wheels of a train. Duffy finds in the fecal train the image of his loneliness, rejection of life, and despair:

Beyond the river he saw a goods train winding out of Kingsbridge Station, like a worm with a fiery head winding through the darkness, obstinately and laboriously. It passed slowly out of sight; but still he heard in his ears the laborious drone of the engine reiterating the syllables of her name.

He turned back the way he had come, the rhythm of the engine pounding in his ears. He began to doubt the reality of what memory told him. He halted under a tree and allowed the rhythm to die away. He could not feel her near him in the darkness nor her voice touch his ear. He waited for some minutes listening. He could hear nothing: the night was perfectly silent. He listened again: perfectly silent. He felt that he was alone.[20]

In *A Portrait* Stephen has some of the same anesthesia of affect that Duffy has: "He listened without sympathy to his father's evocation of Cork and of scenes of his youth" and "heard but could feel no pity" for his father's "images of the dead" (87).

Nevertheless, this anesthesia covers his anxiety only superficially. When he falls asleep at Maryborough, he awakens filled with the "terror of sleep." Joyce does not tell us what terrorizes him, though awake Stephen associates the terror with hearing "his father's deep breath" and with the unseen sleepers who might "harm him." Again calling on the anal pacifier, he defends his ego by the regressive rhythms of train and words, as if he were reenacting the earflap game:

The terror of sleep fascinated his mind as he watched the silent country or heard from time to time his father's deep breath or sudden sleepy movement. The neighbourhood of unseen sleepers filled him with strange dread as though they could harm him; and he prayed that the day might come quickly. His prayer, addressed neither to God nor saint, began with a shiver, as the chilly morning breeze crept through the chink of the carriage door to his feet, and ended in a trail of foolish words which he made to fit the insistent rhythm of the train; and silently, at intervals of four seconds, the telegraphpoles held the galloping notes of the music between punctual bars. This furious music allayed his dread and, leaning against the windowledge, he let his eyelids close again. (87)

The last repetition of the earflap image is obscure. It would be easy to miss if we did not have the *Stephen Hero* fragment to assure us that it *is* a repetition and a very significant one. It explicitly joins the themes that we have been discussing: (1) the earflap-train image; (2) the impregnation of the virgin mother; (3) the problem of giving birth to the self; (4) the relation of rhythmical art to the reconstitution of the mother's destroyed body and the body of the self threatened with talionic destruction or "castration."

The moment occurs as Stephen and Lynch complete their aesthetic walk in chapter 5 by seeking shelter from the rain on the porch of the National Library. The words of Stephen's famous peroration—"The artist, like the God of the creation, remains within or behind or beyond or above his handiwork, invisible, refined out of existence, indifferent, paring his fingernails" (215)—are his last: he becomes all ears. "Your beloved is here," says Lynch. Stephen's "mind, emptied of theory and courage, lapsed into a listless peace" (216). He listens to the students on the porch talk about obstetrics:

Their voices reached his ears as if from a distance in interrupted pulsation. She was preparing to go away with her companions.

The quick light shower had drawn off, tarrying in clusters of diamonds among the shrubs of the quadrangle where an exhalation was breathed forth by the blackened earth. Their trim boots prattled as they stood on the steps of the colonnade, talking quietly and gaily, glancing at the clouds, holding their umbrellas at cunning angles against the few last raindrops, closing them again, holding their skirts demurely.

And if he had judged her harshly? If her life were a simple rosary of hours, her life simple and strange as a bird's life, gay in the morning, restless all day, tired at sundown? Her heart simple and wilful as a bird's heart? (216)

The corresponding moment in *Stephen Hero* includes not only the "interrupted pulsation" of the voices that reach Stephen's ears, but also the identification of the pulsating noises with the earflap fiddling in the refectory at Clongowes. The talk is about "the first number of MacCann's paper," rather than about obstetrics, and Emma is not imaged as a bird. As we shall see, these differences are of the first order of significance in our understanding of the earflap game:

The babble of the young students reached him as if from a distance, in broken pulsations, and lifting his eyes he saw the high rain-clouds retreating across the rain-swept country. The quick light shower was over, tarrying, a cluster of diamonds, among the shrubs of the quadrangle where an exhalation ascended from the blackened earth. The company in the colonnade was leaving shelter, with many a doubting glance, with a prattle of trim boots, a pretty rescue of petticoats, under umbrellas, a light armoury, upheld at cunning angles. He saw them returning to the convent—demure corridors and simple dormitories, a quiet rosary of hours—while the rain-clouds retreated towards the west and the babble of the young men reached him in regular pulsations. He saw far away amid a flat rain-swept country a high plain building with windows that filtered the obscure daylight. Three hundred boys, noisy and hungry, sat at long tables eating beef fringed with green fat like blubber and junks of white damp bread, and one young boy, leaning upon his elbows, opened and closed the flaps of his ears while the noise of the diners reached him rhythmically as the wild gabble of animals. (*SH*, 183–84)

The corresponding epiphany also omits the obstetrics and

the bird image. While it includes the reference to the refectory at Clongowes, it omits the earflaps.

In *A Portrait* the passage is followed by the composition of the villanelle. It becomes clear that the earflap game leads us to precisely the same destination—and, from a psychoanalytic view, for the same reasons—as the enuresis-eyeplucking game: the urethral-anal "artpeatrick," as Joyce calls it on the first page of *Finnegans Wake,* that sponsors the birth of the poem.[21] The "life simple and strange as a bird's life" and the "heart simple and wilful as a bird's heart" are added in *A Portrait* to turn Emma into the pigeon that is at once the Holy Ghost and Gabriel, His voice, who will impregnate Stephen as Blessed Virgin. The bird-girl of the end of chapter 4, seen as seabird, crane, and "darkplumaged dove" (171) and later as "wild angel" and "angel of mortal youth and beauty" (172), has been subsumed in the "dove's eyes" (220) and "bird's life" and "bird's heart" of Emma as male god and angel. In composing the villanelle Stephen is able to solve the parental riddles, dispatch and recreate the parents and the self at once, and in short have all of his infantile cake after he has incorporated it. The Emma-mother-father-bird can penetrate the "virgin's chamber" of Stephen-mother-father-BVM, and with his androgynous and autoerotic pencil he can excrete the "liquid letters of speech," making a new wet womb for himself and his creation.

V

Before concluding this discussion of the features of Joyce-Stephen's infancy with a single glance forward to the return of the earflap game in *Ulysses,* we will look briefly at the letters Joyce wrote to Nora in 1909, when he was in Dublin for several months while she remained in Trieste. About four thousand words of these letters have not been published and quotation from them is forbidden.[22] We will have to paraphrase.

These letters leave no doubt that Joyce's basic fantasy in

relation to his wife was that she was the mother with a penis or penises. He says this literally. He imagines himself as her female love-object and as her child and husband, too. He figures forth her penis in many and diverse ways, making both partners androgynous and thus defending himself doubly against the threat of castration.

Merely to list the phallic emblems given to Nora is instructive. Bodily, they are her clitoris, tongue, hair, fingers, feet, buttocks, feces, flatulence, sweat, odors, and noises—all these named, of course, with "dirty" words or metaphors. Thus, he imagines her playing with her little penis over the toilet bowl, which becomes its vagina, as it does for the feces that he pictures hanging from her anus. Words are but an extension or displacement upward of rectal noises and odors: he wants to hear a dirty word spluttered by her lips at the same time that the smell of flatulence curls up to his nose. Emblems further removed from the body are the cane with which he wishes her to beat him, the crimson flower that he imagines sticking from her anus as she mounts him, and the boots, hat, stockings, drawers with frills, and so on, to be worn during intercourse.

It is clear that in his intricate fantasy Joyce as feminized self wants to introject his little phallic mother in every way possible—through his ears, eyes, nose, mouth, and anus. He wants to give her multiple penises, so that he can receive her in many ways at once, being ridden by her while she is defecating and breaking wind, at the same time that she is making obscene noises with tongue and lips.

Rather curiously, her buttocks, too, become a penis. He repeatedly likes to imagine opening the slit in her underwear to discover her buttocks. Similarly, her entire body—regularly described in diminutives—is a little naked thing hidden and then revealed beneath her dressing-gown and wiggling as he licks her genitals. Conversely, his trouser fly becomes his vagina through which her extended fingers enter like vermin to find his penis and manipulate it. This activity was their initial sexual relation in June 1904. Apparently they did not have complete genital intercourse until 11 October 1904, in Zürich.

In the fall and winter of 1909 this fantasizing was used to help Joyce masturbate or ejaculate as a consequence of the writing itself; while much of it would have been in the service of heterosexual intercourse had they been together, and considered by psychoanalysts as no more perverse than anyone's sexual foreplay, something a little different may be involved in Joyce's considering his real penis as being a symbolic gift for Nora. He wants to be a part of her, with not only his penis, but also his entire body *as* penis inside her womb as a baby. As in the other aspects of his fantasy life so directly portrayed in these letters, his basic wish is less to enter her than to have her enter him—riding him like a man with her thighs between his, provided with the gift of his penis. The other gifts that he actually gives her at this time or imagines giving her—a gold and ivory necklace, money for drawers, a copy of the *Chamber Music* poems written in India ink on parchment, shell cocoa, gloves, sable furs, and a fur cap, stole, and muff—would seem to serve the same purpose of the restoration of the damaged body of the little mother.

He prefers her bottom to her breasts because it defecates, and he likes her vagina less because it receives his penis than because it urinates. Her breasts, in fact, figure very little in Joyce's fantasies, partly, it would seem, because they are not large enough. He wants her to drink cocoa daily—he had sent her some as Swift sent chocolate to Stella—to make them fuller. He even tells her in one of the letters that has been published, in part, that he is laughing as he thinks of "those little girl breasts of yours," and in the same letter quotes his poem beginning "I would in that sweet bosom be."[23] One of his desires is to penetrate her breasts, to treat them as a vagina, and this wish would seem to stem from a more archaic level of his infantile development than the level of the other fantasies: sadistic rather than masochistic. Thus, on 6 December, he writes sadistically that he wants to have intercourse with her between her breasts, to ejaculate on various parts of her head, and then to have anal intercourse with her. The extremes of his ambivalence are indicated when, on 13 December, he has an extended narrative fantasy of being beaten by Nora as his angry nurse in punishment for one of his dirty habits. She is to pull him across her lap like a little child, expose his bottom, and whip him with a cane, while her very large breasts almost touch him.

So he is both sadistic and masochistic toward the breasts of his little mother. As is true in anyone's fantasy life, he has his emotional cake after he has eaten it. In the instance just summarized he is almost delusional about it, substituting Dante or some other big-breasted nurse from his childhood for the girlish, thin-breasted Nora.

It should be emphasized, however, that a similar sadism is expressed in his masochism generally speaking, as I have argued above, in the wish to incorporate Nora's multiple penises through eye, ear, nose, mouth, and anus. To accomplish this, Joyce quite literally imagines fucking her insides out; the farts that he gives masculine common names seem clearly to represent for him the introjected penises of the father, the babies, and the power of the Holy Ghost at once. On the Feast of the Immaculate Conception he concentrates his letter on this multiple theme, dwelling at length on the joys of driving the assorted and personified noises and odors from her anus.

It is in this letter, too, that Joyce first uses the word "fuck-bird." Grammatically, it stands in apposition to "farting Nora," and it seems certain that Joyce has associated her as "bird" with the Holy Ghost as dove or pigeon uttering the anal word of the archangel-seraphim Gabriel, just as he does more discreetly in relation to Emma in *A Portrait* when he has Stephen compose his villanelle. He finds the word a satisfying epithet for Nora. His salutation the next day uses the same word, and he also ends the letter with it, having asked her to write her dirty words larger and to underline them, to smear them with her vaginal secretions, to break wind on them, and to wipe her rectum with them.

In all this the dirty *word* is the main fetish—preferably heard rather than seen and clearly identified with flatulence and excrements. Similarly, it is the sound of defecation, even more than the sight of it, that arouses Joyce. It is as if defecation, too, were a dirty word, the total reality in the image rather than in the actual event. Thus, in the 20 December letter, he reports that Nora has offered to let him have intercourse with her while she defecates in her underclothes. But he would rather talk obscenely in the dark and *hear* her defecate while she embraces him before going on to sexual congress. As he discusses this distinction in the letter, he ejaculates.

VI

The last return of the earflap-train game in *Ulysses* makes all of this clearer, maybe. It is tantalizing in its specificity and occasion. It occurs in the "Circe" episode, during that moment to which we referred at the opening of this discussion, when Stephen's dead mother rises through the floor of the brothel, using her maiden name and wearing her bridal veil. With her *"hollow eyesockets"* and *"toothless mouth"* she is the very image of castration and death (*U*, 579). Stephen is *"Horror-struck"* and *"Choking with fright, remorse and horror,"* as the stage directions tell us. Nevertheless, when his mother recalls his having sung, as she lay dying, Yeats's "Who Goes with Fergus?" he momentarily forgets his extreme anxiety and *"eagerly"* asks her to "tell me the word, mother, if you know now. The word known to all men." (*U*, 581).

That is, here is a loved one back from that undiscovered bourne. Surely she knows the answer now that will satisfy at last the epistemophilic sublimation of pregenital sadism and restore at last the threatened bodies of parents and son at once. But what is her response? It is a question! "Who saved you the night you jumped into the train at Dalkey with Paddy Lee?" (*U*, 581). The "word known to all men," the answer to the riddle of the sphinx, to the epistemophilic quest and question, is another question! And who *is* Paddy Lee? We do not know. His name occurs nowhere else in Joyce's work. Apparently

Stephen's mother refers to the same "train at Dalkey" that he had recalled as part of his repetition-compulsion version of the earflap game: "That night at Dalkey the train had roared" (13). The momentous trauma of that moment is confirmed, but the memory itself is barely enlarged. Does "into the train" mean into the path of the train? Or does it mean into a car on the train? How did the mother save him? Was Paddy Lee another child or a man?

We can, of course, abstract from the dead mother's reply a final assertion of her love. She "saved" him in childhood, and she adds that she had "pity" on him when he was "sad among the strangers." In the "Circe" scene this nurturing love quickly turns, as it had on the first page of *A Portrait,* to a demand by the mother-as-terrifying-superego for repentance and to a threat of "the fire of hell."

The point Joyce makes in the overture of *A Portrait* (and then substantiates by writing the book and the Stephen parts of *Ulysses*) is that by the climax of the oedipal stage of development, given his pregenital fixations, there really is no further defensive move for Stephen to make to shield his ego from the awesome attack by the superego allied with the id from which it sprang. He tries in the overture every kind of reparation for pregenital attacks on the mother's body: story, song, urine, dance, tissue paper, and the feminizing of the self. But the last act of restitution—the arrangement of the threat of eye-plucking into the chiasmic poem—is as far as a boy child can go. It is as far as a man artist can go, too.

He has to do it again and again. He tries a poem for Parnell after Bad Mother Dante chops him up and reduces Simon to childish tears. He tries a poem to E—— C——, after which he looks in the mirror of his mother's dressing table to see the whole body of the mended mother-self. He becomes his own virgin mother, accepting the phallic woman as his male consort, and composes the villanelle. It helps but it does not help. In neurotic Stephen the restoration of the mother can never be adequate, for the repeated expression of the conflict does not eliminate it.

Joyce says as much in "Circe." Stephen manages a kind of phallic assertion and identification with the appreciated father when he smashes the chandelier with his ashplant, calling out the name of *"Nothung"* (Siegfried's father's sword) as he does so (*U*, 583). But the Gasjet flatulates, and Stephen's assertion leads nowhere. He appropriately greets Lynch, Kitty, Cissy Caffrey and the "soldiers and civilians" with the words "Hail, Sisyphus" (*U*, 587), for the labor of rescue from the guilt of having killed the mother is a Sisyphean enterprise entirely. One of the soldiers, Private Carr, as superego, strikes Stephen in the face. He collapses and *"falls stunned"* (*U*, 601). As Bloom tries to rouse him, Stephen, *"doubling himself together,"* *"curls his body"* in a foetal position and mutters Yeats's poem.

Joyce's point is that this is the limit of the possibilities. His most succinct statement of all that I have been arguing comes in ALP's last letter about the old man working: "He'll want all his fury gutmurdherers to redress him" (*FW*, 617). "How small it's all!" as his feminine self says at the end of *Finnegans Wake*, taking the "fluid succession of presents" out to sea for the last time, thirty-five years later. He had arrived at this same destination by the age of six, under the table in Bray.

A friend of mine calls Melanie Klein the "Ann Radcliffe of psychoanalysts," and I am rather painfully aware as I come to the end of this disjointed essay that there is something gothic about it. It is the kind of treatment of literature that Joyce satirizes in the analysis of the "debts and dishes perplex" by the schizzi professors Duff-Muggli and Tung-Toyd (*FW*, 123), or Flann O'Brien in having Professor Unternehmer call the problem of Dermot Trellis (the imaginary Irish author) "an inverted sow neurosis wherein the farrow eat their dam."[24] But O'Brien's wit corrects a common misunderstanding of Stephen Dedalus's more famous statement that "Ireland is the old sow that eats her farrow" (203). Stephen is half right, and Joyce knew it: the fear that Stephen expresses conceals the wish that precedes it—a wish and fear that we all share and handle in our different ways.

The wonder of it is, of course, that Stephen could grow into Bloom and Molly, Earwicker and ALP; that Joyce could turn the features of his infancy into four prose masterpieces.

NOTES

1. *"A Portrait of the Artist as a Young Man": Text, Criticism, and Notes*, ed. Chester G. Anderson (New York: Viking Press, 1968), pp. 252–53. Further references to *A Portrait*, to "A Portrait of the Artist," and to epiphanies will be cited in the text.

2. *Ulysses* (New York: Random House, 1961), p. 16. Further citations, to be included in the text, will be to this edition.

3. "The Relation of the Poet to Day-Dreaming" (1908); rpt. in *Character and Culture*, ed. Philip Rieff (New York: Collier Books, 1963), p. 36.

4. "Early Stages of the Oedipus Conflict and of Super-Ego Formation" (1928); rpt. in *The Psycho-Analysis of Children* (London: Hogarth Press, 1954), p. 187. The summary of Klein's theory that follows relies on this essay and book, as well as on her *Contributions to Psycho-Analysis* (London: Hogarth Press, 1968). The quotations below are from "Early Stages."

5. Sigmund Freud, *Three Contributions to the Theory of Sex* (New York: E. P. Dutton, 1962), p. 57.

6. "*Ulysses*: A Monologue," trans. W. Stanley Dell, *Nimbus 2* (June–Aug. 1953). Originally published as "*Ulysses*, Ein Monolog," in *Wirklichkeit der Seele, Anwendungen und Fortschritte der Neueren Psychologie* (Zurich: Rascher Verlag, 1934), pp. 132–69.

7. For the biographical information that follows I rely on Richard Ellmann's *James Joyce* (New York: Oxford University Press, 1959).

8. *Finnegans Wake* (New York: Viking Press, 1939), p. 340. Further citations, to be included in the text, will be to this edition.

9. John Joyce's version of the story, written in a letter to his first son on 31 January 1931, seems to suggest this latent subject: "I wonder do you recollect the old days in Brighton Square, when you were Babie Tuckoo, and I used to take you out in the Square and tell you all about the moo-cow that used to come down from the mountain and take little boys across?" (*Letters of James Joyce*, vol. 3, ed. Richard Ellmann [New York: Viking Press, 1966], p. 212.)

The moocow is generally a nice, maternal, philic animal who gives us milk to eat on apple tart. In that sense it is here a mollifying substitution for the terrifying and phobic animals of early childhood—the wolves, rats, bugs, eagles, and so on that would devour or invade the child. Stephen represses them—remarkably so—along with the feared revenge of the hostile parent that they represent, but they will return with the eagles at the end of the overture. And that the cow itself is an ambiguous image for Stephen will be made plain in his latency period: "The first sight of the filthy cowyard at Stradbrook with its foul green puddles and clots of liquid dung and steaming brantroughs sickened Stephen's heart. The cattle which had seemed so beautiful in the country on sunny days revolted him and he could not even look at the milk they yielded" (63).

10. See especially Freud's *Three Contributions,* pp. 55 ff., and "On the Sexual Theories of Children" (1908) and "Analysis of a Phobia in a Five-Year-Old Boy" (1909), collected in *The Sexual Enlightenment of Children,* ed. Philip Rieff (New York: Collier Books, 1963); also, chapter 2 of Erik Erikson's *Childhood and Society,* 2nd ed. (New York: Norton, 1963).

11. See "Relation of the Poet to Day-Dreaming."

12. *The Psychoanalytic Theory of Neurosis* (New York: Norton, 1945), p. 232.

13. Fenichel, p. 233.

14. Fenichel, p. 233.

15. See D. D. Paige, ed., *The Letters of Ezra Pound* (New York: Harcourt, Brace & World, 1950), p. 300.

16. "The Madonna's Conception through the Ear" (1914), in *Essays in Applied Psycho-Analysis* (London: Hogarth Press, 1951), 2, 266–357.

17. James Joyce, *Stephen Hero* (New York: New Directions, 1944), pp. 141, 188. Further citations, to be included in the text, will be to this edition.

18. Fenichel, p. 71.

19. *Beyond the Pleasure Principle* (New York: Bantam Books, 1959), p. 39 passim.

20. James Joyce, *Dubliners,* ed. Robert Scholes (New York: Viking Press, 1967), p. 117.

21. I have discussed the meaning of "thuartpeatrick" at length in "On the Sublime and Its Anal Origins in Pope, Eliot, and Joyce," in *Modern Irish Literature,* ed. Raymond J. Porter and James D. Brophy (New York: Iona College Press, 1972), pp. 235–49.

22. The unpublished portions of these letters are in the Cornell University Library.

23. *Letters,* 3, 249.

24. Flann O'Brien, *At Swim-Two-Birds* (New York: Pantheon, 1939), pp. 314–15.

The Cubist
Portrait

HUGH KENNER

8

A PORTRAIT OF THE ARTIST, the title says, *as a Young Man.* If we are to take this title at its face value, then it is unique among Joyce titles; even *Dubliners* varies according as we judge it general or partitive. And since it is too long a title—nine words!—to emboss legibly on the spine of a shortish novel, the sort of detail Joyce didn't overlook, he must have felt sure he needed all those words.

Those nine words do at least three things. First, they impose a pictorial and spatial analogy, an expectation of static repose, on a book in which nothing except the spiritual life of Dublin stands still, a book of fluid transitions in which the central figure is growing older by the page. The book is a becoming which the title tells us to apprehend as a being. Second, they have the same grammatical form as "A Portrait of the Merchant as a Young Man," or "A Portrait of the Blacksmith as a Young Man." The title does not wholly avow that the artist in question is the same being who painted the portrait. It permits us to suppose that we may be regarding the generic artist, the artistic type, the sort of person who sets up as an artist, or acts the artist, or is even described by irreverent friends as The Artist, or as "bullockbefriending bard." [1] And a third thing the title says is that we have before us a portrait of the artist *as a*   ***171*** *young man.* Here there is a clear analogy with Rembrandt, who painted self-portraits nearly every year of his life beginning in his early twenties. Like most Joycean analogies it is an analogy with a tacit difference, because the painter of self-portraits looks in a mirror, but the writer of such a novel as we have before us must look in the mirror of memory.

A Rembrandt portrait of the artist at twenty-two shows the flesh of twenty-two and the features of twenty-two as portrayed by the hand of twenty-two and interpreted by the wisdom of twenty-two. Outlook and insight, subject and perception, feed one another in a little oscillating node of objectified introspection, all locked into an eternalized present moment. What that face knows, that painter knows, and no more. The canvas holds the mirror up to a mirror, and it is not surprising that this situation should have caught the attention of an Irish genius, since the mirror facing a mirror, the book that contains a book, the book (like Swift's *A Tale of a Tub*) which is about a book which is itself, or the book (like Beckett's *Malone Dies*) which is a history of the writing both of itself and of another book like itself, or the poem (like Yeats's "The Phases of the Moon") which is about people who are debating whether to tell the poet things he put into their heads when he created them, and moreover are debating this while he is in the very act of writing the poem about their debate; this theme, "mirror on mirror mirroring-all the show," has been since at least Swift's time an inescapable mode of the Irish literary imagination, which is happiest when it can subsume ethical notions into an epistemological comedy.

So far so good; but Joyce has brooded on the theme more than is customary even in Ireland, and has not been arrested, like Swift or Beckett or Yeats, by the neatness of the logical antinomy. For it inheres in his application of Rembrandt's theme that the portrait of the artist as a young man must be painted, from memory, by an older man, if older only by the time it takes to write a book. Joyce was careful to inform us at the bottom of the last page that this book took ten years. So we have a portrait in which the subject ages from birth to twenty years within the picture space, while the artist lived through ten more years in the course of painting it.

There follows a conclusion of capital importance, that we shall look in vain for analogies to the two principal conventions of a normal portrait, the static subject and the static viewpoint, those data from which all Renaissance theories of painting derive. The one substantial revision I would want to make in the essay I wrote on this book in 1947 is its title. I titled it "The *Portrait* in Perspective" and I now think that the analogies of perspective are simply inapplicable.[2] The laws of perspective place painter and subject in a fixed geometrical relation to one another, in space and by analogy in time. Here both of them are moving, one twice as fast as the other. Joyce's *Portrait* may be the first piece of cubism in literary history.

When we open it, though, what do we discover? We discover, behind and around the central figure, what Wyndham Lewis described as a swept and tidied naturalism, and nowhere more completely than in the places, the accessory figures, the sights and sounds, the speeches and the names. The names. Joyce is famous for his care with fact: "He is a bold man," he once wrote, "who dares to alter . . . whatever he has seen and heard,"[3] and he used, in *Dubliners*, the unaltered names of real people, so often that their concerted determination to sue him the moment he should step off the boat became an implacable, efficient cause for his long exile from Ireland, which commenced virtually on the eve of the publication of *Dubliners*.

Not quite to digress, a Dubliner once told me a story. The BBC, he said, had had an unfortunate experience. They had broadcast in all Sassenach innocence a radio transcription of the funeral episode in *Ulysses*, with its story about the pawnbroker Reuben J. Dodd whose son underwent love's pangs and had to be fished out of the Liffey on the end of a boathook. His father rewarded the boatman with two shillings, and a party to Joyce's dialogue judged this "one and eightpence too much"

(*U*, 95). These words emerged from United Kingdom and also from Irish loudspeakers; whereafter there arrived at Broadcasting House a letter signed "Reuben J. Dodd, Jr." Since one does not receive letters from fictional characters, the BBC dismissed it as a joke until, my man said, "they were persuaded, to their heavy cost, that it was no joke."

For Joyce authenticity of detail was of overriding moment. If actual names were artistically correct, he used them at whatever risk. If they were not, he supplied better ones, but always plausible ones. Yes. And what stares us in the face wherever we open the first book-length narrative of this ferocious and uncompromising realist? Why, a name like a huge smudged fingerprint: the most implausible name that could conceivably be devised for a denizen of lower-class Catholic Dublin: a name that no accident of immigration, no freak of etymology, no canon of naturalism however stretched can justify: the name of Stephen Dedalus.

It seems odd that we accept this name without protest; it is given to no eccentric accessory figure, but to the central character himself. Perhaps it has never had the effect Joyce counted on. For would he not have meant it to arrest speculation at the outset, detaching his central figure at a stroke from the conventions of quiet naturalism? Instead Joyce himself, the Satanic antinomian, attracted attention almost as soon as the book did, and the book was received as no more than thinly veiled autobiography. It was natural to scrutinize the name of Stephen Dedalus for a piece of indulgent symbolism, which (with Stephen's own help to be sure) it yielded quite readily. The strange name (Joyce's text says "strange") seemed a figure of "prophecy" (168), prophecy of light and escape, and of fabulous artifice.

"Fabulous artificer," we read in *Ulysses*, "the hawklike man" (*U*, 201). On the last page of *A Portrait* Stephen invokes him as his new saint, his name-saint, borrowed from an older religion than Catholic Dublin's. In Crete, Daedalus had made Pasiphaë's wooden cow, not by "hacking in fury at a block of wood" like the man who made the cow in Stephen's parable

(214), but by disposing sensible matter for a kinetic end, the relief of the queen's monstrous lust. Then he made the labyrinth to contain her offspring; when Cretans sought to detain him with its secret, *ignotas animum dimittit in artes,* he set his mind to truly arcane arts and made wings to fly away. And in 1903, in December, only months before Joyce had commenced the first of the many drafts of the story of Stephen Dedalus, two brothers, sons of a bishop of the Church of the United Brethren in Christ, had flown on man-made wings at Kitty Hawk, North Carolina. Their feat was like Schliemann's validation of the story of Troy. Their motor developed 16 h.p., and the aeronaut lay prone.

If we think of Dedalus with the help of the Wrights, his triumph consists less in the Shelleyan flight than in the artifice. *Et ignotas animum dimittit in artes.* Orthodoxy's saints had, some of them, invoked God and been levitated. This one had contrived, using lore as arcane, no doubt, as aerodynamics and the new science of the wind tunnel. Insofar as the name of Dedalus carries some manifesto from Joyce, it would seem to be this, that intricate disciplines, *ignotae artes,* must henceforth supplant the enthusiast's *O Altitudo!*

But that does not explain the name's presence, not altogether. The man who could maneuver any Greek hero he liked into Bloom's Dublin without so much as mentioning Odyssean names could have exploited the Daedalus symbolism all he pleased without asking us to believe that Dublin at the drab end of the nineteenth century contained somebody named Stephen Dedalus. That name, simply looked at as the name of a character, is so odd it seems a pseudonym. And indeed it seems to have been modeled on a pseudonym. It combines a Christian martyr with a fabulous artificer, and was very likely based on another name constructed in the same way, a name adopted by a famous Irishman, in fact the most lurid Dubliner of them all. During the brief time of his continental exile, Oscar Wilde joined a Christian martyr's name with a fabulous wanderer's, and called himself Sebastian Melmoth.

Wilde built his pseudonym of exile deliberately. Saint Sebas-

tian was the fashionable martyr of nineteenth-century aestheticism. Melmoth—*Melmoth the Wanderer*—was the hero of a
novel that yet another Irish romancer, Charles Maturin, had
written eighty years before. The two names joined the Christian and the pagan, the sufferer and the exile. In combination
they vibrate with heavy exoticism, linking Wilde with the
creed of beleaguered beauty and with the land of his ancestors,
affirming at the same time something richer and stranger about
this shuffling Celtic scapegoat than would seem possible
(Wilde thought) to a countryman of people with names like
Casey, Sullivan, and Moonan. It is a haunted, homeless name,
crying for exegesis, deliberately assumed by a haunted, homeless man. He was a man, furthermore, in whom Joyce did not
fail to see enacted one of his own preoccupations, the artist as
scapegoat for middle-class rectitude. And if Joyce modeled, as
seems likely, the name of the hero of his novel on the pseudonym of the fallen Oscar Wilde, then he was invoking a
Wildean parallel for Dublin readers to recognize.

Once we recognize it, *A Portrait* acquires a new paradigm,
quite as useful as the autobiographical paradigm that did
service for so long. If it is probably in the long run no more
sufficient (no map is the territory), that is no reason not to
explore it. Different maps show different things.

We may state the new paradigm as follows. *A Portrait* is a
sort of Euclidean demonstration, in five parts, of how a
provincial capital—Dublin, though Toronto or Melbourne
would do—goes about converting talent into rebellious bohe-
mianism. Once converted, the talent exhausts its energies
striking poses. This demonstration is completed in *Ulysses,*
where the bourgeois misfit *par excellence* turns out to be the
bohemian's spiritual father. Dublin, by the time Joyce came to
look back on the process to which he had barely escaped
falling victim, had already extruded the arch-bohemian of a
generation, Oscar Wilde, who had completed the Icarian myth
by falling forever. If we are going to be consistent about the
symbolism of names, we should reflect that Stephen is the son

of Daedalus-Joyce much as Hamlet is the son of Claudius-Shakespeare, and in the myth the son's role is to fall. It seems clear that Joyce sees Stephen as a lad who is going to fall, not as a chrysalis from which the author himself is about to wing forth. He remarked to Frank Budgen that Stephen had "a shape that can't be changed," which appears to mean that by Bloomsday his metamorphoses have ended.[4] He no longer says, "Welcome, O life" (252). He is "displeased and sleepy" in the morning (U, 3), a *bricoleur* of theories in the afternoon, and drunk in the evening: in short, a character about Dublin, the artist-fellow. That is Dublin's accomplishment, to have turned him into that.

How Dublin goes about manufacturing Dubliners is the theme of Joyce's first book of fiction. Character after character in *Dubliners* is shown us at a moment when we can guess how he is going to turn out, what he will be like when he finally acquires "a shape that can't be changed." (In *Ulysses*, as though to validate our foresight, we are shown how Bob Doran for one turned out, after Polly married him; he is a periodic drunk.) And a surprising number of the characters in *Dubliners*, caught by Joyce's stroboscope en route to immutability, resemble Joyce himself about as strikingly as Stephen Dedalus does.

Mr. James Duffy, for instance, in "A Painful Case," has been endowed with the author's Christian name and a surname with just as many letters in it as there are in Joyce. He has moved out of Dublin, but not far, only as far as suburban Chapelizod, which he elected because he judged the other suburbs "mean, modern and pretentious" (D, 107). Like his creator, who kept a notebook labeled "Epiphanies," he keeps on his desk a sheaf of papers labeled "Bile Beans." The woman with whom he attempts to strike up a relationship is named Mrs. Sinico, after a singing teacher Joyce frequented in Trieste. He has even translated *Michael Kramer*, as Joyce did in the summer of 1901. The manuscript of his translation is exceptionally tidy. And he listens, as did the author of *Exiles* and of the final pages of *Finnegans Wake,* to "the strange impersonal voice which he recognized as his own, insisting on the soul's incurable loneliness. We cannot give ourselves, it said: we are our own" (*D*, 111). "Ourselves, oursouls alone," echoes Anna Livia across thirty years (*FW*, 623). Mr. Duffy is "A Portrait of the Artist as Dublin Bank-clerk."

Or consider Jimmy Doyle, in "After the Race," whose name is Jimmy Joyce's with two letters altered. Jimmy Doyle, who becomes infatuated with continental swish and hangs around racing drivers, owes detail after detail of his taste for the anti-Dublin to the life of Jimmy Joyce, who even made a few shillings that first bleak Paris winter by interviewing a French motor-racing driver for the *Irish Times.* Or consider Little Chandler in "A Little Cloud," with his taste for Byron, his yearning after a literary career, his poverty, his fascination with escape from Dublin, his wife and baby. Almost every detail of his story has its source in the author's life. Or consider Gabriel Conroy in "The Dead."

Gabriel Conroy, who is sick of his own country and has "visited not a few places abroad" (*D*, 203), who writes book reviews, as did Joyce, for the *Daily Express,* teaches language, as did Joyce, parts his hair in the middle, as did Joyce, wears rimmed glasses, as did Joyce, has taken a west-county wife, as did Joyce, snubs people unexpectedly, as did Joyce, and is eternally preoccupied, as was Joyce, with the notion that his wife has had earlier lovers: Gabriel Conroy, attending a festivity in a house that belonged to Joyce's great-aunts, and restive in his patent-leather cosmopolitanism among the provincials of the capital by the Liffey, is pretty clearly modeled on his author by rather the same sort of process that was later to produce the Stephen Dedalus of the final *Portrait.*

These Dubliners who are modeled on the author can enlighten us in two ways. They can remind us that Stephen Dedalus is in that respect not privileged; Joyce's works contain many variations on himself. And they can help us see what Joycean shadow-selves are. They are not the author. They are potentialities contained within the author. They are what he has not become.

The sharpest exegetical instrument we can bring to the work of Joyce is Aristotle's great conception of potency and act. His awareness of it helps distinguish Joyce from every other writer who has used the conventions of naturalist fiction. Naturalism as it was developed in France was based on scientific positivism, which affirms that realities are bounded by phenomena, persons by behavior, that what seems is, that what is must be. But Joyce is always concerned with multiple possibilities. For a Zola, a Maupassant, a Flaubert, it is always meaningless to consider what might have been; since it was not, to say that it might have been is without meaning. But in the mind of Joyce there hung a radiant field of multiple possibilities, ways in which a man may go, and corresponding selves he may become, bounding him by one outward form or another while he remains the same person in the eye of God. The events of history, Stephen considers in *Ulysses*, are branded by time and hung fettered "in the room of the infinite possibilities they have ousted" (*U*, 25). Pathos, the subdominant Joycean emotion, inheres in the inspection of such limits: men longing to become what they can never be, though it lies in them to be it, simply because they have become something else.

All potentiality is bounded by alien and circumstantial limits. For the people in *Dubliners* it is bounded by the city. They sense this, all of them, and yearn to remove themselves, but in their yearning they reveal their subjection to the axiom that we cannot desire what we do not know. If they have notions of what it would be like to live another way, in another place, they confect these notions out of what Dublin makes available. Ignatius Gallaher, who is Little Chandler's image of liberation, is a walking anthology of Dublin's tavern gestures of rebellion. The sailor called Frank—"kind, manly, open-hearted" (*D*, 38)— is a sailor-doll Eveline's imagination has pieced together from a list supplied to her by Dublin escapism, and which she has projected onto the fellow who tries and fails to talk her onto the boat to Liverpool. The Frank with whom she fancies what she calls marriage is a chimera of her own mind, and when she refuses to flee she refuses herself. "Eveline" is another Irish mirror-story; it may help us understand Stephen's remark in *Ulysses*, that if Socrates step forth from his house today, it is to Socrates that his steps will tend (*U*, 213).

And so it is with Stephen, whom we are shown electing, by a hundred small acts of election, to become what Dublin will permit "the artist" to be: a wastrel, a heavy drinker, a spongers' victim, a bitterly incandescent talker. Joyce might have been that. Like anyone else in Dublin or anywhere else, Joyce was confronted every day of his life with decisions and choices, courses of conduct elected or not elected, each of which if he elects it branches into a branching family of further choices. If the nose on Cleopatra's face had been shorter, the destiny of the world would have altered. If the swan had not come to Leda, Troy would not have fallen nor Homer therefore educated Greece, nor Greece in turn Rome, and we should none of us perhaps exist. So there lies before a man an indefinitely large potentiality of events he may set in motion, ways he may go, or selves he may become. (For Joyce no self is immutable, it is a costume; hence the costume changes in "Circe.") But each way, each self, each branching from a branch, is supplied to Dubliners by Dublin. The field therefore, however large, is closed. In Dublin one can only become a Dubliner. As for a Dubliner in exile, since his exile was elected within Dublin and is situated along one of the many paths that lead out of Dublin and so are connected to Dublin, he is a Dubliner still.

Joyce contained, then, within him, multitudes. All the men in *Dubliners* are men he might have been, all imprisoned in devious ways by the city, all come to terms of some sort with it, all meeting or refusing shadow selves who taunt them with the specter of another course once possible but now possible no longer. *Dubliners* is a portrait of the artist as many terminated men. And it foreshadows the more famous *Portrait* in another way, having one subject who does not stay still in time.

The boy in "The Sisters" does not become Gabriel Conroy, but he might. Eveline does not become the Maria of "Clay," but she might. Bob Doran does not become Little Chandler, but he might. And none of the men becomes James Joyce, nor none of the women Nora, but they contain those possibilities also. Joyce thought of his genius rather as patient persistence than as a divine gift; he even toyed with delegating to another man, James Stephens, the work of finishing *Finnegans Wake*.

Only by a series of accidents, such as checking into Mrs. Mooney's boarding house, does anyone become what he does become, and though he can be only what he is, he can look back along the way to what he is and test it for branching points now obsolete. So the subject of *Dubliners* is a single subject, metamorphosing along many lines of potentiality as the circle of light directed by the storyteller picks out, successively, a small boy (three small boys?) of the time when he was a small boy, or adolescents of the time when he was an adolescent. Each story lets us think that it obeys the pictorial convention of a fixed perspective, subject and viewer set in place until the work of portrayal is finished. But the book is a succession of such pictures, or the trace of a moving metamorphosing subject, seen from a viewpoint that is always very close to him.

This in turns yields the formula for *A Portrait of the Artist as a Young Man:* the moving point of view, product not only of a book ten years in the writing, but of a standpoint which remains close to the subject as he moves; the moving subject, passing from infancy forward for twenty years; and the subject himself, like the characters in *Dubliners*, a potentiality drawn from within the author, the most fully developed of the alternative selves he projected during a long life with careful labor.

If the differences between Stephen and Joyce seem small, all differences are small, all decisive ones especially. One has only to accept or refuse some opportunity, and the curve of one's life commences a long slow bending away from what otherwise might have been. This line of argument is not only Aristotelian, but wholly familiar to a man brought up, like Joyce, amid clerical exhortations. From the time he could first remember hearing human words, he must have listened to hundreds of homilies, ruminations, admonitions, to the effect that little sins prepare the habit great sins will later gratify, or that the destiny of the soul is prepared in early youth because there is nothing that does not matter.

So Stephen Dedalus is a perfectly normal Joyce character, not the intimate image of what Joyce in fact was, but a figure he generated by his natural way of working. Stephen, unlike a character in *Dubliners*, is followed for twenty years instead of being caught in one posture on one day by stroboscope. But like the characters in *Dubliners*, who also do many things Joyce did, he leaves undone many others things Joyce did, and does many things Joyce did not. These are not trivial divergences. They are the many small points of decision that inhibit him from being Joyce.

Fascinated by Dublin's lifelong hold on its citizens, Joyce himself made no pretence of having escaped it except in body. To the last he kept in repair his knowledge of its shops and streets, pressing visitors for news of alterations, making note of the fact that a business had changed hands. Stephen's talk of flying by nets remains Stephen's talk. One does not fly by such nets, though the illusion that one may fly by them may be one variety of Dublin birdlime.

But Stephen Dedalus is a young man who imagines that he is going to put the city behind him. He is going to fly, like Shelley's skylark. (When Joyce flew, it was like Orville Wright.) Stephen will fall into cold water, like Icarus or like Oscar Wilde. (That is one reason *Ulysses* describes him as "hydrophobe" [*U*, 673].)

Given this formula for his principal character, Joyce used everything he could find or remember that was relevant, all the time fabricating liberally—even the sermon, it is now well known, was fabricated—in order to simplify and heighten a being whose entire emotional life is an act of ruthless simplification. Considered as a genius, the finished Stephen is a tedious cliché, weary, disdainful, sterile. He writes one exceedingly conventional poem, not a *Chamber Music* kind of poem but a poem in the idiom of the empurpled nineties, a poem of which Wilde might perhaps have acknowledged the paternity, and a poem unlikely to outlive its decade. He has, as Joyce said, a shape that can't be changed.

Or has by the end of the book. The Stephen of most of the book is an interaction between that changing subject and that changing viewpoint. To *end* such a book is a difficulty. It is less difficult when the perspective is fixed. What we call "tone"— the writer's attitude to his subject—is the product of a fixed relationship between writer and subject. It is the exact analogy of perspective in painting. Its two familiar modes are sympathy and irony. Irony says, "I see very well what is going on here and know how to value it." But Joyce's view of Stephen is not ironic; it is not determined by a standpoint of immovable superiority. Sympathy says, "Withhold your judgment; if you undervalue this man you will offend *me*." Joyce's view of Stephen is not sympathetic either, not in that sense: not defensive, nor self-defensive. Like a Chinese or a medieval painter, he expects our viewpoint to move as the subject moves. We are to be detached from Stephen, however profoundly we comprehend; we are not to reject him nor defend him, nor feel a kind of embarrassment on the writer's behalf. We have not "irony," we have simply the truth. This is so until the end. At the end, when Stephen's development ceases, when he has very nearly acquired the shape that can't be changed, then he is troubling, and behind the device of the diary entries we may sense, a little, Joyce determined to withhold judgment.

It is a terrible, a shaking story. It brings Stephen where so many other potential Joyces have been brought, into a fixed role: into paralysis, or frustration, or a sorry, endlessly painful coming to terms. The most broken of the genre of beings to which Stephen belongs will be objects of pity and ridicule, like Bob Doran. The more fortunate will meditate on restful symbols, as Gabriel Conroy, cuckolded by a shade, turns toward the snow. All the potential selves we can admire stop short of what we are, and this is true however little we may be satisfied with what we are. Dubliner after Dubliner suffers panic, thinks to escape, and accepts paralysis. It is the premise of the most sensitive of them, such as Stephen Dedalus, that the indispensable thing is to escape. It was Joyce's fortune that having carried through Stephen's resolve and having escaped, he saw the exile he accepted as a means of being more thoroughly a Dubliner, a citizen of the city that cannot be escaped but need not be obliterated from the mind. He celebrated it all his life and projected the moods through which he had passed, and for which he retained an active sympathy, into fictional characters for each of whom the drab city by the Liffey, whatever else it is, is nothing at all to celebrate.

NOTES

This essay is based on one I contributed to the *University of Windsor Review*, Spring, 1965.

1. James Joyce, *Ulysses* (New York: Random House, 1961), p. 36. Other Joyce editions cited in the text are: *Dubliners* (New York: Viking Press, 1967); *Finnegans Wake* (New York: Viking Press, 1939); and *A Portrait of the Artist as a Young Man* (New York: Viking Press, 1964).

2. Published in *James Joyce: Two Decades of Criticism*, ed. Seon Givens (New York: Vanguard Press, 1948), pp. 132–74.

3. *Letters of James Joyce*, vol. 2, ed. Richard Ellmann (New York: Viking Press, 1966), p. 134.

4. Frank Budgen, *James Joyce and the Making of "Ulysses"* (New York: Harrison Smith and Robert Haas, 1934), p. 105.

A Light from
Some Other World:
Symbolic Structure in
A Portrait of the Artist

BERNARD BENSTOCK

9

IN THE AUTUMN of 1907, after a bout of rheumatic fever and amid the chaos of his pauperish household, James Joyce embarked upon his New Economic Policy. Over a thousand pages of *Stephen Hero* were unceremoniously set aside for a new plan of attack, a short novel in five long chapters. The nineteenth century was scrapped and the twentieth century ushered in. Long episodic scenes, fully developed confrontations between the characters, lengthy explanations of Stephen Daedalus's motivations—these were to be replaced by quick, deft strokes of character sketching, a series of related scenes in chronological order but with gaps of varying length, and a maze of minor characters with only one central focus, that of Stephen himself. In essence every aspect of the life of the young hero was deleted that did not in some way contribute to his direct development as an artist. And to replace the narrative and descriptive functions of the auctorial voice Joyce evolved a complicated set of "symbols and portents" as the structural device of his novel.

On the simplest level Joyce's symbolism is strictly denotative, a shorthand for characterization. From Stephen's initial fear of rats with "black shiny eyes,"[1] there follows a legion of dark-eyed persons; some of the parallels are no more than casual, while others suggest patterned possibilities. The dark-eyed are Mr. Casey, Emma, Father Arnall, Cranly, Temple, and the consumptive student; the important linking here is between Emma and Cranly, a parallel that will be discussed later in a larger symbolic context. Joyce's descriptive technique frequently is to "plant" the first adjective and augment it with another soon after. Early in the Christmas dinner argument Casey is described as having "dark eyes" (35), but when the argument is at its fiercest they are "dark flaming eyes" (39)—in the interim he had narrated his tale of having spit his tobacco juice into the harridan's eye ("I'm blinded and drownded!" [37]). Cranly develops from "dark eyes" (194) to "large dark eyes" (245); Temple modulates from "dark, oval eyes" (197) to "dark gipsy eyes" (229) once his gipsylike personality is established. The only designation for Father Arnall during his sermon is of "dark stern eyes" (108), but the change in his face color takes on symbolic proportions, from the first classroom appearance, where it "looked very black but he was not in a wax; he was laughing" (12), to the second when Fleming is exposed as a dullard and "Father Arnall's dark face . . . was a little red from the wax he was in" (48), to the sermon where "his pale face was drawn and his voice broken with rheum" (108).

Expanded adjectives and variations are used throughout. For Davin there is some editorialization since Stephen sees his eyes as "mild" (238) but reports his father as saying "he had a good honest eye" (250), the singular here being not only literal idiom but a reflection of the monocular view of the elder Dedalus who sees the world through his "eyeglass" (29). The dean of studies has "pale" eyes at first (185), but soon after they are "pale loveless eyes" (186) as Stephen's mind further dissociates him from the passion and fire that mark the true intensity of the priestly vocation. With Lynch the change is actually startling: his eyes are first described as "humbled" (205), and then Stephen sees him as a reptile, his eyes "reptilelike in glint and gaze" (206). But the two most important augmentations are found in the first and last chapters—for Father Dolan and for the old man in the west of Ireland. The priest's eyes are twice termed "nocoloured" (50, 52) by Stephen, both before and after the pandying. On the third occasion, as the injustice rankles, the "objective" description is enhanced with the pejorative verdict: "He thought of the baldy head of the prefect of studies with the cruel nocoloured eyes" (55). The final adversary of the novel has "red eyes" (251) according to Mulrennan, yet once Stephen has transformed him into a figure of fear he has "redrimmed horny eyes" (252). These descriptive terms, ostensibly coming from the narrative voice, are actually the reflections of Stephen's highly subjective attitudes.

The most important eyes in *A Portrait,* however, are Stephen's. Their color is never revealed by the narrator, but their condition is often referred to. At almost a dozen places throughout the first four chapters the tender condition of Stephen's eyesight is mentioned, especially that they are "weak and watery" (8). Four times during the pandying we are told that tears "scalded" Stephen's eyes (50–51); in his disappointment at not seeing Emma after the Whitsuntide play, "pride and hope and desire like crushed herbs in his heart sent up vapours of maddening incense before the eyes of his mind," causing his eyes to be "anguished" while a film "veiled his eyes" (86); as a result of the first retreat sermon "he felt the deathchill touch his extremities and creep onward towards the heart, the film of death veiling the eyes" (112). There is a direct link for Stephen Dedalus between the heart and the eyes, the two areas of sensitivity through which the torments of the outer world reach him with full force. In the final chapter, stress is placed on the attitudes that his eyes betray, the reactions that are mirrored in his eyes. Here Stephen's eyes are "smiling" (181, 196)—he's Irish after all!—"soothed" (224), "jaded" (226), and "idle" (232).

Even the simplest Joycean technique rarely remains simple for very long. The vulnerability of young Stephen's eyes enlarges the symbolic possibilities and makes eyes a focus of terror from the first suggestion that "the eagles will come and pull out his eyes" (8). Nót only have the Clongowes rats black shiny eyes, but the dog ghost has "eyes as big as carriagelamps" and human ghosts have "great eyes like carriagelamps" (19). The adolescent Stephen imagines the lascivious women of the night as having "eyes bright with brutish joy" (99), and once he has succumbed to them he imagines that the equation in his scribbler has a tail "eyed and starred like a peacock's" (103), the eyes constantly opening and closing. His guilty dreams then include "goatish creatures," whose "malice of evil glittered in their hard eyes" (137). It is understandable that the mature Stephen should find himself learning to read the message in the eyes of others: looking into the mild eyes of gentle Davin he is repelled by "a dull stare of terror in the eyes, the terror of soul of a starving Irish village in which the curfew was still a nightly fear" (180–81).

But mostly his eye contact relates to his experiences with women. The rise of sexual desire in Stephen can be tracked from the photograph of the beautiful Mabel Hunter with "demurely taunting eyes" (67) to the whore with "frank uplifted eyes" (101) who first seduces him, to the imagined harlots in his guilty mind with "gleaming jewel eyes" (116). Because of the sexual menace in the eyes of the whores (and their supernatural extensions in his guilt-ridden imagination) the reformed Stephen mortifies his sense of sight by keeping his painful eyes "downcast," and "his eyes shunned every encounter with the eyes of women" (150) until his eventful confrontation with the wading girl. There is no verbal contact between them; instead, "when she felt his presence and the worship of his eyes her eyes turned to him in quiet sufferance of his gaze, without shame or wantonness" (171). The perfect stasis has been established, that aesthetic balance between the two extremes of the taunting-frank-jewel-brutish and the mortified-downcast-shunned. This static beauty is reflected in the inspiration for the villanelle where the temptress's sexuality is tempered by a pre-Raphaelite aura: "Her eyes, dark and with a look of languor, were opening to his eyes" (223).

The ambivalence that still exists derives from Stephen's mythic fantasy about women, that they embody the soul of the race, that their basically sexual natures are at the same time profoundly spiritual. Davin's tale of the seductive approaches of the country wife has burned deep into Stephen's consciousness as he conflates the narrated scene with his own childhood recollections of cottage doors in Clane. At first it is the secondhand report of an older Clongowes pupil ("he had seen a woman standing at the halfdoor of a cottage with a child in her arms" [18]) which is quickly transposed as his own ("the peasant women stood at the halfdoors" [20]). Then comes Davin's story, which includes his inference, "I thought by her figure and by something in the look in her eyes that she must be carrying a child" (182–83). Finally there is Stephen's conclusion that although Davin's mild eyes might well attract these women, "him no woman's eyes had wooed" (238). Two diary entries reveal the dichotomy still within him. In his dream "strange figures" (no gender given, but "they are not as tall as men") "peer at me and their eyes seem to ask me something. They do not speak" (249–50). This is once again a troubled dream, but it obliquely parallels the contact with the wading girl in that eyes look at each other without speaking. The later entry is a burst of idyllic rapture of "swirling bogwater" with "eyes of girls among the leaves" (250)—both the bright and the dark sides of the eyes of women are still present in Stephen's mind.

Most important is that women's eyes are primarily associated with Emma. During the composition of the villanelle it is her dark eyes that are the temptress's, and Stephen feels that "perhaps the secret of her race lay behind those dark eyes" (221). That the young Emma has reached puberty excites Stephen since it gives her status as a mature woman capable of child-bearing, engendering the race: "A tender compassion filled his heart as he remembered her frail pallor and her eyes, humbled and saddened by the dark shame of womanhood" (222–23). In Stephen's mind Emma's dark eyes are invariably imagined as peering from her cowled head. Our first view of Emma on the tram steps is of her head in her shawl; Stephen's heart is excited as the party ends and now "his heart danced" as "he heard what her eyes said to him from beneath their cowl and knew that in some dim past, whether in life or in revery, he had heard their tale before" (69). Years later, as he anticipates encountering her after his stage performance, he remembers "only that she had worn a shawl about her head like a cowl and that her dark eyes had invited and unnerved him" (82). Later still, as he lies in bed writing his villanelle, Stephen wraps his head in his blanket, "making a cowl of the blanket" (221). His "closely cowled head" soon reminds him again that she had "worn her shawl cowlwise about her head" (222), and still later, in his diary entry, he contemplates the menstruating Emma as sitting "at the fire perhaps with mamma's shawl on her shoulders" (248).

That Emma and Cranly both have dark eyes suggests the important link made between them in Stephen's mind. Emma has become wary of Stephen and he sees her as flirting with the priest, Father Moran of the dove's eyes; Cranly has argued that Stephen should remain within the church and perform his Easter duty; Emma acknowledges Cranly and ignores Stephen, and it is reported that Cranly has been invited home by Emma's brother. As he associates them together Stephen is preparing himself to be betrayed and abandoned by both his beloved and his friend. His first thought of Cranly as he walked toward the university had been of a bodiless head and face, the "face of a severed head or deathmask" (178); when he encounters him he notices that "from under the wide falling leaf of a soft hat Cranly's dark eyes were watching him" (194); in the final conversation with him, "his hat had come down on his forehead. He shoved it back: and in the shadow of the trees Stephen saw his pale face, framed by the dark, and his large dark eyes" (245). In the diary Stephen concludes that Cranly is the Precursor and now understands why he always sees him as "a stern severed head or deathmask as if outlined on a ˌgrey curtain or veronica. Decollation they call it in the fold" (248). Emma's cowled head is aptly paralleled by the decapitated Cranly as John the Baptist.

Eyes and heart are the prevalent anatomical symbols in *A Portrait*, on important occasions working together much like hands and head in *Exiles*. They are easily overlooked as they blend into descriptive narrative and idiomatic expressions, but even in the most ordinary circumstances they carry symbolic weight dependent upon context. In over a hundred "heart" references in *A Portrait* only two are related to broken hearts. During the Christmas confrontation Mr. Casey cries that "the priests and priests' pawns broke Parnell's heart" (33–34), which has an ironic echo in the diary when that staunch Parnellite, Mr. Dedalus, while advising his graduating son about his future, gratuitously comments about some insignificant incident from his own past: "Told me then how he broke Pennyfeather's heart" (250). This unknown Pennyfeather is certainly intended as an absurd reduction of the great Parnell.

The condition of Stephen Dedalus's heart is of paramount importance in *A Portrait of the Artist*. At Clongowes Stephen locates his sickness in his heart, "if you could be sick in that place" (13). Although not physically weak like his eyes, his heart is nonetheless vulnerable. The first serious challenge comes during the pandybat incident: as soon as Father Dolan's presence is felt in the classroom "Stephen's heart leaped up in fear" (48); it is "beating and fluttering" during Fleming's punishment and "jumped suddenly" when the priest addressed Stephen (49). After the pandying, when his classmates surround him, "Stephen felt his heart filled by Fleming's words and he did not answer" (52); he steels himself for the journey to the rector's office and once again "his heart jumped" when he heard Father Conmee's voice and is "beating fast" when he approaches his desk (56). The condition of Stephen's heart during early adolescence ranges from further contact with the realities of life to the anticipations of imagined pleasures. His heart is "sickened" by the sight of the filthy cowyard (63), ruining his illusions about the beauty of the countryside, but this soon proves to be a metaphor for the disintegration of his father's household, and his heart is once again "sickened" (64). The removal from suburban Blackrock to a north Dublin tenement makes "his heart heavy" (68), but Stephen has begun the substitution of new illusions for sordid reality. His "restless heart" (64) is affected by the imaginary Mercedes whom he had tracked down suburban roads; the real Emma soon replaces Mercedes, and he feels her glance "flattering, taunting, searching, exciting his heart" (69). The colloquy on the tram steps sets his heart "dancing" (69), yet Emma is destined to disappoint his expectations. After the play he rushes through the dark streets of Dublin until he comes to the morgue where the smell of "horse piss and rotted straw" (a reality like the smell of the cowyard) calms his heart: "It is a good odour to breathe. It will calm my heart. My heart is calm now. I will go back" (86). Stephen counters the mundane reality of Emma's prissiness with such sordid realities, and instead of the "innocent" excitement of his infatuation he turns to lechery to "appease the fierce longings in his heart" (98).

During the crucial days of the religious retreat Stephen's heart is bombarded. As the retreat is announced he gazes at Father Arnall's "dark stern eyes. In the silence their dark fire kindled the dusk into a tawny glow. Stephen's heart had withered up" (108). Fire is the primary symbol of the chapter, and the fear of burning in hell torments Stephen's mind. Throughout the sermons his heart is "touched" by the innocence of his fellow students at the retreat (126), "a tremulous chill blew round his heart" and he feels his heart "close and quail" (126). The "boyish hearts about him" (126) awaken further anxieties, and he seeks to be "humble of heart" like Jesus: "He bowed his head upon his hands, bidding his heart be meek and humble" (141). The final attack upon his heart, therefore, comes with his furtive trip to the Church Street chapel to confess. "His heart bounded from his breast" when he entered the confessional, and absolution from the old priest falls like rain "upon his quaking parching heart" (145).

During Stephen's darkest moments of fear and contrition it is his fantasy of Emma which provides him with possible redemption. After the first sermon he walks through the city, "not daring to lift his eyes. . . . Shame rose from his smitten heart. . . . The image of Emma appeared before him and, under her eyes, the flood of shame rushed forth anew from his heart" (115). He imagines a spiritual union in heaven with her, blessed by the Blessed Virgin, whose "eyes were not offended . . . nor reproachful" (116). In his desire for spiritual salvation Stephen has assumed that Emma shares his blame and is an equal partner in his sin, a transfer that allows for mutual redemption: "It is one heart that loves another heart," the Virgin says to them. "Take hands together, my dear children, and you will be happy together and your hearts will love each other" (116). The writing of his poem affords him another opportunity to project his own emotions into Emma's heart. The vignette is bracketed by Stephen's thoughts of birds. Feeling that he might have judged Emma unfairly he wonders whether she is not like a bird, "her heart simple and wilful as a bird's heart" (216); after writing the villanelle he stands on the steps of the National Library and conjectures on the meaning of the birds flying over Molesworth Street: "He felt that the augury he had sought in the wheeling darting birds . . . had come forth from his heart like a bird from a turret quietly and swiftly" (226). In the interim he has had his sexual fantasy and written poetry from its inspiration. Emma and the Virgin coalesce into an inspirational figure from whom emanates a "roselike glow," and he concludes that the "rose and ardent light" was her strange wilful heart (217). That its "rays . . . consumed the hearts of men and angels" leads him to the second tercet of his villanelle, "*Your eyes have set man's heart ablaze*" (218), but he soon finds his inspiration flagging as the aura of his erotic dream begins to wear off and the uncomfortable reality of the world around him intrudes. His own heart has now become the subject of his awareness. "The cry of his heart was broken," he feels, and reiterates, "the heart's cry was broken" (218). The bells and birdsong of early morning, accompanied by the first faint light of dawn, invade his room, "covering the roselight in his heart" (218).

Joyce's purposeful confusion of religious and sexual symbolism is not without its ironic intensity. The adolescent Stephen who tortures himself for his lechery realizes that he is sinning against the "sacred and loving heart" of Christ (134). Yet when he is lying in his bed at dawn trying to recapture the impetus for his poem, the mundane world has taken over his thoughts, and he remembers the scene at Emma's home where he found himself "displeased with her and with himself, confounded by the print of the Sacred Heart above the untenanted sideboard" (219). The gap between the sacred and loving heart of Christ and the cheap reproduction of the sacred heart impresses itself upon him. In lieu of the artificially contrived heart he has discovered Luigi Galvani's "enchantment of the heart," which he transfers from its scientific origins (213) to his own poetic creativity (217). Holding fast to his own concept of the sacredness of the heart, Stephen is nonetheless in danger, at the other extreme, of losing touch with the human and the ordinary. In his diary he notes his mother's concern over his detachment: "She prays now, she says, that I may learn in my own life and away from home and friends what the heart is and what it feels. Amen" (252).

The momentous meeting with the wading girl takes also its toll on Stephen's heart. He had approached the sea with a certain trepidation ("a faint click at his heart") but no longer are his eyes downcast in shame or piety; although "disheartened, he raised his eyes towards the slowdrifting clouds" (167). In anticipation of the as yet unknown experience, but already aware of winged forms flying over him, a "prophecy" and a "symbol," his heart trembles in ecstasy (169). He feels himself "near to the wild heart of life . . . alone and young and wilful and wildhearted" (171)—a significant anticipation of Emma as a bird with a wild and wilful heart.

An important stress has often been given to the colors of the wading girl's costume, "the white fringes of her drawers . . . [and] slateblue skirts" (171). Joyce's color symbolism here is traditional, the colors specifically of the Blessed Virgin, with whom the association is therefore established. On other occasions in *A Portrait* Joyce employs colors symbolically according to associations that he establishes uniquely for the particular context, and it is from that context that its meaning derives.

The antiphony of green (and emerald) with red (and maroon) is basic to the first chapter of *A Portrait*, although almost nonexistent thereafter. Its function is to parallel the dissension developing in Stephen's world, the disintegration of the promise of unity and harmony which would have given security to the child Stephen. Like many of the *Portrait* motifs it is established immediately in the opening segment of the chapter: "Dante had two brushes in her press. The brush with the maroon velvet back was for Michael Davitt and the brush with the green velvet back was for Parnell" (7). Dante Riordan's loyalty to the leaders of the Land League and the Irish Parliamentary Party would be considered coherent and consistent in the 1880s, but after the scandal that engulfed Parnell at the end of the decade a staunch Catholic like Mrs. Riordan would understandably desert Parnell—as did Davitt. Her action is symbolically definitive: "Dante had ripped the green velvet back off the brush that was for Parnell one day with her scissors and had told him that Parnell was a bad man" (16). But her simplistic explanation hardly satisfies the child, who "wondered which was right, to be for the green or for the maroon" (16). His loyalties are subliminally with Parnell, and he dreams of Parnell's death while in the school infirmary: "And he saw Dante in a maroon velvet dress and with a green velvet mantle hanging from her shoulders walking proudly and silently past the people who knelt by the waters' edge" (27). His innocent mind has brought about a reconciliation with the death of

Parnell, and the next scene is Christmas: "A great fire, banked high and red, flamed in the grate and under the ivytwined branches of the chandelier the Christmas dinner was spread" (27). The innocence proves short-lived.

The Christmas colors of red and green are alluded to often during the dinner scene: "There were coloured lanterns in the hall of his father's house and ropes of green branches. There were holly and ivy round the pierglass and holly and ivy, green and red, twined round the chandeliers. There were red holly and green ivy round the old portraits on the walls. Holly and ivy for him and for Christmas" (20). The almost hypnotic litany of this passage reflects Stephen's search for unity and harmony, his hopes for a tranquil Christmas dinner, which he bases on the peaceful coexistence of red and green seen on the table, although the turkey at first introduces an element of fear from his recollection of his few months at school:

Why did Mr Barrett in Clongowes call his pandybat a turkey? But Clongowes was far away: and the warm heavy smell of turkey and ham and celery rose from the plates and dishes and the great fire was banked high and red in the grate and the green ivy and red holly made you feel so happy and when dinner was ended the big plumpudding would be carried in, studded with peeled almonds and springs of holly, with bluish fire running around it and a little green flag flying from the top. (30)

The flag emphasizes the political dichotomy: green for Ireland, red for England (or maroon for the Catholic church). The explosive Christmas quarrel leaves Stephen in a shambles; his known world is seriously dismembered, the family split, religion and nationalism at odds, adults unable to command his continued respect. During his later days at Clongowes he finds himself still yearning for reconciliation as he admires Simon Moonan's ball of sweets which "was made just like a red and green apple only it opened and it was fully of creamy sweets" (42). Like an interlocked Yin and Yang the ball can be put back together, but the same is not true of the red and the green. The disastrous Christmas meal had opened a Pandora's box of evils for Stephen that could never be shut again. Before it, Stephen had obeyed the code insisted upon by the parental figure and refused to "peach" on Wells; afterward he rejects the code and reports Father Dolan to the rector. A faint suggestion that unity and harmony can still be recaptured occurs at the sight of the wading girl: her colors are the Virgin's, but "an emerald trail of seaweed had fashioned itself as a sign upon her flesh" and when she sees Stephen "a faint flame trembled on her cheek" (171). These signs of green and red upon the flesh may represent the possibility of artistic balance and harmony for the embryonic aesthete.

A corollary color contrast, and a possible directional signal toward an even more important emblem, is the conflict between red and white initiated by the schoolroom War of the Roses. As utilized by the Jesuits at Clongowes, this English symbol of internecine warfare pits two segments of the class against each other in competitive exercise. Stephen is a Yorkist with a white badge, but in the battle of the sums the red rose of Lancaster wins. More important to Stephen than the outcome is the beauty of the contrasting colors. "White roses and red roses: those were beautiful colours to think of" (12). Whiteness (and coolness) is most specifically associated with Eileen Vance and her hands, *"Tower of Ivory,"* as Stephen attempts to concentrate on them during the passion of the Christmas dinner debacle, the cool whiteness standing aloof above the battle of the red and the green. The image returns to Stephen at Clongowes as he remembers first Simon Moonan's red and green ball of sweets and then Tusker Boyle's nails. Again Stephen's troubled mind escapes to the comforting coolness, but it soon returns to the transgression in the square. He is forced to contemplate the slimy urinal wall with its smells and its graffiti, particularly a pencil drawing in red of a bearded Roman, not really a face at all but a segment of female anatomy designed to look like one. "Some fellows had drawn it there for a cod. It had a funny face but it was very like a man with a beard" (43). Stephen is as naïve about this sexual totem as he is about Eileen's cool white hands in his pocket.

These two lines of symbolism intersect during Stephen's fantasies over Mercedes, his superimposition of the romance that is Marseilles on the reality that is Blackrock: "Outside Blackrock, on the road that led to the mountains, stood a small whitewashed house in the garden of which grew many rose-bushes" (62-63). Here in the bliss of his reveries white and red are reconciled into a single aspect of passion and tranquillity. Yet passion is rarely tranquil, as the new rioting of sexual emotions proves, and the fear of hell drives Stephen once again to seek inner peace at the confessional on Church Street where absolution is granted by the old priest. "His prayers ascended to heaven from his purified heart like perfume streaming upwards from a heart of white rose" (145). Yet neither the red rose of passion nor the white rose of purity is Stephen's ultimate goal but lead to an impossible concept born of his initial awareness of the symbology of roses. While red and white are both beautiful colors to the Clongowes pupil, he nonetheless aspires to something more: "The cards for first place and second place and third place were beautiful colours too: pink and cream and lavender. Lavender and cream and pink roses were beautiful to think of. Perhaps a wild rose might be like those colours and he remembered the song about the wild rose blossoms on the little green place. But you could not have a green rose. But perhaps somewhere in the world you could" (12).

The quest for the green rose is one of the three significant journeys of the medieval allegory that is *A Portrait of the Artist as a Young Man* (along with the trek to ancient Greece and Rome with Peter Parley and the pursuit of the moocow that is the lore of his fathers). As a symbolic image it glows briefly within the childlike mind, from its origins as a "green wothe" (7) to the hope momentarily sparked when his mind plays truant from the hard sums on the board at Clongowes. There-after it goes underground; no longer does the maturing brain

conjure up green roses, except in muted longings for fulfillment with a Mercedes or for absolution from an aged priest. In
its place, stemming from the same desire for the unattainable,
the Belvedere boy gauges the journey of his soul "going forth
to experience, unfolding itself sin by sin, spreading abroad the
balefire of its burning stars and folding back upon itself, fading
slowly, quenching its own lights and fires" (103). The real
world of experience is wedded to the fantasy of stars and fires,
the stars of the imagined peacock's tail (the guilt from sinful
experiences in the brothels) and the fires of hell soon to be
kindled for him by Father Arnall. Once he has conquered sin
and been offered an ecclesiastical future Stephen further
contemplates the attaining of the impossible: "In vague sacrificial or sacramental acts alone his will seemed drawn to go forth
to encounter reality" (159). It remains only for the symbol of
the winged spirit to work its magic on Stephen's dream; visions
of the "hawklike man flying sunward above the sea" produce a
prophecy of "a symbol of the artist forging anew in his
workshop out of the sluggish matter of the earth a new soaring
impalpable imperishable being" (169), and a view of the
wading birdlike girl causes his soul to leap so that he is
determined "to live, to err, to fall, to triumph, to recreate life
out of life" (172). Running counter to Stephen's expectations
that something will approach him if he but stand and wait is
this insistence that he must actively venture into the unknown
(*et ignotas animum dimittit in artes*), that existing reality will
come to him but that he must strive toward that reality which
has never existed before. His culminating determination is
embodied in the diary entry for 26 April: "Welcome, O life! I
go to encounter for the millionth time the reality of experience
and to forge in the smithy of my soul the uncreated conscience
of my race" (252-53). The green rose of childish admiration
evolves into the as yet uncreated conscience sought by the
artist.

Multiple aspects of the immediate environment conspire to
keep Stephen's soul from soaring and creating—the sky, the

air, the earth, the weather, natural conditions in general. Joyce
develops a symbology of mood like an invisible shield to
complement the tangible forces of nationality, language, religion. The basic color in *A Portrait* is gray; the most powerful
contrast is between coldness and warmth; the essential substance is the sluggish matter of the earth, filth and slime. It is
against this conspiracy of ambiance that Stephen struggles to
attain wings.

Throughout the Clongowes experience, from the first
glimpse of Stephen on the playing field through his repeated
recollections of the scene, the light and air are specified as
"grey" (8, 22, 26, 41, 45). The effect is oppressive throughout,
yet once Stephen has scored his victory over Father Dolan and
won the admiration of his schoolfellows, he finds himself again
on the playground and the air now is "soft grey" and even "soft
and grey and mild" (59). But the triumph is short-lived and the
sinful adolescent is obsessed with the specter of goatish
creatures whose faces, "lightly bearded and grey," are "lit up
greyly" with cruelty (137); he hurries off to confess to a
Capuchin with a "long grey beard" (142). The sky is gray once
again in Dollymount when he encounters the wading girl, but
counterbalancing influences are already present. There had
been a "sad quiet greyblue glow" to the dying day as he looked
out the window in the preceding episode (163); now as he
crosses the bridge the "veiled sunlight lit up faintly the grey
sheet of water" (167), and when he awakens on the beach at
evening, a "rim of the young moon cleft the pale waste of sky
like the rim of a silver hoop embedded in grey sand" (173)—
the blue of sky, the light of the sun, the silver of the moon now
invade the dominant grayness.

Grayness predominates in the last chapter as Stephen confronts numerous adversaries at University College. He walks to
school in "the grey morning light" (176), and only associative
devices along the way that recall his favorite writers relieve his
soul's miseries. Gloom returns when he thinks of the university
and of Cranly's face as a severed head "against the grey curtain

of the morning" (178). Trinity College is a "grey block" (180) that he must circumvent to get to the Catholic university, and his first encounter upon arrival is with the dean of studies: "He opened the door of the theatre and halted in the chilly grey light that struggled through the dusty windows. A figure was crouching before the large grate and by its leanness and greyness he knew that it was the dean of studies" (184). He sees the priest's "aging body" as "spare and sinewy, greyed with a silverpointed down" (185). The physics theatre is gloomy "under the grey cobwebbed windows" (190–91); Moynihan's "snoutish" face is "outlined on the grey light" (191); "O the grey dull day!" Stephen's mind exclaims; the bursar has a "cap of grey hair" (192); and even Cranly's handball is gray (196). The grayness is associated in Stephen's mind with the incestuous love that presumably engendered the dwarf who likes Scott; rain and wet trees, aspects of his morning's walk to school, recur in the mood-fantasy where the lake lay "grey like a shield" and the sister wore a "grey woollen cloak" (228). As reality surrounding him the gray taints everyone Stephen meets: the dean of studies, the bursar, Cranly, Moynihan, Temple (who refers to hell as "the grey spouse of Satan" [236]), and Lynch. As Stephen walks along with him "a crude grey light, mirrored in the sluggish water, and a smell of wet branches over their heads seemed to war against the course of Stephen's thought" and Lynch makes a "grimace at the raw grey sky" (207). Lynch and Cranly are the two primary antagonists, and the symbology of gray ultimately embraces both of them. Cranly's decapitated head is now viewed as outlined on "a grey curtain or veronica" (248), Emma's cowl, while Lynch soon after is recorded as having lured Stephen into following a hospital nurse: "Two lean hungry greyhounds walking after a heifer" (248), recalling the dean of studies, spare and sinewy and gray.

Whereas the air in *Dubliners* is brown (and dry as dust), the air in *A Portrait* is gray and damp, aspects of larger patterns of cold-hot, cold-damp, and cold-damp-dark, intricate patterns that form a complicated symbolic system connotatively more important than its denotative significance. The contrast of hot and cold is not as relevant as the sequential and interactive relationship between the extremes, as in the infant's reaction to wetting the bed: "first it is warm then it gets cold" (7). And from the warmth of childhood Stephen is thrust out into the cold of Clongowes Wood College. On the playground the air is chilly and Stephen's hands are blue (8, 9); the sky is "pale and cold" and he yearns to be inside the warm buildings, yet in the corridors and the stairways he feels the cold even "inside his clothes" (14). He longs to be in his warm bed but even there the sheets are cold at first (17). In his thoughts the cold is general all over Ireland: "There was the cold night air in the chapel and the marbles were the colour of the sea at night. The sea was cold day and night: but it was colder at night. It was cold and dark under the seawall beside his father's house" (17). In his thoughts the life at home has lost its warmth as all things turn cold for Stephen. He has undergone a rude baptismal at Clongowes, shouldered into the "cold slime of the ditch" by Wells (14), an event that triggers both the fear of cold, slime, and rats and the fever that makes Stephen turn hot. Between the chill of the playing field and the feverish night in bed, the confusion of hot and cold persists in an amalgam of general discomfort: the white tiles of the lavatory "made him feel cold and then hot" (11); the bread and tablecloth and the scullion's apron are all damp, but the tea although weak is hot, and he wonders "whether all white things were cold and damp" (13). His thoughts are of cold chapels and the warmth of peasant cottages, of the white cloak of the dead marshal which also conjures up the cold: "O how cold and strange it was to think of that! All the dark was cold and strange" (19). And with morning he is consumed with fever, "his forehead warm and damp against the prefect's cold damp hand. That was the way a rat felt, slimy and damp and cold" (22). In the infirmary the cold sunlight that he sees from his window (23, 24) is balanced by the fire burning in the grate (23, 26).

Adolescent Stephen is almost totally a victim of coldness; cold elements surround him, and he adopts coldness for his own protection. This attitude perhaps originates in the child's reaction to corporal punishment at Clongowes—the sound of the cane cleaving the air made him "shivery . . . and cold" (45). At moments of crisis Stephen relied on thoughts of Eileen's cool, white hands, but here it is Mr. Gleeson who has "clean white wrists and fattish white hands" and long nails, and Stephen trembles "with cold and fright to think of the cruel long nails and of the high whistling sound of the cane and of the chill you felt at the end of your shirt when you undressed yourself yet he felt a feeling of queer quiet pleasure inside him to think of the white fattish hands" (45). By contrast the actual pandying results in hot, scalding tears and "flaming cheeks" (51) and a "hot burning stinging tingling blow" that "made his hand crumple together like a leaf in the fire" (50). Thereafter Stephen cloaks himself in a protective coldness. He separates himself from his elders, his mind shining "coldly on their strifes and happiness and regrets like a moon" (95); "nothing stirred within his soul but a cold and cruel and loveless lust" (96), and Shelley's lines in their "alternation of sad human ineffectualness with vast inhuman cycles of activity chilled him" (96). The coldness of his sexual lust, once it has been realized, becomes the cold hell of Milton and Dante, where the fires are quenched by "the cold darkness" (103) which fills the chaos. "A cold lucid indifference reigned in his soul," and "the chaos in which his ardour extinguished itself was a cold indifferent knowledge of himself" (103). With icy Luciferism he can glance coldly with contempt at the Sunday worshippers, until Father Arnall's dark eyes peer into his heart like "dark fire" kindling "the dusk into a tawny glow" (108).

With the new terror over his sinful life the dry cold of indifference and aloofness gives way to a damp cold of fear. His mind is encompassed by a "thick fog" (111) and a "cold sweat" breaks out on his forehead (116) in response to the hellfire sermons; his heart is affected by a "tremulous chill" and his flesh is pierced by a "cold shining rapier" that is the need for confession (126); "his hands were cold and damp and his limbs ached with chill" (136). He attempts to hide in his room, but his vision of the goatish creatures sends him into a paroxysm of vomiting as he clasps "his cold forehead wildly" (138). The world outside, when he ventures forth to confession, mirrors the thick fog within him. He encounters the "damp dark air" (139), a correlative of the death of his soul in the "black cold void waste" (141).

His new sanctity restores to Stephen a clinical coldness in which he views his possible vocation as a priest, washing in "cold water" and wearing "clean cold linen" (156). Emerging from the director's office, Stephen recalls his tenure at Clongowes from the "gasflames" of the corridors to the "warm moist unsustaining air" of the baths, and a reaction against entering the priesthood takes hold of him. "The chill and order of the life repelled him. He saw himself rising in the cold of the morning" (161). Metaphoric coldness and literal coldness again interact; his mind attempts to focus on a sensation which lacks warmth, "like a changing glow of pallid red brick. Was it the raw reddish glow he had so often seen on wintry mornings on the shaven gills of the priests?" (161). In his retreat Stephen crosses a bridge (a foreshadowing of the bridge to North Bull Island in the next sequence) and he turns "his eyes coldly for an instant towards the faded blue shrine of the Blessed Virgin" (162).

The crucial confrontation on North Bull Island contrasts warmth and cold in a strange fantasy. At first "the air was chilled" and "his flesh dreaded the cold infrahuman odours of the sea" (167)—the primordial Clongowes experiences still hold him fast—and his fellow students frolicking in the water reinforce his discomfort: "The mere sight of that medley of wet nakedness chilled him to the bone" (168). Repeated emphasis is laid upon "the wet of the sea . . . cold wet lustre . . . cold seawater . . . cold brine" (168), but the awakening image of Icarus changes the atmosphere to "grey warm air" (168), first imagined and then realized. Stephen reaches a "long oval bank of sand . . . warm and dry amid the wavelets," and the air too is warm and grey (170). It is here that he 'finds his new madonna.

In the final chapter Stephen comes to terms with dampness by luxuriating in its literary and literary-sexual possibilities. The wet muse of the strand has effected the change, so that as he walks toward the university he muses over literary associations. He had had to step carefully through the "wet rubbish" of the "waterlogged" terrace (175) just outside his home (while hearing the screeching of the mad nun) but now the smell of "wet leaves and bark" (176) soothes him: "The rainladen trees of the avenue evoked in him, as always, memories of the girls and women in the plays of Gerhart Hauptmann; and the memory of their pale sorrow and the fragrance falling from the wet branches mingled in a mood of quiet joy" (176). The converse of these associations of women in literature is his own desire to make literature out of his obsession with women; the inspiration for the villanelle comes with his waking after an erotic dream. "His soul was all dewy wet. Over his limbs in sleep pale cool waves of light had passed. He lay still, as if his soul lay amid cool waters" (217). The noctural emission in adulthood duplicates the infantile bed-wetting experience. Stephen's ardor begins to cool toward the end of his creative effort, and he tries "to warm his perishing joy" by remembering Emma: "A gradual warmth, a languorous weariness passed over him, descending along his spine from his closely cowled head" (222). The final inspiration that brings the poem to its conclusion is again generated from his recollections: "Her nakedness yielded to him, radiant, warm, odorous and lavish-limbed, enfolded him like a shining cloud, enfolded him like water with a liquid life: and like a cloud of vapour or like waters circumfluent in space the liquid letters of speech, symbols of the element of mystery, flowed forth over his brain" (223). Yet what began with literary echoes from Hauptmann and evolved into poeticization of his own desire still remains basically unalloyed sexuality. Stephen walking through Dublin thinks of Emma: "Yes, it was her body he smelt: a wild and languid smell: the tepid limbs over which his music had flowed desirously and the secret soft linen upon which her flesh distilled odour and a dew" (233). Coldness, ironically, is now almost exclusively related to Cranly and Stephen's last conversation with him (240, 247).

The pervading dampness in *A Portrait* is most often allied to a basic environmental foulness—as in the wet rubbish Stephen steps gingerly through in the lane—and such elements have usually been considered naturalistic details in the novel. They also form a symbolic understructure, Stephen's Ireland mirrored in the privacy of Stephen's soul. The symbology derives from three areas of Clongowes, the urinal "square" in which the smugging took place (sexual misconduct), the square ditch into which Stephen is pushed by Wells (baptism in the slime), and the communal baths (the world that he must share with others); they are represented respectively by the "queer smell of stale water" (43), "cold slimy water" (10), and "warm turfcoloured bogwater" (22). The relatively innocent bathwater, which causes Stephen a "vague fear" as he passes the baths on the way to the infirmary, eventually forms part of a larger concept in the work. It surfaces when Stephen contemplates his future as a Jesuit priest, recollecting the life at Clongowes; the necessity of being part of a "community" of Jesuits revolts Stephen's sense of individual privacy. Later, viewing the dregs of his meager breakfast, he is reminded of "the dark turfcoloured water in the baths of Clongowes" (174), but the connotation changes when he stands in the dusk and feels "the thoughts and desires of the race to which he belonged flitting like bats, across the dark country lanes, under trees by the edges of streams and near the poolmottled bogs" (238). He has evolved a theory of the birth of the Irish soul spawned by mysteriously sensual country women like those viewed in cottage doorways, and although he admits that among his fears are "the country roads at night" (243), Stephen is strangely fascinated. In his diary he exclaims, "O life! Dark stream of swirling bogwater on which appletrees have cast down their delicate flowers. Eyes of girls among the leaves" (250).

The associative symbolism of slime eventually relates to Stephen's own sexual appetite, the external sign corroborated by his inner self. He circles the edges of the brothel district, wandering down the "dark slimy streets" (99), moving inevitably into its center, and when he is tormented by his self-debasement Stephen visualizes his body being thrown into a grave "to be devoured by scuttling plumpbellied rats" (112). He later wonders if a "torpid snaky life" is not "feeding itself out of the tender marrow of his life and fattening upon the slime of lust" (140). Yet once he has achieved the stasis afforded by his acknowledgment of the bird-girl and his balanced artist's conception of the world about him, Stephen is able to objectify the slime of lust when he contemplates the incestuous relationship under "wet silent trees": "A game of swans flew there and the water and the shore beneath were fouled with their greenwhite slime" (228).

Somewhat more circuitous is the recurrence of the "writing on the wall" that has its origins in the Clongowes closet where a bearded Roman face masks adolescent worship of the female genitalia, accompanied by such oblique schoolboy messages as "*Balbus was building a wall*" and "*Julius Cesar wrote The Calico Belly*" (43). When at Belvedere Stephen is attacked by Heron, Nash, and Boland (with cabbage stumps) for his support of Lord Byron; he turns on Boland, asserting, "All you know about poetry is what you wrote up on the slates in the yard" (81), and Boland's couplet is recounted. Stephen's intellectual superiority, however, does not spare him having to read the handwriting on his own wall, and in the brothel area the cry of sexual longing that issues from him is "but the echo of an obscene scrawl which he had read on the oozing wall of a urinal" (100), the motif having come full circle.

Stephen Dedalus's gradual and unvoiced decision to refuse the priestly calling is anticipated by the subliminal touches throughout the colloquy with the director at Belvedere. The priest's smile, particularly his "indulgent smile" (154), has analogues in other priestly smiles until it eventually becomes a Cranly characteristic; that he has "his back to the light" (153) recalls Simon Dedalus's stance with his back to the firelight both at the Christmas dinner and when the family fortunes have been severely altered; the looping of the "brown cross-blind" (153) by the director is Stephen's own habit when irritated during the theatricals. The major echoes, however, revert back to the unfortunate incident with Father Dolan and then Father Conmee. It is during the interview at Belvedere that Stephen calmly acknowledges to himself that throughout his apprenticeship to the Jesuits "he had received only two pandies and, although these had been dealt him in the wrong, he knew that he had often escaped punishment" (156). Yet as much as his conscious mind seems to have forgiven Father Dolan, unconsciously the unfair pandying still rankles. "The swish of a soutane" (154) that marks the beginning of the interview echoes "the swish of the sleeve of the soutane as the pandybat was lifted to strike" (50). More ominous is the director's association with Father Conmee, who had inflicted the ultimate betrayal by admitting to Simon Dedalus that he joked with Father Dolan about Stephen's gesture of defiance. The skull that sits on Conmee's desk, referred to three times in the short span of the scene in the rector's office (56, 58), reappears as the director's head: "The priest's face was in total shadow but the waning daylight from behind him touched the deeply grooved temples and the curves of the skull" (154). The death's head, also to be affixed on Cranly, accounts for the "grave and cordial voice" (154) of the director, for his chin "gravely" leaning on his hands after he releases the blindcord (157), and for Stephen's thought that it is "a grave and ordered and passionless life that awaited him" with the Jesuits (160).

The director's peripheral discourse on *les jupes* awakens Stephen's mind to the contrast between expectation and reality, most particularly with items of female attire but also in a more symbolic context. "As a boy he had imagined the reins by which horses are driven as slender silken bands and it shocked him to feel at Stradbrook the greasy leather of harness" (155). Although the primary relevance is to the filth in the cowyard (63–64), there is also a muted echo of "the greasy leather orb" (8) that menaced his days on the playing field of Clongowes. The football flies "like a heavy bird through the grey light" (8), a bird of prey that follows immediately after the threat that unless Stephen apologizes, "the eagles will come and pull out his eyes" (8). In the child's mind it soon ceases to be a football and becomes "a heavy bird flying low through the grey light" (22); at Christmas dinner he wonders, "why did Mr Barrett in Clongowes call his pandybat a turkey?" (30). The final swoop of the bird of prey occurs when Heron threatens Stephen, first menacingly over the "heretical" essay, and then with begrudging respect over Emma. Heron's face is "beaked like a bird," Stephen tells himself, "he had often thought it strange that Vincent Heron had a bird's face as well as a bird's name" (76). Stephen manages to outface Heron, having risen to a position in Belvedere that disarmed those who would prey upon him, and although his recital of the Confiteor is intended to be ironic, his hubris will later lead to the actual need for confession.

Bird symbolism during the second phase of Stephen's maturation involves the tandem relationship between the hawklike man and the bird-girl, Stephen's Icarus and his private madonna. She was a "strange and beautiful seabird. Her long slender bare legs were delicate as a crane's. . . . Her slateblue skirts were kilted boldly about her waist and dovetailed behind her. Her bosom was as a bird's, soft and slight, slight and soft as the breast of some darkplumaged dove" (171). Bearing the colors of the Virgin and resembling fragile and ethereal cranes and doves, she arouses neither lust by her partial nakedness nor feelings of guilty contrition. The full spectrum from sacred to profane ecstasy, however, can be seen in Stephen's response: "—Heavenly God! cried Stephen's soul, in an outburst of profane joy" (171). The girl wading along the shore reflects the image of "a winged form flying

above the waves and slowly climbing the air" (169). Not just
the tame and fragile dove-crane, but a fierce and frightening
bird of prey, this totem of Stephen's aspirations derives
directly from the menacing birds of his childhood and adolescence; he yearns to cry aloud "the cry of a hawk or eagle on
high" (169). Stephen has tenaciously pursued Peter Parley
"along the road to Greece and Rome" (53) and arrived at the
myth of Icarus. He questions the significance of the winged
form—"Was it a quaint device opening a page of some
medieval book of prophecies and symbols, a hawklike man
flying sunward above the sea, a prophecy of the end he was
born to serve and had been following through the mists of
childhood and boyhood?" (169)—and goes on to attempt to
read the flights of birds as an augury of his future and attach to
Emma the possibility of birdlike innocence. The latter fails and
the former demands flight from Ireland into exile.

The most tantalizing symbolic cluster in *A Portrait of the
Artist* is the assemblage of cows and bulls, anticipating the
pervading myth-symbol in *Ulysses* of Stephen as "bullockbefriending bard" opposing the slaughter of the sacred oxen of
the sun.[2] One aspect of the pattern specifically involves Cranly.
It is he who is reading *Diseases of the Ox* (227), ostensibly as a
front for his conversation on chess at the library and as an
affront to the offended priest who has been attempting to read
The Tablet; it is Cranly who admits having eaten "cowdung"
(205, 206); and to Cranly the aesthetician argues about the
kinesis of "hacking in fury at a block of wood" to make "an
image of a cow" (214). Is it accidental that when Stephen and
Cranly are walking outward from Dublin Cranly seized his
arm and "steered" him back? (247). Lynch figures in a minor
version: to Stephen's definitions of *integras* and *consonantia* he
exclaims, "Bull's eye!" and "Bull's eye again!" (212) and leads
Stephen in pursuit of the "heifer" (248). Perhaps it is as
"disciples" that Cranly and Lynch are present in the pattern,
since the Christ myth informs an important part of the cattle
associations. In the third sermon Father Arnall notes that "He
was born in a poor cowhouse in Judea" (118); when Stephen

emerges from the sermon and enters the classroom his fellow students sound like "softly browsing cattle" as they "munched their lunches tranquilly" (125). Stephen, who had expected to die as he entered the room, finds himself still alive, resurrected among the cows in the manger.

The quest that had begun "Once upon a time and a very good time it was there was a moocow coming down along the road" (7) had wound up disastrously in "the filthy cowyard at Stradbrook with its foul green puddles and clots of liquid dung and steaming brantroughs. . . . The cattle which had seemed so beautiful in the country on sunny days revolted him and he could not even look at the milk they yielded" (63). Stephen himself will evolve into a member of the bovine family at a crucial instance: in Clontarf ("meadow of the bull") he wanders across the bridge to "the Bull" (165) where his swimming classmates call to him, "Bous Stephanoumenos! Bous Stephaneforos!" (168). As St. Stephen he is the Christian protomartyr, and as the sacrificial ox he is garlanded for the sacrifice, the Greek *bous* reminding us that on King Minos's island of Crete, where Daedalus contrived a labyrinth to contain the Minotaur, he had previously contrived a device in which Pasiphaë could be mounted by the white bull. It is that same Daedalus, carpenter and aeronautical genius, cartographer and sculptor, who hacked in fury at a block of wood to make an orgasm box in the image of a cow. Under the watchful eye of "a bovine god" (111) Stephen rejects kinetic art and pledges himself to the artificer who can raise him above the labyrinth, but who is also the father who committed the original sin and lured him down the road in search of mythic moocows and impossible green roses and the unknown arts.

NOTES

1. James Joyce, *A Portrait of the Artist as a Young Man* (New York: Viking Press, 1964), p. 22. All page references in the text are to this edition.
2. James Joyce, *Ulysses* (New York: Random House, 1961), pp. 36, 389–90.

In Ireland
After *A Portrait*

DARCY O'BRIEN

10

Perhaps the true fascination of Joyce lies in his secretiveness, his ambiguity (his polyguity, perhaps?), his leg-pulling, his dishonesties, his technical skill, his attraction for Americans. His works are a garden in which some of us may play. All that we can claim to know is merely a small bit of that garden.

Brian Nolan[1]

I WISH TO TRACE the effects of *A Portrait of the Artist as a Young Man* on some Irish writers recently or not yet dead. The writers I choose to discuss, Seamus Heaney, Flann O'Brien, Patrick Kavanagh, and Conor Cruise O'Brien, are each so different from one another that they may be said to have little in common other than place of birth; but, being born in that place in 1939, 1911, 1904, and 1917, respectively, they had to confront Joyce in a direct way and to work around him or through him to reach their own styles, forms, and themes, much as Jacobeans had to confront Shakespeare. None actually met Joyce, though Flann O'Brien, whose novel *At Swim-Two-Birds* Joyce admired and praised, is said to have journeyed specially to Paris for an encounter, backing off at the last minute out of shyness. Conor Cruise O'Brien's mother, Kathleen Sheehy, played at charades with Joyce in her parents' parlor, and she appears as Miss Ivors in "The Dead"; Cruise O'Brien's maternal grandmother, Mrs. David Sheehy, is greeted by Father Conmee in the "Wandering Rocks" episode of *Ulysses*; and two of Cruise O'Brien's uncles, Francis Sheehy-Skeffington and Thomas Kettle, knew Joyce well as fellow students at the Royal University, and the former appears as MacCann in *A Portrait*. Of the four writers Cruise O'Brien has the closest personal connections to Joyce, resembles him least literarily but is the most Joycean of all, in an unexpected way. Of him last.

This is not an essay about literary influence in the sense that Henry James was influenced by Jane Austen or Graham Greene by Joseph Conrad. To say that *A Portrait* has influenced subsequent Irish writing is like saying that *A Preface to Lyrical Ballads* influenced the English romantic movement. *A Portrait* and its sequel, the first three chapters of *Ulysses*, synthesized the social, political, religious, and aesthetic issues facing any Irish writer at the start of this century. Some of these issues have begun to go away recently; others seem more alive than ever. Ireland is now changing, and change will accelerate, but it has come lately and slowly. The population has not expanded during this century, owing to emigration and the linked phenomena of alcoholism and chastity; as I write this, the Dail (Parliament) debates whether legalizing contraception will destroy "the quality of Irish life." The mannered prose of *A Portrait* has long since become dated, but as a source of images and ideas the book's life has in Ireland been prolonged. I doubt that this life will continue much longer. *Dubliners* is already a textbook in Irish schools. A few years ago, the hellfire sermons of *A Portrait* were used on their own as inspirational reading in certain educational establishments in Ireland, but shortly the complete text will feed classroom discussion, a sign that it no longer applies as it has to Irish life.

But as recently as 1971 the most important Irish poet now writing, Seamus Heaney, found *A Portrait* applicable to himself and to his art:

THE WOOL TRADE

'How different are the words "home",
"Christ", "ale", "master", on his
lips and on mine.'   Stephen Dedalus

'The wool trade'—the phrase
Rambled warm as a fleece

Out of his hoard.
To shear, to bale and bleach and card

Unwound from the spools
Of his vowels

And square-set men in tunics
Who plied soft names like Bruges

In their talk, merchants
Back from the Netherlands:

O all the hamlets where
Hills and flocks and streams conspired

To a language of waterwheels,
A lost syntax of looms and spindles,

How they hang
Fading, in the gallery of the tongue!

And I must talk of tweed,
A stiff cloth with flecks like blood.[2]

Without the epigraph from Stephen Dedalus, the poem is quite accessible as a lament for language impoverished. The poet, word-merchant, must make do with depleted stocks, the old words museum pieces now, "in the gallery of the tongue." But if we remember the context of the quotation from *A Portrait*, chapter 5, the poem expands into a meditation on the position of the Irish writer in relation to society and history, as well as to language.

Stephen has with some diffidence been discussing aesthetics with the dean of studies at the Royal University, and when the dean, an Englishman, uses the word *funnel*, Stephen questions it, and says that for him the word is *tundish:* "—It is called a tundish in Lower Drumcondra, said Stephen laughing, where they speak the best English."[3] And the dean, mildly disbelieving and expressing a patronizing sort of interest, says that he will look the word up. Later, we learn from Stephen's diary that he has himself looked the word up: "13 *April:* That tundish has been on my mind for a long time. I looked it up and find it English and good old blunt English too. Damn the dean of studies and his funnel! What did he come here for to teach us his own language or to learn it from us? Damn him one way or the other!" (251). The word has been on Stephen's mind because he had been intimidated by the dean's Englishness, for were not the English masters of their language as of the Irish people?

The language in which we are speaking is his before it is mine. How different are the words *home, Christ, ale, master,* on his lips and on mine! I cannot speak or write these words without unrest of spirit. His language, so familiar and so foreign, will always be for me an acquired speech. I have not made or accepted its words. My voice holds them at bay. My soul frets in the shadow of his language. (189)

When, a moment earlier, Stephen had made his laughing remark about the best English being spoken in Lower Drumcondra, his laughter and his comment came from nervous shame and cultural insecurity. Lower Drumcondra was and is a run-down district in North Dublin City to which Simon Dedalus, like John Joyce, had brought his family after successive evictions from more prosperous neighborhoods. Even today when Dubliners say that the best English is spoken in Dublin, there is a touch of defensiveness in the assertion, and the boasters are likely sending their children to elocution classes to iron out their Dublin accents. The best English may well be spoken in Dublin, but what the statement often means is that what people speak in Tralee or Macroom can't be called English at all. Stephen's unease in his conversation with the dean can be better appreciated in tandem with the preceding action of chapter 5: Stephen's morning walk through Dublin, from Lower Drumcondra, along the North Strand Road, into Talbot Place, across the Royal Canal and the Liffey, past Trinity College and under the trees in St. Stephen's Green to the university buildings. It is a long walk, but it saves tram fare and delays going to classes. The sights, sounds, and smells of the poorer quarters, which make up most of the city, repel him, reminding him of the degradation of the people or nation to which he belongs. He distracts himself with phrases from German, Norwegian, Italian, and English authors, and with condescending thoughts of his nationalist friend, Davin, who would have Stephen learn Irish. Reaching the sanctuary of the university, where he can sometimes escape into abstract thoughts and foreign literatures, he must confront the English Jesuit and enter into a disquieting discussion about the language of the conqueror.

All this expresses the humiliation and resentment that have gone with being Irish and the pressures on the Irish writer to choose sides and languages. We can question, as critics have done for many years, Stephen's responses to this situation, but the situation itself is not of his own but history's making. For Seamus Heaney, this section of chapter 5 is a many-faceted description of the situation of the Irish writer. Political independence for most of the island has not ended the language problem, and as Heaney comes from Derry, which remains part of the United Kingdom, he feels the problem more acutely. His responses, in "The Wool Trade," are from the angle of Stephen's diary entry, after *tundish* has been identified as purer English than its Latinate synonym, *funnel.* The issue for him is not so much the purity of words, for many of those he cherishes in the poem are themselves Latinate, but the resonances and connotations of certain words used naturally and practically by men in their craft, without reference to university or dictionary. The word for the finished cloth, *tweed,* seems as flat, stiff, and unevocative as its sound. The redundant old man is entangled in the very roots of his vocabulary; it is a learning, a "lost syntax," from which the poet feels excluded. But he can celebrate it, and he can take at least vicarious pride in a beauty of language which was once to hand and still lingers, if one would notice it.

The poem implies respect for the language of Lower Drumcondra or its country equivalent. Heaney's invoking of Stephen Dedalus prompts one to note that Stephen's definition of the artistic process—"to try slowly and humbly and constantly to express, to press out again, from the gross earth or what it brings forth, from sound and shape and colour which are the prison gates of our soul, an image of the beauty we have come to understand" (207)—fits very well as a description of what Heaney has done in "The Wool Trade." And many others of his poems may be said to reflect Stephen's priestly idea of art as transubstantiation. But a companion poem to "The Wool Trade" exhibits a different sort of Joycean influence:

TRADITIONS

For Tom Flanagan

I

Our guttural muse
was bulled long ago
by the alliterative tradition,
her uvula grows

vestigial, forgotten
like the coccyx
or a Brigid's Cross
yellowing in some outhouse

while custom, that 'most
soverign mistress',
beds us down into
the British isles.

II

We are to be proud
of our Elizabethan English:
'varsity', for example,
is grass-roots stuff with us;

we 'deem' or we 'allow'
when we suppose
and some cherished archaisms
are correct Shakespearean.

Not to speak of the furled
consonants of lowlanders
shuttling obstinately
between bawn and mossland.

III

MacMorris, gallivanting
round the Globe, whinged
to courtier and groundling
who had heard tell of us

as going very bare
of learning, as wild hares,
as anatomies of death:
'What ish my nation?'

And sensibly, though so much
later, the wandering Bloom
replied, 'Ireland,' said Bloom,
'I was born here. Ireland.'[4]

"Traditions" muses again over questions raised by Stephen's
walk across Dublin and his conversation with the dean of
studies. What is the relation between Ireland and Britain? What
is the language of Ireland? "What ish my nation?" It is a highly
ordered and compact poem. Each of the three sections comments on a separate tradition in Irish language and literature.
Section 1 refers to the alliterative tradition of poetry in the Irish
language, which flourished during the Middle Ages, began to
wane as the English influence spread beyond the Pale, was
almost completely wiped out by the end of the eighteenth and
beginning of the nineteenth century, was to some extent
revived at the end of the last century, and survives in vestigial
though often impressive form today. Heaney describes the
destruction of this tradition as a kind of rape. Section 2 admits
a nasty sort of irony, mocking the idea that Irishmen should be

proud of their Elizabethan English, "correct Shakespearean" archaisms, for these are but reminders of the rape. The last stanza of this section alludes to certain pockets of the country in which the linguistic conquest was never quite complete, *bawn* being an Irish word meaning, approximately, "mossland." Section 3 explains the dedication of the poem and gives us Seamus Heaney's attitude to the mixture of traditions which Ireland has become. Tom Flanagan chose as the epigraph for his splendid book on nineteenth-century Irish novelists the words of Shakespeare's only Irish character, MacMorris: "What ish my nation?"[5] A major theme of Professor Flanagan's book is the linguistic confusion of these Irish novelists, who sometimes caused, to unintentionally ludicrous effect, Irish characters to jump from native dialect into standard British English. This phenomenon, together with religious and political confusions, indicates how alive MacMorris's question was then, as it is now. Finally Seamus Heaney looks to Joyce, here to *Ulysses*, for an answer, choosing Bloom's simple declarative.

"The Wool Trade" and "Traditions" make a transition for the poet from *A Portrait* to *Ulysses*, as complications of national and linguistic identity become at last accepted and encompassed, having been to begin with sources of torment, rancor, and self-doubt. The religious, sexual, and national ambiguities of Bloom's nature seem to Heaney as they did to Joyce an apt definition of Ireland. Or to put the matter another way, accepting Bloom as an Irishman precludes exclusive definitions of Ireland.

It is worth noting both the powerful effect of Joyce on these poems and also the ways in which Heaney shapes that effect, adapts it to his own use, and passes through it to his own form, style, and statement. The influence of *A Portrait, Ulysses,* and even *Finnegans Wake* on Flann O'Brien is greater in degree and different in kind from that on Seamus Heaney. Heaney has been able to appreciate the clarity of Joyce's definition of the position of the Irish writer, to make use of it, and to pass on in other poems to a multiplicity of things irrelevant to this essay. He has never read *Finnegans Wake*, being unattracted by its quicksands. With Flann O'Brien, the Joycean presence was ever immanent. In two recent essays, J. C. C. May's, of University College, Dublin, has argued that what grew into an obsession with Joyce was destructive to Flann O'Brien's talent.[6] Dr. Mays is probably correct, although I am sure he would agree that the limitations of a talent are its own and not the work of some foreign agent. A theory common in Dublin literary circles today is that writers hit the skids when they switch from stout to whiskey, but it could easily be argued the other way around, as in the case of Scott Fitzgerald, who was never worse off than when he changed from gin to thirty bottles of beer a day. Any addiction, whether to Joyce or to alcohol, is a symptom long before it becomes a contributing cause. Flann O'Brien's use of Joyce was at any rate highly successful to begin with, much less so only at the end of his life, when various afflictions, including cancer of the throat, were taking their toll.[7]

Dr. Mays notes some of the many Joycean elements in *At Swim-Two-Birds*, published in 1939:

Dubliners and *Ulysses* are echoed on a number of occasions, for instance the Circe episode is transposed into a minor key in the trial of Dermot Trellis and the values of the Cyclops citizen reappear in Jem Casey. The use of *A Portrait of the Artist as A Young Man* and *Finnegans Wake* is even more important, and supplies the principle of *At Swim-Two-Birds's* entire organization. Section V of the *Portrait* becomes the reference point for the verminous dissolute University College student and the *Wake* for his 'work in progress'. The book that [Flann O'Brien's] Stephen-figure is writing centres on the dreams of a publican, a 'night-logic' world which obeys its own laws and appears to be liberated from customary physical restraints, all its characters merging into one another around a small core of fixed types.[8]

We are alerted to the possibility of such analogies or borrowings by the Stephen-figure narrator of *At Swim-Two-Birds* who advises that

a satisfactory novel should be a self-evident sham to which the reader could regulate at will the degree of his credulity.... Characters should be interchangeable as between one book and another. The entire corpus of existing literature should be regarded as a limbo from which discerning authors could draw their characters as required, creating only when they failed to find a suitably existing puppet. The modern novel should be largely a work of reference.[9]

Yet a point vital to any understanding of the influence of Joyce on Flann O'Brien is that *At Swim-Two-Birds*, for all its borrowing of characters, situations, and literary projects from Joyce, is a mockery and a parody of Joyce's works, particularly of *A Portrait*. Stephen Dedalus gets a drubbing. The Stephen-figure narrator regards his own literary pursuits as no better than a spare-time diversion, at best a distraction from the boredom, squalor, and futility of life. Stephen Dedalus proclaims, "I desire to press in my arms the loveliness which has not yet come into the world" (251). Flann O'Brien's Stephen-figure creates a novelist, who in turn creates a lovely female, whom he, the novelist, rapes. The issue of this union gives the novelist a lot of trouble. At length, after the novelist's characters throw him out the window, it is suggested that he suffers from "an inverted sow neurosis wherein the farrow eat their dam": this inversion vitiates Stephen's remark that Ireland is an old sow that devours her young. The more that we see chapter 5 of *A Portrait* as a reference point for *At Swim-Two-Birds*, the more Stephen Dedalus appears a pretentious ass. To the extent that the Stephen-figure narrator does take himself and his literary work seriously, he is rebuked. Near the end of the book, his uncle, hitherto described contemptuously as an ignorant, tedious fool, below the level of a philistine, gives him a watch as a present for passing his examinations. The Stephen-figure is embarrassed: "My uncle had evinced unsuspected traits of character and had induced in me an emotion of surprise and contrition extremely difficult of literary rendition or description."[10]

It has been argued that Joyce himself saw Stephen as an ass. Professor Hugh Kenner has been so effective an advocate of this interpretation that it has become the mark of a naif to take seriously much of anything that Stephen says or does. Flann O'Brien seems to accept Stephen as Joyce's persona and to delight in ridiculing the high claims for art which Stephen makes, which Joyce's work seems to make, and which most of Joyce's admirers certainly make. Most of us would probably agree that there was little cause to mock a writer so full of self-mockery as Joyce: what can one add to the "Shem" chapter of the *Wake?* But *At Swim-Two-Birds* is at least a healthy kick where it counts to "the four thousand strong corps of American simpletons now in Dublin doing a thesis on James Joyce" who would use *Finnegans Wake* as a prayer book and refer to its author at St. James.[11] *At Swim-Two-Birds* is also, on its own, a comic masterpiece, showing word skill second only to Joyce's in the history of Irish literature; as Joyce said, it is "a really funny book." [12]

As closely as Flann O'Brien's talent resembles Joyce's, the two writers diverge in their abilities to control or to avoid the kind of cynicism which makes life so bleak that the writing of books becomes a pointless gesture against futility. To keep going, Joyce held to the idea of rebirth, renewal, regeneration. It is little enough but it is the most mankind has come up with since the beginning of death. Joyce played this idea for perhaps more than it is worth; it is after all the only idea in the whole of *Finnegans Wake.* But it kept him going, and it made of him a singer and a praiser of life, as all the great poets have been. If Flann O'Brien has a central or controlling idea one would have to term it the Futilitarian Ethic. By comparison, Samuel Beckett is an apostle of hope, going on, waiting, or playing a tape. To Flann O'Brien writing is the barking of a dog: "When a dog barks late at night and then retires again to bed, he punctuates and gives majesty to the serial enigma of the dark, laying it more evenly and heavily upon the fabric of the mind." [13] The bark or the book only punctuates the enigma and the darkness, lending perhaps the transient majesty of articulation; but the final sentence like the last bark amplifies the silence. Meticulously he frustrates any attempt to discover meaning in his work. At the conclusion, *"ultimate,"* to *At Swim-Two-Birds,* he dismisses all possible explanations of his characters' actions, contemplates the eccentricity of human behavior, and scorns one of humankind's most pathetic compulsions, that of imagining significance in the coincidence of numbers:

> Well-known, alas, is the case of the poor German who was very fond of three and who made each aspect of his life a thing of triads. He went home one evening and drank three cups of tea with three lumps of sugar in each cup, cut his jugular with a razor three times and scrawled with a dying hand on a picture of his wife good-bye, good-bye, good-bye.[14]

I wish Flann O'Brien had lived to read the following item which I came upon in the Los Angeles *Times* of 25 October 1972, just as I was finishing *At Swim-Two-Birds* for the third time:

Triple Mishap Kills German

BERLIN (AP)—A man fell out of a taxi and died after he was struck by a passing train, West Berlin police reported Saturday.

The man, a 33-year-old West German from Frankfurt, was in the cab with a woman companion when the cab skidded, police said. Lutz-Dieter Hesse, the woman and the cab driver were thrown from the taxi when it hit a wall.

Hesse fell upon the track of an elevated railway and a train rolled over him, severing both legs below the knee.

On the way to a hospital, an ambulance carrying Hesse, the badly injured woman and the slightly injured cab driver collided with another car. The ambulance turned over.

Another ambulance was called to take them, and the driver of the second car, to the hospital, where Hesse was declared dead.

It is instructive to compare the endings of Joyce's with Flann O'Brien's novels. The meditation on Teutonic triads closes *At Swim-Two-Birds.* In *The Third Policeman*[15] the narrator-protagonist has been killed before the novel begins, is already in hell, and is doomed to repeat the absurdities of his life eternally: this he begins to do on the last page. *An Béal Bocht,*[16] subtitled *A Bad Story About the Hard Life,* ends with the hero-narrator going to jail, probably forever. On the way, he meets for the first time his father, who is just getting out of jail. In *The Hard Life*[17] an impecunious philanthropist tries unsuccessfully to interest the Pope in a scheme to provide women's lavatories throughout Dublin. Bloom worried along these lines, you will recall, but did not sacrifice his life to the cause. The philanthropist, who has gained 500 pounds · because of the evil stupidity of a nephew, is killed when he crashes through the stairway of a Roman concert hall. The book ends with the narrator, another nephew of the misfortunate philanthropist, entering the lavatory of a pub: "There, everything inside me came up in a tidal surge of vomit." The novel is subtitled *An Exegesis of Squalor.* Finally we have *The Dalkey Archive,*[18] the least grim but also the least of these comedies, in which James Joyce appears as an applicant to the Jesuits and settles in the penultimate chapter for a job repairing their underwear. The digs at Joyce are faintly amusing, but on the whole they do not come off; they are noteworthy here as evidence of how much Flann O'Brien, but two years from his death, still felt the weight of Joyce upon him and at last resorted to enfeebled satire, where twenty-five years before he had produced *At Swim-Two-Birds.* It is as if he thought he could turn Joyce back into Stephen Dedalus once again, for the sake of one more swipe. The last chapter has no teeth; one Mary announces she will have one Mick's baby. Set against Joyce's, all of these endings, and the "plots" which they terminate, are signs of the misanthropy which made Flann O'Brien's achievement so different from that of Joyce.

In terms of language and technique, Patrick Kavanagh, who was until his death in 1967 Ireland's best poet after Yeats, wrote as though Joyce had never existed. For Kavanagh cared nothing for experiment, cleverness, or verbal play; he strove

rather for power of expression through simplicity and direct-
ness of language. He achieved this power, and it is beginning
to be recognized. Thematically, however, his relation to Joyce,
especially to *A Portrait*, is close.

Kavanagh did in poetry and prose for the Irish countryside
what Joyce did in prose for Dublin City. Again, I am not
referring to technique here but to the revelation of the *quidditas* of a place and its people. Joyce and his characters appear in
Kavanagh's verse, which I shall discuss further on, but it is in
the prose that connections with *A Portrait* are most apparent.
He wrote two autobiographical novels, both of which are
"portraits of the artist as a young man," *The Green Fool* (1938)
and *Tarry Flynn* (1948).[19] The first was published and then
quickly withdrawn because of a libel action by Oliver St. John
Gogarty.[20] Kavanagh seems to have matured as a personality,
though not as an artist, rather earlier in life than Joyce, perhaps
because he did not have the benefits of a university or even a
high school education, having quit school at the age of twelve
to apprentice himself to his father as a shoemaker and to help
farm the few stony, watery family acres in County Monaghan.
Both books depict a child and a youth full of poetic feeling and
sensitivity but without the callow posings and gratuitous
intellectual jeers of a Stephen Dedalus or, as we know from
biographical accounts, of a young James Joyce. *The Green
Fool* shows as much interest, love and, when appropriate,
acute observation and judgment of the people around him as
of himself. *Tarry Flynn* is more like *A Portrait* in its concentration on the artist figure. Aesthetically, *A Portrait* is by far the
more dazzling; as a human document, *Tarry Flynn* is more
balanced, complete, and emotionally moving.

I can illustrate differences between the two by comparing
parallel sections from *Tarry Flynn* and *A Portrait*. Both describe a religious crisis brought on by hellfire sermons, and
both end with the artist figure taking leave of family and
friends. The retreat sermons scare hell into Stephen Dedalus;
he makes his confession, (after finding a sympathetic priest)

and falls into a short-lived religious mania which is broken off by his interview with the sinister director of studies and his sight of the girl with the soft white down drawers. In *Tarry Flynn* the religious crisis is more of a communal experience. In a village in County Cavan a girl has been knocked off her bicycle by some mildly rowdy youths. The incident outrages the parish priest. He speaks of it in his sermon as a vile, lewd, lustful, intolerable act; he depicts it as only the latest, most outward, and most grotesque example of the carnal laxity which has spread throughout the townland. From the sermon one would gather that there are fornicators behind every hedge. The priest announces that desperate measures will be taken, and he calls in a Redemptorist to give a mission on the evils of sex, a subject on which the Redemptorists have the reputation of being more vigorously conversant than any other order.

The effect of these hellfire sermons is quite different from those of *A Portrait*. In truth, the people of this little corner of County Cavan hardly ever think about sex at all, and still more rarely do they do anything about or with it. Occasional masturbation, perhaps the odd go at bestiality are about the sum of their abandon. But when the Redemptorist starts talking, the people, Tarry Flynn among them, start thinking, and never have the farmhouses and roadways so steamed with desire. Tarry's love for Mary quickens, and he has to write poems to keep himself in check.

The chief difference between the incidents in the two books, aside from the one being handled comically and the other seriously though with some irony, lies in the contrast between the positions of the artist figures in relation to the people around them. Tarry is more alert, sensitive, and lazy than the other villagers, but he is one of them, he is no Zarathustra-Dedalus. He experiences no important conflicts with his family, only the sometimes painful distance which his perceptions and sensibilities impose. Through his reading he becomes aware of a literary world in Dublin which he does not under-

stand but which he begins to feel he must see and try. When he
takes at last his chance to leave, it is with no Dedalian sense of
mission, but rather with complicated misgivings, regrets, and a
finally decisive sense that he must go, or never know himself.
Kavanagh treats the artist's departure as in essence no different
from the departure of any son or daughter who would make a
way in the world, doubtful but driven and pulled out of the
home. He ends the novel with one of Tarry's poems, summing
up his feelings for the home place, and in part it reads:

> On an apple-ripe September morning
> Through the mist-chill fields I went
> With a pitch-fork on my shoulder
> Less for use than for devilment.
> . . . .
>
> As I crossed the wooden bridge I wondered
> As I looked into the drain
> If ever a summer morning should find me
> Shoveling up eels again.[21]

Six years before *Tarry Flynn*, in 1942, Kavanagh published
"The Great Hunger,"[22] the most powerful, or to put it less
ambiguously, the best long poem written by an Irishman since
"The Deserted Village." It is more scathing about the Irish
countryside than anything Joyce wrote in *Dubliners* about city
life, and it was meant as a retort to the sentimental treatment of
the Irish peasant which Kavanagh saw in Yeats, Lady Gregory,
and Synge. Of the peasant-protagonist:

> O he loved his mother
> Above all others.
> O he loved his ploughs
> And he loved his cows
> And his happiest dream
> Was to clean his arse
> With perennial grass
> On the bank of some summer stream;
> To smoke his pipe
> In a sheltered gripe

In the middle of July—
His face in a mist
And two stones on his fist
And an impotent worm on his thigh.[23]

"The Great Hunger" must be read along with *Tarry Flynn*
and *The Green Fool* if one is to know the hate which, like
Joyce, Kavanagh felt for his native place; but it is not the whole
Kavanagh any more than *Dubliners* and the "Cyclops" episode
of *Ulysses* are the whole Joyce. Hatred and resentment often
characterized Kavanagh's verse, and his conversation, but it is
a wonder that they did not dominate altogether, for he, unlike
Joyce, endured Dublin's spite from his early thirties until his
death, leaving only for occasional holidays in Monaghan and
London. It is intriguing to note that, although in his *Portrait*-
like novels there is little resemblance between the artist-
protagonist and Stephen Dedalus, Kavanagh often saw himself
as a latter-day Stephen Dedalus in Dublin, fending off philis-
tines, literary ruffians, and pernicious dullards of every description, protecting his art and himself from the cheap, flashy,
vulgar, and sentimental. He railed most Dedalus-like against
what he termed "the Irish thing": the promotion of bogus
literature by means of its association with an artificial national
identity. In "The Paddiad" (1949), a verse satire on Dublin
literary circles, he casts himself as Paddy Conscience, who
shows up Paddy Mist, Paddy Frog, and the other Paddies as
frauds:

This is Paddy Conscience, this
Is Stephen Dedalus,
This is Yeats who ranted to
Knave and fool before he knew.
This is Sean O'Casey saying,
Fare thee well to Inishfallen.[24]

Paddy Conscience gets himself thrown out by the other
Paddies, but another Paddy Conscience will come to take his
place. It would be missing the point somewhat, however, to

see Kavanagh here as Stephen Dedalus cut-and-dried, because
the poem is a farce, though it sometimes bites.

Kavanagh's view of himself in relation to Joyce was as a
kindred spirit, a truth-teller who would be honored in death,
for the wrong reasons, as he was vilified in life, again for the
wrong reasons. In "Who Killed James Joyce?" (1951)—a
satirical piece done to the rhythms of "Who Killed Cock
Robin?"—the confessing murderers are writers of academic
theses, and the funeral is a broadcast symposium, led by W. R.
Rodgers, a Presbyterian minister who became a poet and
broadcaster. But Joyce at least had great renown while he was
alive. Kavanagh never did. He was honestly and openly bitter
about it, but his bitterness never took the form of envy of
Joyce. Kavanagh could mock his own failures at the same time
that he excoriated people too thick to appreciate his talent. His
sense of spiritual kinship with Joyce helped his courage and his
wit, as in

PORTRAIT OF THE ARTIST

I never lived, I have no history,
I left no wife to take another,
I rotted in a room and leave—this message.

The morning newspapers and the radio
Announced his death in a few horrid words:
—A man of talent who lacked the little more
That makes the difference
Between success and failure.

The biographer turned away disgusted from
A theme that had no plot
And wrote instead the life of Reilly.[25]

I risk laboring the obvious to suggest that the title becomes as
the poem goes on a bitter, joking reversal of Joyce's title, or,
perhaps, of Stephen's romantic idea of the artist and of
himself. The self-mockery of the poem is a little like the ironies
(assuming they exist) with which Joyce treats Stephen in *A
Portrait* and still more like the self-lacerations of the "Shem"

chapter of *Finnegans Wake*. But, as with Joyce's cuts at himself, one has always the sense with Kavanagh that beneath the self-ridicule there is invulnerable self-respect, and that the artist will have the last laugh, though he may be too dead to enjoy it.

I have traced some of the different ways in which Seamus Heaney, Flann O'Brien, and Patrick Kavanagh have been affected by *A Portrait* and by other facets of Joyce. Each has had different sorts of reactions: Seamus Heaney precise and meditative, incorporating Stephen Dedalus and Bloom into his own intricate verbal world; Flann O'Brien diabolically imaginative, yet haunted by Joyce as a rival, trying in the end to consume him with satire; Kavanagh bearing the Joycean burden lightly, sensing Joyce as a friendly, helpful ghost. But all have in common the apprehension of Joyce and his Stephen as presences palpably close, familiar, easily met and known, almost as older brothers, loved, mistrusted. Only a common nationality can account for this closeness, the sometimes offhand intimacy with which these writers allude to Joyce and Stephen. I am ignorant of apt analogies in other literatures, although Allen Ginsberg's

> I saw you, Walt Whitman, childless, lonely old grubber, poking among the meats in the refrigerator and eyeing the grocery boys [26]

comes close.

First readers of *A Portrait* discover that they cannot comprehend the eighth paragraph of the book without knowing something of Charles Stewart Parnell and that the Christmas dinner scene in chapter 1 is vague unless they find out that Parnell was the leader of the Irish Parliamentary party during the late nineteenth century; that he almost succeeded in getting the Home Rule Bill through Parliament, until his being named in the divorce action brought against Mrs. Katharine O'Shea by her husband destroyed his leadership; and that the role of the church in Parnell's fall is what the fighting is about at the Christmas dinner table. Richard Ellmann's biography and

Joyce's *Critical Writings*[27] tell us that "Et Tu Healy," a (lost) poem casting Parnell in the role of Caesar, was Joyce's first known work, written when he was nine, and that Parnell haunted Joyce's imagination.

Besides the connections mentioned earlier in this essay, Conor Cruise O'Brien is linked to Joyce by a fascination with Parnell. In his autobiographical *States of Ireland*, Cruise O'Brien writes:

The Parnell split occurred twenty-seven years before I was born, and it must have been about forty years in the past by the time I became involved in it. In between, there had been the Rising of 1916, the Black-and-Tans, the Civil War of 1922, the coming of independence (or was it independence?) and the partition of the country. There had also been the First World War, but that seemed a side issue, in terms of the only history that really counted. And in that history, as far as it affected my imagination, the great primal and puzzling event was the fall of Parnell.[28]

Joyce, it can be said, took Parnell for his hero, the archetype of the betrayed leader, politician or artist, and he justified to himself his policy of silence, exile, and cunning with reference to Parnell's fate. His treatment of Oliver St. John Gogarty as Buck Mulligan in *Ulysses* was a way of stabbing Brutus first, and the cold dismissal of Cranly in *A Portrait* is another instance of the *Et tu* syndrome in Joyce's work and life. Cruise O'Brien, not a hero-worshiper, has taken a more disinterested approach and has made of himself, among several other things, the leading authority on Parnell. A serious student of *A Portrait* should read the first chapter of *States of Ireland*, "The Fall of Parnell," which throws into doubt the version we get in *A Portrait* and in Joyce's essay "The Shade of Parnell."[29] This is not the place for a discussion of Cruise O'Brien's argument, except to say that it must now be taken into account in any assessment of Joyce's metamorphosis of historical material for his own private, psychological, and aesthetic reasons.

In 1910 Cruise O'Brien's uncle, Thomas Kettle, advised his fellow countrymen: "My only counsel to Ireland is, that in order to become more deeply Irish, she must become European."[30] What Kettle feared was that the attempts to rediscover a native, Gaelic culture in Ireland would result in isolation and provincialism were these attempts not coupled with discovery of the outside world; that the worthy efforts to escape British domination, culturally as well as politically, must mean the admission of other foreign influences and the assimilation of them, for "a national literature that seeks to found itself in isolation from the general life of humanity can only produce the pale and waxen growth of a plant isolated from the sunlight."[31] Kettle's sentiments are of course entirely Joycean in spirit, reflected in Stephen's aspirations to penetrate beyond Irish horizons, fulfilled in *Ulysses* and *Finnegans Wake*, where Ireland, recaptured through Joyce's breadth of learning and experience, refracted through the lenses of a multinational culture, becomes in Kettle's sense "more deeply Irish." It was Joyce's greatest legacy to his fellow countrymen that he showed them ways in which this new Irish literature might be created.

It is in this sense or spirit that Cruise O'Brien, of the four writers discussed here, is the most Joycean. As impatient as Stephen Dedalus with the old Irish issues, rancors and enthusiasms alike, he has tried to bring to Ireland's literature as to its politics an energy and an intelligence aware of the past but free from its domination. His studies of Parnell have been efforts as much to free the imagination from that ghost as to understand it, for of Parnell's fall Cruise O'Brien observes:

The event was one thing, the way the event was imagined another thing, and more powerful. And there were men and women who lived through the event, *and* through the imagining of the event. Their lives, marked by this double experience, marked mine. And both the event and its imagining, and the consequences of the way in which it was imagined, helped powerfully to shape what happened in Ireland in the early twentieth century, and what is happening now.[32]

His revisions of the study of Parnell and the Parnell myth have been made possible by the detachment he, like Joyce, has achieved by becoming "more European," which in Cruise O'Brien's case means also more African and more American. Two of his works, *Maria Cross*[33] and *Albert Camus*,[34] show depth of insight into foreign cultures and understanding of interactions among politics, economics, and literature in places remote from Ireland. It has been the curse of the worst elements in Irish culture, that a well-founded resentment of everything British has too often led to xenophobia and the cultural asphyxiation which that disease induces. One would hope that Joyce's example would be tonic, and in Cruise O'Brien there is proof that it has been. The titles of two of his other works, *United Nations: Sacred Drama* and *To Katanga and Back*[35] speak for themselves in this regard. His play *Murderous Angels*[36] concerns clashes between white Western-ers and black Africans: it is certainly the first African chapter in the history of Irish dramatic literature, yet as a study of some of the aftereffects of colonialism it has a more than passing application to the Irish scene. We remember an Irish novel structured on a tale from ancient Greece and given as its hero a Jew with a Hungarian father. Since entering Irish politics—he was elected to the Dail in 1969 and became a cabinet minister in the new coalition government in 1973—Cruise O'Brien has advised the Irish in speech after speech to stop behaving as if they were essentially different from the people of other nations and to cease murdering each other for the sake of what mythical differences exist among them. Contemplating the lethal absurdities of Catholic-Protestant antagonisms, with each side regarding itself as God-chosen and the other as creatures of the devil, he has written: "One could say that Ireland was inhabited, not really by Protestants and Catholics but by two sets of imaginary Jews."[37]

To the question What is an Irishman? Cruise O'Brien has given his own version of Bloom's answer to the cyclops citizen of *Ulysses:* "Irishness is not primarily a question of birth or blood or language: it is the condition of being involved in the Irish situation, and usually of being mauled by it."[38] In Ireland after *A Portrait*, as I began by saying, the questions and situations posed by Joyce with such dramatic clarity have not yet gone away, and Joyce's early works retain their relevance. In "The Dead" Joyce has Miss Ivors, the militant nationalist, lecture Gabriel Conroy about the primacy of Gaelic culture and the Irish language. There is wonderful Joycean irony in that Cruise O'Brien, the son of the woman Joyce called Miss Ivors, should recently ask his fellow Irishmen, "Is the language in which I am now speaking not part of the national culture? If so, it is very agreeably spread throughout the world." [39] If so, one can include Joyce as part of the national culture. If not? And what of *En Attendant Godot?* "What ish my nation?"

> I know you Dubliners have had a Jewish
>   Mayor
> But when have you had a Jewish
>   Archbishop of Dublin? [40]

NOTES

1. "A Bash in the Tunnel," in *A Bash in the Tunnel*, ed. John Ryan (London: Clifton Books, 1970), p. 20. Brian Nolan (or O'Nolan) is the given name of the man who wrote novels under the name Flann O'Brien and a newspaper column under the name Myles Na gCopaleen (or Na Gopaleen). Since I discuss only the novels here, I refer to him henceforth as Flann O'Brien.

2. From *Wintering Out* (London: Faber and Faber; New York: Oxford University Press, 1972), p. 37, Mr. Heaney's third collection of poetry. His fourth, *North*, appeared in 1975 from the same publishers.

3. James Joyce, *A Portrait of the Artist as a Young Man* (New York: Viking Press, 1964), p. 188. All page references in the text are to this edition.

4. *Wintering Out*, pp. 31–32.

5. See Thomas Flanagan, *The Irish Novelists* (New York: Columbia University Press, 1959).

6. The two essays are "Brian O'Nolan: Literalist of the Imagination," in *Myles: Portraits of Brian O'Nolan*, ed. Timothy O'Keeffe (London: Martin Brian & O'Keeffe, 1973), pp. 77–119; and "Brian O'Nolan and James Joyce on Life and on Art," *James Joyce Quarterly* 11 (Spring 1974): 238–56.

7. For some sense of these afflictions, see the essays by John Garvin and Jack White in *Myles*.

8. "Brian O'Nolan: Literalist of the Imagination," p. 106.

9. *At Swim-Two-Birds* (London: MacGibbon & Kee, 1968), p. 33.

10. P. 312.

11. Phrases borrowed from Myles Na gCopaleen, quoted by Dr. Mays in "Brian O'Nolan: Literalist of the Imagination," p. 107.

12. Joyce to Niall Sheridan, quoted in a letter from Sheridan to Timothy O'Keeffe dated 4 March 1960. See Anne Clissmann, *Flann O'Brien: A Critical Introduction to His Writings* (Dublin: Gill and Macmillan, 1975), p. 79. See also Sheridan's essay in *Myles*, pp. 48–49.

13. *At Swim-Two-Birds*, p. 314.

14. *At Swim-Two-Birds*, p. 316.

15. (London: MacGibbon & Kee, 1967). It was written 1939–40, but O'Nolan, discouraged by a rejection from Longmans, threw the manuscript into a trunk, where it was discovered after the author's death in 1966 by Niall Sheridan.

16. (Dublin: An Preas Náisiúnta, 1941), translated from the Irish by Patrick C. Power as *The Poor Mouth* (London: Martin Brian & O'Keeffe, 1973).

17. (London: MacGibbon & Kee, 1962).

18. (London: MacGibbon & Kee, 1964).

19. *The Green Fool* makes no pretence at being fiction but was called a novel when reissued in 1971 by Martin Brian & O'Keeffe. *Tarry Flynn* (London: MacGibbon & Kee, 1965); subsequent quotations are from that edition.

20. The run-in with Gogarty provides a biographical link with Joyce. For background see my *Patrick Kavanagh* (Lewisburg: Bucknell University Press, 1975), chapter 2.

21. *Tarry Flynn*, pp. 255–56.

22. Reprinted in Kavanagh's *Collected Poems* (New York: Norton, 1975), pp. 34–55.

23. *Collected Poems*, p. 37.

24. *Collected Poems*, p. 91.

25. *Collected Poems*, p. 121. Dated 1951.

26. From "A Supermarket in California," in *Howl and Other Poems* (San Francisco: City Lights, 1956), p. 27. For other examples of a personal reaction to *A Portrait* by recent Irish writers, see my interview with Benedict Kiely in *James Joyce Quarterly* 11 (Spring 1974): 189–94, and John Jordan's essay, "Joyce Without Fears," in *A Bash in the Tunnel*, pp. 135–46.

27. Richard Ellmann, *James Joyce* (New York: Oxford University Press, 1959); *The Critical Writings of James Joyce*, ed. Ellsworth Mason and Richard Ellmann (New York: Viking Press, 1959).

28. *States of Ireland* (London: Hutchinson, 1972), p. 21.

29. *Critical Writings*, pp. 223–80.

30. *The Day's Burden* (Dublin, 1910), p. xxi. Kettle, a member of the nationalist Parliamentary party, was killed in World War I, serving as a lieutenant in the British army. He felt the war against Germany more important than his nationalist scruples. His brother-in-law, Francis Sheehy-Skeffington, a pacifist, was murdered by the British in 1916, after he was arrested trying to help the wounded. As mentioned earlier, Sheehy-Skeffington appears as MacCann in *A Portrait*.

31. *The Day's Burden*, p. xii.

32. *States of Ireland*, p. 23. See also his *Parnell and his Party* (London: Oxford University Press, 1957), pp. 347-56.

33. (London: Chatto and Windus, 1954).

34. (London: Fontana, 1970).

35. (New York: Pantheon, 1968); (New York: Simon and Schuster, 1962).

36. (London: Hutchinson, 1969). The play has been produced in Los Angeles, Hanover, Paris, Dublin, and New York.

37. *States of Ireland*, p. 309.

38. *Writers and Politics* (New York: Pantheon, 1965), pp. 98-99.

39. Address at Waterford, 16 February 1974. Cruise O'Brien was attacking the legal fiction that Irish is the "first" national language. He advocates equal status for English.

40. *King Herod Explains*, an unpublished play by Conor Cruise O'Brien, written 1969-70, produced at the Dublin Drama Festival, 1970. King Herod reminds the audience of their political-religious prejudices. Script supplied me by the author.

Biographical
Notes

CHESTER G. ANDERSON, professor of English at the University of Minnesota, is the author of *James Joyce and His World* and the editor of the Viking Critical Edition of Joyce's *Portrait*. His most recent essays on Joyce have been psychoanalytic, appearing in *Modern Irish Literature* and the journals *Mosaic* and the *James Joyce Quarterly*.

BERNARD BENSTOCK is professor of English and comparative literature at the University of Illinois at Urbana-Champaign. He is the author of *Joyce-again's Wake: An Analysis of Finnegans Wake*, *Sean O'Casey, Paycocks and Others: Sean O'Casey's World,* and the forthcoming *James Joyce: The Undiscover'd Country*, as well as coeditor of *Approaches to Ulysses: Ten Essays*. His articles on Joyce have appeared in the *James Joyce Quarterly*, *Southern Review*, *PMLA*, *Modern Fiction Studies*, and other journals.

MARGARET CHURCH, professor of English and chairman of comparative literature at Purdue University, is coeditor of *Modern Fiction Studies*. Her publications include *Time and Reality: Studies in Contemporary Fiction* (which contains a chapter on James Joyce), *Don Quixote: The Knight of La Mancha*, and articles on modern fiction. She has published on Joyce in the *James Joyce Quarterly* and *College Literature*, and is currently preparing a book-length study of structure and its relation to meaning in fiction; the final chapter will discuss the works of James Joyce.

HANS WALTER GABLER, Dr. phil., formerly Librarian of the Munich Shakespeare Library and Harkness Fellow of the Commonwealth

Fund of New York, is now wissenschaftlicher Assistent in the Department of English, University of Munich. He has written on Elizabethan drama and Shakespeare, translation, bibliography, and Joyce. He currently serves as advisory editor of the *James Joyce Quarterly* and is exploring the textual problems in James Joyce in view of a scholarly edition.

RICHARD M. KAIN is professor emeritus of English at the University of Louisville. His books include *Fabulous Voyager,* an early study of *Ulysses,* and *Dublin in the Age of W. B. Yeats and James Joyce.* He is coauthor with Marvin Magalaner of *Joyce: the Man, the Work, the Reputation,* and coeditor with Robert Scholes of *The Workshop of Daedalus.* He has contributed critical articles, reviews, and notes to numerous books and periodicals.

HUGH KENNER is Andrew W. Mellon Professor of the Humanities at The Johns Hopkins University. His "A Portrait in Perspective" was written for the 1948 Seon Givens volume, *James Joyce, Two Decades of Criticism.* His book *Dublin's Joyce* was published in 1955, and *Joyce's Voices* is scheduled for 1977.

BREON MITCHELL is associate professor of German and comparative literature and associate dean of the College of Arts and Sciences at Indiana University. He is the author of *James Joyce and the German Novel: 1922-1933.* His essays on Anglo-German literary relations and modern literature include studies of Brecht, Beckett, Grass, Kafka, Döblin, W. H. Auden, and others. His current research focuses on novels of the 1930s.

JAMES NAREMORE is associate professor of English at Indiana University. His publications include *The World Without a Self: Virginia Woolf and the Novel,* and various writings on Joyce, modern literature, and film. He is currently working on a book about Orson Welles.

DARCY O'BRIEN is professor of English at Pomona College. He is the author of *The Conscience of James Joyce, W. R. Rodgers,* and *Patrick Kavanagh.* His articles on Joyce and other Irish writers have been published in several periodicals and he is a contributor to the *Irish Times* (Dublin). He is completing a book on Irish writers after Yeats and Joyce.

Thomas F. Staley is Trustees' Professor of Modern Literature and dean of the Graduate School, University of Tulsa, where he also edits the *James Joyce Quarterly*. He has written or edited five books on James Joyce, among them the commemorative volume *Ulysses: Fifty Years*, and with Bernard Benstock *Approaches to Ulysses: Ten Essays*. He has also written widely on modern literature; his essays have appeared in *The Southern Review, Mosaic, Modern Fiction Studies, Commonweal, Studies in the Novel, Etudes Anglaises*, and the *Journal of Modern Literature*. His most recent book is *Dorothy Richardson*.